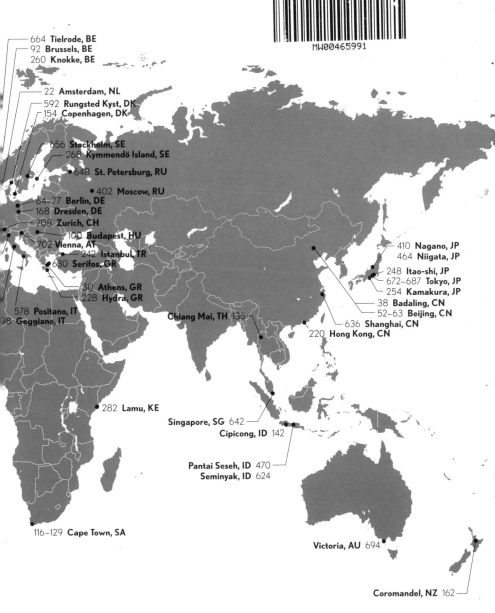

664 Tielrode, BE
92 Brussels, BE
260 Knokke, BE

22 Amsterdam, NL
592 Rungsted Kyst, DK
154 Copenhagen, DK

656 Stockholm, SE
268 Kymmendö Island, SE
648 St. Petersburg, RU
• 402 Moscow, RU

64–77 Berlin, DE
168 Dresden, DE
708 Zurich, CH
100 Budapest, HU
702 Vienna, AT
242 Istanbul, TR
630 Serifos, GR
130 Athens, GR
228 Hydra, GR

578 Positano, IT
98 Geggiano, IT

282 Lamu, KE

Chiang Mai, TH 136

410 Nagano, JP
464 Niigata, JP
248 Itao-shi, JP
672–687 Tokyo, JP
254 Kamakura, JP
38 Badaling, CN
52–63 Beijing, CN
636 Shanghai, CN
220 Hong Kong, CN

Singapore, SG 642
Cipicong, ID 142

Pantai Seseh, ID 470
Seminyak, ID 624

116–129 Cape Town, SA

Victoria, AU 694

Coromandel, NZ 162

MW00465991

100

INTERIORS AROUND THE WORLD

TASCHEN

Bibliotheca Universalis

100

INTERIORS AROUND THE WORLD
So wohnt die Welt · Un tour du monde des intérieurs

BALTHAZAR & LASZLO TASCHEN (Eds.)

TASCHEN
Bibliotheca Universalis

CONTENTS

CONTENTS

INTRODUCTION

One hundred interiors on five continents

Successful interiors tell stories—be they of an industrial loft, a luxury penthouse, or a grand old villa. When presented together, as in this book, they tell us much more besides, providing insights into how the world of the early 21st century chooses to live. What does a Zurich dining room look like? Or a bathroom in Niigata, Japan? How might a Miami art collector paint his bungalow's walls? And what awaits you in a St. Petersburg apartment? We went inside a hundred homes around the globe and found answers that amazed, intrigued, and enchanted us.

The locations could hardly be more diverse—nor could the views. They range from the urban skyline seen from a Singapore tower block to the idyllic island landscape of rocks, pine trees, and water surrounding one family's holiday home near Stockholm. Whatever the topography, the external environment inevitably influences the ambience inside— it's with good reason, for example, that Sylvia Avontuur describes her windows overlooking Amsterdam's docklands as the most important picture in her apartment. Just as crucial to the character of an interior is the era of its architecture. From Istanbul via Paris to Barcelona, a great many of the spaces featured on the following pages are in apartments dating from the late 19th century, whose occupants-cum-curators have breathed new life into old walls. Elsewhere, we find others taking similar care of bold Modernist houses built in the revolutionary spirit of the International Style. And then there are the contemporary homes, with all their clever technical innovations, designed to meet the specific needs of their owners—such as the riverside villa in Dresden or the house on stilts in Nagano. But whether their shells are historic or brand-new, interiors all over the world exhibit the effects of an aesthetic evolution that has been shaping our built world for over a hundred years.

How did we get here

So many design projects take their cue from famous interiors of the past, thus ensuring the ideas contained within them live on. The homes in this book are no exception—although their sources of inspiration vary greatly. One such influence is the Red House in the English town of Bexleyheath. Built in 1859 for William Morris, it was the cradle of the Arts and Crafts Movement. Morris aimed to counter the tide of inferior industrial products with high-quality workmanship, and decorated the rooms of his own home with finely crafted furniture and hand-made accessories in the Neo-Gothic style. Our featured apartment in Moscow is an homage to the impact of his colorful reform.

Ludwig Mies van der Rohe's 1929 Barcelona Pavilion, on the other hand, broke with convention and heralded the arrival of Modernism. A grid of narrow steel supports allowed for an open-plan layout, in which the space seemed to flow around the panel-like walls. Marble, onyx, and travertine lent it an air of dignity, calling to mind an ancient temple, while the architect's purpose-designed leather-upholstered steel chair and stool have long since become classics. Now a São Paulo villa has eloquently extended the design repertoire established by Mies's pavilion.

Around the same time, Le Corbusier was developing his plans for the Villa Savoye near Paris. His design, on which work had begun in 1928, combined white walls, wide ribbon windows, and glass frontages with elegantly pared-back interiors, and featured delicate supporting columns, a ramp leading to the upper floor, and a roof terrace that adds outdoor living space—something since copied in countless city apartments. We found his ideas echoed in a 1950s-built house in Havana.

With his municipal library of 1933, in the then Finnish city of Viipuri, Alvar Aalto subsequently presented a softer, Scandinavian version of Modernism: details such as the undulating wood-paneled ceiling, the three-legged stools made of plywood rather than tubular steel, and the similarly organic and now famous cylindrical skylights result in a warmer ambience that takes the edge off modern austerity. In Rungsted Kyst, Hanne Kjærholm later created a house for herself and her husband, Poul, another Scandinavian design pioneer, that perfectly embodies this philosophy.

Back in 1928, meanwhile, Michel Roux-Spitz had devised an interior for the Salon des Artistes Décorateurs in Paris that acted as a catalyst for the emerging Art Deco style. In addition to drawing inspiration from Bauhaus Modernism, this new movement also incorporated influences such as Cubism and African art. Steel, chrome, and Bakelite were the preferred materials, while the defining characteristics included the incorporation of mirrors and the use of stepped profiles for furniture. Art Deco was the collective expression of a playful yet elegant vision of the future. Jean-Louis Deniot's tastefully hued Parisian apartment and a restored Budapest villa offer contemporary takes on this theme. Among those who gave Modernism a new impetus in the mid-20th century were the American designers Charles and Ray Eames. Their ergonomically shaped fiberglass chairs introduced plastic to the mix and can now be found in homes as wide-ranging as Madrid and Buenos Aires, either as vintage originals or in the form of re-editions by Vitra. Concrete interiors were built both by Louis Kahn, who developed his signature style in the 1950s, and, two decades later, by Japan's Tadao Ando, who created structures that, in contrast to the pronounced heft of the former's work, are as poetic as the paper panels of traditional Japanese screens. This is the architectural context that gave rise to Hijiri, a small concrete residence near Ito-shi.

In the early 1990s, the designs of Zaha Hadid brought new energy to architecture. Her forms are distorted, broken up: in short, deconstructed. The invigorating effect her furniture has on a room can be seen in William Sawaya's apartment in Milan. A few years later, sometime around the turn of the millennium, the concept of the "white cube" exhibition space took hold, although its roots can be traced back to Modernism. The use of all-white rooms to allow objects to speak for themselves has now spread to living spaces, to the Milanese studio residence of Elia Mangia, for instance, or the former shipyard building in Tielrode, in which artists Sofie Lachaert and Luc d'Hanis have established their gallery and home.

Individual, interconnected, and global—A new international style emerges

Traditionally, however, the main factor in interior design has been the cultural frame of reference rather than the ideas of the creative avant-garde. Hamwood House in the Irish countryside, for instance, is typical of the Anglo-Saxon elegance. A very different aesthetic, yet one equally influenced by the local vernacular, defines the home of artist Shao Fan, who has filled his newly built home in Beijing with antique furniture from his native land, thus creating a new take on Chinese decorative idioms.

There are, on the other hand, also interiors that don't necessarily follow from their surroundings—such as the featured houses in Biarritz and Monte: despite being in France and Argentina, respectively, and thus hardly near neighbors, they have a similarly rustic, cozy charm. We also came across a whole host of projects that, although scattered around the globe, might almost have been created in concert. They include the Athens home of architect Penny Loukakou—with its space-defining trompe-l'œil tiles and black designer furniture, it could just as easily be in Milan. As could Filippa Knutsson's apartment in an old Stockholm townhouse and Simon de Pury's majestic Parisian pied-à-terre. It's not hard to imagine them in any number of alternative locations. Likewise, the New York loft transformed by Deborah Berke and the panoramic penthouse in Brussels. They all share a common aesthetic vocabulary that suggests the existence of a new international or global style.

Another clear sign is the regular recurrence on the following pages of certain items of furniture: Eero Saarinen's Tulip chairs and table, for example, those plastic-shelled Eames designs, or the plywood chairs of Arne Jacobsen's Series 7 range. Perhaps this internationalization can be put down to our collective travel fever, perhaps it's also influenced by the reach of today's style magazines. They, in particular, ensure that trendsetting apartments such as Christian Liaigre's duplex in Paris serve as inspiration the world over. Liaigre and style pioneers like him have begun to write a new interior design story for today, the latest chapter of which is recorded in this TASCHEN collection. What will the next chapter bring? We'll keep you posted.

EINLEITUNG

Hundert Interieurs auf fünf Kontinenten

Gelungene Einrichtungen erzählen immer Geschichten – vom Industrieloft, vom luxuriösen Penthouse oder von der Sehnsucht nach der klassischen Villa. So wie in diesem Buch zur Anthologie versammelt, berichten sie aber auch von der Geschichte. Im konkreten Fall kreist unser Bilderreport um die Frage, wie die Welt am Beginn des 21. Jahrhunderts wohnt. Wie sieht ein Zürcher Esszimmer aus und wie ein Bad im japanischen Niigata? Welche Farben tragen die Wände im Bungalow eines Kunstsammlers in Miami und welche erwarten einen zur Teestunde in St. Petersburg? An hundert ausgewählten Orten mit allen möglichen Längen- und Breitenkoordinaten öffnen sich die Türen. Und wir staunen.

So unterschiedlich die Standorte, so verschieden auch ihr Blick. Urbane Apartments, wie jenes in einem Wohnblock mit Aussicht über die Skyline von Singapur, wechseln sich mit landschaftlichen Traumkulissen ab – etwa an der Schärenküste bei Stockholm, wo ein Ferienhaus nur von Felsen, Kiefernwald und Wasser umgeben ist. Wie auch immer die Topografie beschaffen sein mag: Sie nimmt Einfluss auf die atmosphärische Gesamtstimmung im Hausinneren. Völlig zu Recht bezeichnet Sylvia Avontuur den Blick aus den Panoramafenstern zum Hafen von Amsterdam als wichtigstes Kunstwerk ihrer Wohnung. Ebenso prägend für den Charakter der Räume sind die Epochen, aus denen die Architektur stammt. Eine ganze Reihe von Apartments auf den Folgeseiten befindet sich in Gebäuden aus dem späten 19. Jahrhundert, ob nun in Istanbul, Paris oder Barcelona. Ihre Bewohner könnte man als Kuratoren bezeichnen, die der alten Substanz neues Leben eingehaucht haben. Ähnlich bewahrend widmen sich andere den Häusern der Moderne, die im revolutionären Duktus des International Style erbaut wurden und für ihre Kühnheit geliebt werden. Und dann wären natürlich die zeitgenössischen Bauten zu nennen, technisch innovativ und maßgeschneidert für die Bedürfnisse ihrer Besitzer, wie die Villa in Dresden oder das Haus auf Stützen in Nagano. Doch egal ob frisch gemauerte oder denkmalgeschützte Hülle – in der Raumgestaltung spürt man allseits die Einflüsse einer Wohnevolution, die seit etwas mehr als hundert Jahren auf die bebaute Welt wirkt.

Wie das Wohnen wurde, was es heute ist

Berühmte Interieurs der Vergangenheit dienten immer wieder als Stilmatrizen für die Gestaltung aktueller Projekte und leben mit ihren Ideen in deren Räumen fort. Das gilt auch für die Interieurs in diesem Buch – wobei ihre Einflüsse ausgesprochen vielfältig sind. Darunter findet sich etwa William Morris' Red House im englischen Bexleyheath, das 1859 den baulichen Beginn des Arts and Crafts Movement markierte. Morris bekämpfte den Ramsch billig produzierter Industrieprodukte mit Handwerkskunst in höchster Qualität. Die Zimmer seines Hauses stattete er mit geschreinertem Mobiliar und handgemachten Accessoires im neugotischen Stil aus. Einflüsse seiner farbenfrohen Reformbewegung zeigt das Moskauer Apartment.

Ludwig Mies van der Rohes Barcelona-Pavillon wiederum brach 1929 mit den tradierten Wohnvorstellungen und läutete die Moderne ein. Während eine Konstruktion mit filigranen Stahlstützen den Grundriss offen lässt, scheint das Raumgefüge um die scheibenartig aufgestellten Wände zu fließen. Marmor, Onyx und Travertin verleihen dieser Architektur eine Würde, die an antike Tempel erinnert. Ein lederbezogener Sessel und der zugehörige Hocker, die für die Innenausstattung des Pavillons geschaffen wurden, sind heute Klassiker. In São Paulo fand eine Stadtvilla zur eloquent weiterentwickelten Variante des damals geschaffenen Formenrepertoires.

Le Corbusier baute zur selben Zeit, ab 1928, die Villa Savoye bei Paris. Weiße Wände mit breiten Fensterbändern, Glasfronten und eine Innenraumgestaltung, die durch eine auf das Wesentliche reduzierte Eleganz geprägt war, bildeten seine gestalterischen Prämissen. Eine Rampe führt zum ersten Geschoss des von Stützen getragenen Baus hinauf. Die zum Wohnbereich gehörende Dachterrasse ist heute in vielen Cityapartments zum Standard geworden. In Havanna nimmt ein Wohnhaus aus den 1950er Jahren genau diese Impulse Le Corbusiers auf.

Alvar Aalto entwarf 1933 die Stadtbibliothek im damals finnischen Viipuri, an der sich maßgeblich seine weichere skandinavische Variante der Moderne zeigt: Mit Holzpaneelen ist die wellenförmig geschwungene Decke verkleidet, und auch für die dreibeinigen Hocker verwendete er Schichtholz statt Stahlrohr. Entsprechend organisch, nämlich kreisrund, entwarf Aalto die berühmt gewordenen Oberlichter. Behaglichkeit bestimmt die Räume und nimmt der Sachlichkeit ihre Strenge. Das Haus Poul Kjærholms, der selbst zur skandinavischen Designavantgarde zählte, verkörpert, von seiner Frau Hanne Kjærholm entworfen, in Rungsted Kyst diese Philosophie. Michel Roux-Spitz schuf 1928 im Pariser Salon des Artistes Décorateurs einen Raum, der als Substrat des beginnenden Art déco gelten kann. Von der Bauhaus-Moderne beeinflusst, nahm diese Strömung auch andere Einflüsse wie den Kubismus oder afrikanische Ethnokunst in ihren dekorativen Stil auf. Möbel mit abgetrepptem Profil und der Einsatz von Spiegeln wurden stilbildend. Bevorzugte Materialien waren Stahl, Chrom und Bakelit, die Entwürfe sind kollektiver Ausdruck einer verspielteleganten Zukunftsvision. Das Pariser Apartment von Jean-Louis Deniot in seiner raffinierten Farbigkeit und eine Villa in Budapest spielen Variationen dieses Themas durch.

Weiterentwickler der Moderne in der Mitte des vergangenen Jahrhunderts waren Charles und Ray Eames in den USA. Kunststoffe spielen eine große Rolle bei der Entwicklung ihrer ergonomisch geformten Fiberglasstühle, die sich heute als Vintage-Möbel oder Neuauflagen von Vitra in Wohnungen von Madrid bis Buenos Aires finden. Der amerikanische Architekt Louis Kahn, der in den 1950ern seinen Stil entwickelte, und zwanzig Jahre später auch Tadao Ando in Japan kreierten Interieurs in Beton. Während diese bei Kahn etwas Gewichtiges haben, werden sie bei Ando so poetisch wie die Papierwände der traditionellen japanischen Raumteiler. Hijiri, ein kleines Wohnhaus bei Ito, fügt sich in diesen Kontext ein. Zaha Hadid bringt zu Beginn der 1990er Jahre mit ihren Entwürfen ein neues Tempo in die Architektur. Bei ihr werden Formen gebrochen und verzerrt, kurz: dekonstruiert. Wie ihre Möbel einen Wohnraum beschleunigen, sieht man in William Sawayas Mailänder Apartment. Der White Cube als Ausstellungskonzept nimmt seinen Anfang schon in der Moderne, doch in den Jahren um 2000 erlebte er einen wahren Boom. Die Idee, Objekte in weißen Räumen für sich allein sprechen zu lassen, schlägt sich auch in Wohnkonzepten nieder, so zum Beispiel bei dem Atelierhaus, das sich Elia Mangia in Mailand einrichtete, oder bei der alten Werfthalle, die das Künstlerpaar Sofie Lachaert und Luc d'Hanis in Tielrode zur Galerie mit Wohnräumen umfunktionierte.

Individuell, vernetzt, global – ein neuer international style entsteht

Traditionell ist es aber weniger das Wirken der Designavantgarde als der jeweilige Kulturkreis, der sich in der Gestaltung von Interieurs niederschlägt. So ist der irische Landsitz Hamwood ein typischer Vertreter des angelsächsischen Stils. Ganz anders, und doch mindestens genauso stark von Lokalkolorit geprägt, zeigt sich das Pekinger Haus des chinesischen Künstlers Shao Fan, der den Neubau mit antikem Mobiliar aus seiner Heimat füllte und durch diese Kombination ein Update chinesischer Wohnkultur schuf.

Doch gibt es auch Innenräume, die nicht unweigerlich auf ihre Umgebung schließen lassen, wie die nicht eben benachbarten Häuser im französischen Biarritz und im argentinischen Monte: Beide prägt ein rustikaler Look voller Charme. Und schließlich fanden wir eine ganze Reihe von Projekten, die wie aufeinander abgestimmt erscheinen, obwohl sie sich über den ganzen Globus verteilen. Da wäre zum Beispiel das Zuhause der Architektin Penny Loukakou in Athen: Mit seinen raumprägenden Trompe-l'œil-Fliesen und den schwarzen Designermöbeln könnte es sich ohne Weiteres in Mailand befinden. Dasselbe gilt für Filippa Knutssons Wohnung in einem historischen Stockholmer Stadthaus oder für Simon de Purys feudales Pied-à-terre in Paris. Man könnte sie gedanklich vielerorts ansiedeln, wie auch das von Deborah Berke gestaltete Loft in New York oder das Penthouse in Brüssel. Sie alle haben ein stilistisches Vokabular gemeinsam, an dem sich ein neuer Internationaler, ein Global Style ablesen lässt.

Ein weiteres Indiz für dessen Existenz: Gewissen Möbelstücken begegnet man auf den folgenden Seiten immer wieder, rund um die Welt. Die Stühle und der Tisch der Tulip-Sitzgruppe von Eero Saarinen gehören dazu, ebenso wie die Schalensitze des Ehepaars Eames oder Arne Jacobsens Stühle der Serie 7 aus Schichtholz. Vielleicht verdankt sich diese Internationalisierung unser aller Reisewut, vielleicht auch der Verbreitung von Designmagazinen. Gerade sie sorgen dafür, dass wegweisende Wohnungen wie die von Christian Liaigre in Paris rund um den Erdball gesehen und als Inspiration genutzt werden können. Liaigre und andere heute wirkende Designpioniere haben begonnen, eine zeitgenössische Wohnweltgeschichte zu schreiben, deren aktuellstes Kapitel diese TASCHEN-Kollektion festhält. Wie die Story wohl weitergehen wird? Wir halten Sie auf dem Laufenden.

INTRODUCTION

Cent intérieurs sur cinq continents

Des aménagements réussis ont toujours une histoire à raconter – celle du loft industriel, celle du penthouse luxueux ou celle d'un propriétaire rêvant d'une villa classique. Mais – et c'est le cas de cet ouvrage qui offre une véritable anthologie des intérieurs –, ils parlent aussi de l'Histoire. Concrètement, notre reportage en images tente d'analyser comment les hommes vivent dans leurs demeures au début du 21e siècle. À quoi ressemblent une salle à manger zurichoise et une salle de bains à Niigata, au Japon ? De quelle couleur sont les murs du bungalow du collectionneur d'art à Miami et quelles sont celles qui nous attendent pour le thé de cinq heures à Saint-Pétersbourg ? Les portes s'ouvrent dans cent endroits sélectionnés sous toutes les latitudes. Et l'étonnement nous saisit.

Qui dit emplacement différent, dit perspective différente. Les appartements de ville, ceux qui se trouvent dans un bloc d'habitation avec vue sur le panorama de Singapour, alternent avec des paysages de rêve, par exemple les archipels de la côte suédoise, près de Stockholm, là où une maison de vacances n'est entourée que de rochers, de forêts de pins et d'eau. Quelle que soit la topographie, elle influence l'atmosphère qui règne dans la maison. Sylvia Avontuut qualifie à juste titre d'œuvre d'art totale les fenêtres panoramiques de son appartement, qui donnent sur le port d'Amsterdam. Quant à l'époque de construction, elle est tout aussi importante pour le caractère des pièces. De nombreux appartements présentés sur les pages qui suivent se trouvent dans des bâtiments construits à la fin du 19e siècle, que ce soit à Istanbul, à Paris ou Barcelone. Leurs occupants sont en quelque sorte des conservateurs qui ont insufflé une vie nouvelle aux vieilles pierres. D'autres veillent, dans le même esprit de préservation, sur les maisons de l'époque moderne, construites durant le mouvement révolutionnaire du Style International et qui sont appréciées pour cette audace. Et il faut bien sûr nommer ensuite les constructions contemporaines, innovantes sur le plan technique et fabriquées sur mesure pour les besoins des propriétaires, telle la villa de Dresde ou la maison sur pilotis de Nagano. Mais qu'il s'agisse d'un bâtiment flambant neuf ou classé monument historique, la décoration historique est partout influencée par une révolution de l'habitat dont on observe les effets depuis plus d'un siècle.

Comment l'habitat est devenu ce qu'il est

Lorsqu'il s'agit de décorer une maison aujourd'hui, de célèbres intérieurs d'autrefois servent sans cesse de matrices stylistiques et les idées qu'ils propagent continuent ainsi de vivre. Cela vaut aussi pour les intérieurs présentés dans cet livre, les influences auxquelles ils sont soumis étant extrêmement variées. On trouve ici par exemple la Red House de William Morris à Bexleyheath, en Angleterre, une maison qui marque en 1859 le début du mouvement Arts and Crafts sur le plan de la construction. Morris se bat contre les produits industriels médiocres en leur opposant de l'artisanat de la meilleure qualité. Il meuble sa maison de pièces réalisées par des menuisiers et d'objets de style néogothique fabriqués à la main. L'appartement moscovite montre les influences d'un mouvement réformateur haut en couleur.

En revanche, le pavillon de Barcelone de Ludwig Mies van der Rohe rompt en 1929 avec les idées reçues et sonne l'avènement de l'ère moderne. Tandis qu'une construction aux fines poutres d'acier ouvre les espaces, les volumes semblent s'écouler autour des fines parois. Le marbre, l'onyx et le travertin donnent au bâtiment une dignité qui évoque celle des temples antiques. La chauffeuse de cuir et le tabouret assorti, créés pour le pavillon, sont aujourd'hui des classiques. Une villa de São Paulo abrite une version élaborée du vocabulaire formel créé à cette époque.

Le Corbusier construit à la même époque, à partir de 1928, la Villa Savoye près de Paris. Des murs blancs et leurs fenêtres courant d'un bout à l'autre, les façades vitrées et une décoration intérieure que caractérise une élégance réduite à l'essentiel constituent les prémisses de son travail d'architecte. Une rampe mène au premier étage du bâtiment sur pilotis. Le toit-jardin qui faisait partie de l'espace de vie est aujourd'hui la norme dans de nombreux appartements de ville. À La Havane, une maison d'habitation des années 1950 reprend exactement ces idées de Le Corbusier. En 1933, Alvar Aalto a dessiné la bibliothèque municipale de Viipuri, ville finlandaise à l'époque, qui concrétise sa version scandinave, plus douce, du mouvement moderne : le plafond ondulé est revêtu de panneaux de bois, et il a aussi utilisé du bois lamellé et non du tube d'acier pour les tabourets à trois pieds. Aalto a dessiné des ouvertures zénithales circulaires, devenues célèbres, dans cet esprit organique. Les pièces sont caractérisées par un confort qui ôte de leur sévérité à ces espaces fonctionnels. Dessinée par sa femme Hanne Kjærholm, la maison de Poul Kjærholm – lui-même l'un des designers scandinaves d'avant-garde –, incarne cette philosophie à Rungsted Kyst. Michel Roux-Spitz a créé en

1928 à Paris, au Salon des Artistes Décorateurs, une pièce qui peut être considérée comme le substrat de l'Art Déco tout jeune alors. Influencé par le modernisme du Bauhaus, ce mouvement intègre aussi d'autres influences, telles le cubisme ou l'art africain. L'utilisation de miroirs et de meubles aux angles étagés fera école. Les matériaux de prédilection sont l'acier, le chrome et la bakélite, les créations sont l'expression collective d'une vision du futur à la fois élégante et ludique. L'appartement parisien aux couleurs raffinées de Jean-Louis Deniot et une villa de Budapest jouent intensément des variations sur ce thème.

Au milieu du siècle dernier, Charles et Ray Eames vont plus loin encore aux États-Unis. Les matériaux synthétiques jouent un grand rôle dans l'élaboration de leurs chaises ergonomiques en fibre de verre que l'on trouve aujourd'hui dans nombre d'appartements, de Madrid à Buenos Aires, achetées comme meubles vintage ou nouvelles éditions de Vitra. L'architecte américain Louis Kahn qui a mis son style au point au cours des années 1950 et, vingt ans plus tard, Tadao Ando au Japon, créent des intérieurs en béton. S'ils ont quelque chose de monumental chez Kahn, ils deviennent chez Ando aussi poétiques que les cloisons de papier des maisons japonaises traditionnelles. Higiri, une petite maison d'habitation à Ito-shi, trouve sa place dans ce contexte. Au début des années 1990, Zaha Hadid donne un nouveau rythme à l'architecture. Chez elles, les formes sont rompues, déformées, en un mot déconstruites. On peut voir dans l'appartement milanais de William Sawayas comment ses meubles « accélèrent » un espace d'habitation. Le White Cube vu comme un concept d'exposition apparaît déjà à l'époque moderne, mais il va connaître un véritable boom autour de l'an 2000. L'idée de laisser parler pour eux-mêmes des objets dans des espaces blancs se répercute aussi dans l'habitation, par exemple dans l'atelier que s'est aménagé Elia Mangia à Milan ou dans l'ancien hall de chantier naval transformé en galerie avec pièces à vivre par le couple d'artistes Sofie Lachaert et Luc d'Hanis à Tielrode

Individuel, connecté, global – la naissance d'un nouveau Style International

Il n'empêche que la décoration des intérieurs est traditionnellement moins marquée par les effets de l'avant-garde du design que par ceux de l'aire culturelle. Ainsi le manoir irlandais Hamwood est un représentant typique du style anglo-saxon. Tout à fait différente, mais reflétant là aussi la couleur locale, la nouvelle maison de l'artiste chinois Shao Fan à Pékin : il l'a remplie de meubles anciens de son pays, mettant à jour la culture de l'habitat chinois par ce mariage du moderne et de l'ancien. Il existe toutefois aussi des intérieurs dont on ne saurait dire où ils sont situés. C'est le cas de maisons qui ne sont vraiment pas voisines, l'une à Biarritz, l'autre à Monte, en Argentine, toutes deux caractérisées par un confort rustique. Et nous avons finalement trouvé une série de constructions dont le vocabulaire formel semble concorder, bien qu'elles soient réparties aux quatre coins de la planète. Ce serait par exemple la demeure de l'architecte Penny Loukalou à Athènes : avec ses carreaux en trompe-l'œil qui définissent les pièces et ses meubles design noirs, elle pourrait très bien se trouver à Milan. De même l'appartement de Filippa Knutsson dans une maison historique de Stockholm ou le pied-à-terre féodal de Simon de Pury à Paris – on les imaginerait très bien dans d'autres endroits. Qu'il s'agisse du loft new-yorkais de Deborah Berke ou du penthouse de Bruxelles, ils ont un vocabulaire stylistique commun dans lequel on découvre la présence d'un nouveau style international, un style global. Un autre signe de son existence : sur les pages qui suivent, on retrouve sans cesse certains meubles, dans des demeures très éloignées l'une de l'autre. Les chaises et la table Tulip d'Eero Saarinen ainsi que les sièges des Eames ou encore les chaises de la série 7 en bois lamellé d'Arne Jacobsen. Cette globalisation est éventuellement le fruit de notre goût des voyages, elle est peut-être aussi due à la généralisation des magazines de design. Grâce à eux, en effet, des appartements novateurs comme celui de Christian Liaigre à Paris sont vus dans le monde entier et servent d'inspiration. Liaigre et d'autres pionniers du design actifs aujourd'hui ont commencé à écrire une histoire mondiale de l'habitat contemporain dont cette collection TASCHEN présente le chapitre du jour. Et ensuite ? Que va-t-il se passer ? Nous vous tenons au courant.

ACAPULCO
MEXICO

Bold is Beautiful

Perched high above Acapulco Bay, architect John Lautner's Arango Residence is vertiginous, dramatic and original. For Lautner expert Frank Escher, "what is so beautiful is that it feels like an extension of the topography." The upper level is cantilevered out from the steep slope. Below, boulders thrust inside to become bedroom walls. Completed in 1973, the house was conceived as a weekend retreat. The initial intent was to enclose the upper living deck with glass. The client, however, decided the climate was so mild that it should be left open. Instead, Lautner ringed it with a moat. "He wanted to create the feeling of water flowing into the bay below," recalls Helena Arahuete, who assisted on the project. The free-flowing platform, meanwhile, was devised to block out views of certain buildings. "The concept," she adds, "was to create a feeling of unlimited, open space."

Hoch über der Bucht von Acapulco erhebt sich schwindelerregend, dramatisch und in überwältigender Originalität das Bauwerk Arango Residence des Architekten John Lautner. Für den Lautner-Experten Frank Escher ist „das Schöne daran, dass man es als Erweiterung der Landschaft empfindet". Die obere Ebene ist in den steilen Abhang hineinge-schnitten. Unterhalb wurde Felsgestein zur Bildung der Schlafzimmerwände in das Innere einbezogen. Das 1973 voll-endete Haus war als Feriendomizil geplant. Ursprünglich sollte der obere Wohnbereich verglast werden. Der Auftraggeber beschloss jedoch, ihn angesichts des milden Klimas offen zu lassen. Lautner umgab ihn daraufhin statt-dessen mit einem Wasserlauf. „Er wollte den Eindruck von in die Bucht hinabfließendem Wasser hervorrufen", erinnert sich Helena Arahuete, die Lautner bei dem Projekt assistierte. Die frei schwebende Anlage der Plattform wiederum sollte den Blick auf bestimmte Gebäude verstellen. „Das Konzept war, ein Gefühl grenzenloser Weite zu erzeugen."

Haut perchée au-dessus de la baie d'Acapulco, Arango Residence, de l'architecte John Lautner, est vertigineuse, spec-taculaire et originale. Pour Frank Escher, spécialiste de Lautner : « Ce qui est superbe, c'est qu'on dirait une extension de la topographie. » Le niveau supérieur saille de la pente escarpée. Plus bas, des rochers ont été intégrés pour servir de murs aux chambres. Achevée en 1973, la maison fut conçue comme une retraite pour les week-ends. Le niveau supé-rieur devait être protégé par des baies vitrées mais, compte tenu de la douceur du climat, le propriétaire a décidé de le laisser ouvert aux éléments. Lautner l'a ceint de douves afin, selon Helena Arahuete qui l'a assisté, « de donner une impression d'eau s'écoulant dans la baie en contrebas ». Les formes fluides de la plateforme cachent la vue de certains bâtiments, le concept étant de « créer un espace ouvert et infini ».

P. 15 A painting by Jordi Boldó hangs above a copper cabinet created by interior designer Arthur Elrod, for whom Lautner built another famous house, in Palm Springs. • Ein Gemälde von Jordi Boldó hängt über einem Sideboard aus Kupfer nach einem Design von Arthur Elrod. Für den Innenarchitekten und Designer Elrod entwarf Lautner ein nicht weniger berühmtes Haus in Palm Springs. • Une toile de Jordi Boldó au-dessus d'un meuble en cuivre créé par le décorateur Arthur Elrod, pour qui Lautner a construit une autre maison célèbre à Palm Springs.

PP. 16–17 The upper level is home to an open concrete living terrace, surrounded by a six-foot-wide moat, in which you can swim. The platform is accessed at the entrance by a small bridge. • Die obere Ebene nimmt eine offene Wohnterrasse ein, umgeben von einem 1,80 Meter breiten Wasserlauf, in dem man sogar schwimmen kann. Zu dieser Ebene gelangt man vom Eingang her über eine geschwungene Brücke. • Le niveau supérieur accueille une terrasse en béton servant de séjour ouvert aux éléments, entourée d'une douve de 1,80 m de large dans laquelle on peut nager. On y accède depuis l'entrée par une passerelle aux lignes ondoyantes.

↖ Mexican artist Antonio Farreny created a number of built-in elements for the house. Among them, this geometric metal sideboard. • Der mexikanische Künstler Antonio Farreny schuf für das Haus eine Reihe von Einbau-Elementen, darunter dieses Sideboard aus Metall. • L'artiste mexicain Antonio Farreny a créé plusieurs éléments encastrés pour la maison, dont cette console géométrique en métal.

→ A steel sculpture by Eduardo Wegman mirrors the architecture's curvaceous lines. • Eine Stahlskulptur des Künstlers Eduardo Wegman wiederholt den Kurvenschwung der Architektur. • Une sculpture en acier d'Eduardo Wegman reprend les courbes de l'architecture.

← Geometric forms such as these on concrete are a trademark of architect John Lautner's work. • Geometrische Formen, hier auf Beton, sind das Markenzeichen des Architekten John Lautner. • Les formes géométriques, ici sur béton, sont la marque de fabrique de l'architecte John Lautner.

↓ The curved, sloping concrete roof is anchored into the hill on both ends. The roof is low on the hill side and high on the Bay side, allowing a great view of the sky and the ocean. • Das geschwungene und geneigte Betondach ist auf der Hangseite im Boden verankert, während es auf der Meerseite weit nach oben gezogen ist und so eine einzigartige Sicht auf den Ozean und Himmel ermöglicht. • Le toit en béton courbe et pentu est ancré dans le sol, bas du côté de la colline et tiré vers le haut du côté de la mer, ce qui permet une vue unique sur l'océan et le ciel.

AMSTERDAM
THE NETHERLANDS

Rooms with a View

In 2002, no architecture magazine was complete without pictures of MVRDV's rectangular Silodam block, which calls to mind a cargo ship stacked with containers. One of those lucky enough to live in the building is Sylvia Avontuur, director of PR agency Press Only, who shares the apartment with her two daughters. "Inside, the focal point is the North Sea Canal," she says. "The passing ships are the most important part of the decor." Bespoke mahogany units and contemporary designs provide a restrained counterpoint to the unique panorama, while shades of beige and dark wood selected by interior designer Marius Haverkamp create a palette reminiscent of sepia-toned vintage photographs.

Bilder des Gebäuderiegels Silodam von MVRDV, der wie ein großes Containerschiff am Hafen liegt, waren 2002 in jedem Architekturmagazin abgedruckt. Glücklich, wer darin wohnt – wie die Direktorin der PR-Agentur Press Only, Sylvia Avontuur, mit ihren beiden Töchtern. „Im Inneren dreht sich alles um den Nordseekanal", sagt sie. „Die vorbeifahrenden Schiffe sind das wichtigste Dekor." Mit maßgeschreinerten Mahagoni-Einbauten und zeitgenössischem Mobiliar wurde dieses einzigartige Panorama zurückhaltend ergänzt. Interiordesigner Marius Haverkamp kombinierte Beige und dunkle Holztöne zu Raumensembles, die an historische Fotografien denken lassen.

En 2002, on pouvait voir dans tous les magazines d'architecture des photos de la barre d'immeuble de MVRDV, qui semble amarrée au quai comme un grand bateau conteneur. Sylvia Avontuur, directrice de l'agence de relations publiques Press Only, et ses deux filles ont la chance d'y habiter. « À l'intérieur, le centre d'intérêt est le canal de la mer du Nord », dit-elle. Le plus important dans le décor, ce sont les bateaux qui passent. » Des meubles intégrés fabriqués sur mesure en acajou et des pièces au design contemporain complètent avec retenue ce panorama unique. L'architecte d'intérieur Marius Haverkamp a combiné le beige et les teintes de bois foncées pour créer des ensembles évoquant les photographies historiques.

P. 23 In the bedroom, only the horns of passing ships can be heard. The Mushroom chair and matching footstool were designed by Pierre Paulin for Artifort. • Im Schlafzimmer hört man nur das Tuten der vorbeiziehenden Schiffe. Den Mushroom-Sessel mit Fußhocker entwarf Pierre Paulin für Artifort. • Dans la chambre à coucher, on n'entend que les avertisseurs des navires qui passent. Le fauteuil Mushroom et son pouf sont signés Pierre Paulin pour Artifort.

↑ Hung above the Meridiani sofa is a photograph from the series *Hidden Beauty* by Mirjam Bleeker. • Eine Arbeit aus der Fotoserie *Hidden Beauty* von Mirjam Bleeker hängt über dem Sofa von Meridiani. • Une photo de la série *Hidden Beauty* de Mirjam Bleeker au-dessus du canapé de Meridiani.

→ Next to the double doors leading to the bedroom is a Casala chair by Alexander Begge. • Der Stuhl neben der zweiflügeligen Tür zum Schlafzimmer ist ein Entwurf von Alexander Begge für Casala. • La chaise à côté de la porte à deux battants qui mène à la chambre à coucher est un projet d'Alexander Begge pour Casala.

← For the kitchen, Piet-Jan van den Kommer combined acid-treated mahogany with Wolf appliances from the US. • Die Küche entwarf Piet-Jan van den Kommer. Er kombinierte dabei säurebehandeltes Mahagoni mit den wuchtigen Geräten der US-Marke Wolf. • Piet-Jan van den Kommer a dessiné la cuisine, combinant de l'acajou décapé à l'acide à des appareils de la marque américaine Wolf.

↖ A mahogany staircase joins the lower and upper floors; the windows are east-facing. • Eine Mahagonitreppe führt vom ersten ins zweite Geschoss, die Fenster orientieren sich nach Osten. • Un escalier en acajou relie le premier au second étage, les fenêtres sont orientées vers l'est.

↓ An Artemide pendant light hangs over the custom-made table. The Knoll chairs were designed by Harry Bertoia. • Die Leuchte von Artemide hängt über einem maßgeschreinerten Tisch. Die Stühle entwarf Harry Bertoia für Knoll. • Un plafonnier d'Artemide au-dessus d'une table fabriquée sur mesure. Les chaises sont Harry Bertoia pour Knoll.

← The bar stools next to the granite-topped kitchen island are from the 1950s, the photograph is by Mirjam Bleeker. • Am Küchenblock mit Granitarbeitsplatte stehen Barstühle aus den 1950er Jahren, die Fotoarbeit stammt von Mirjam Bleeker. • Des tabourets de bar des années 1950 devant le bloc cuisine avec plan de travail en granit, la photo sur le mur est de Mirjam Bleeker.

→ Avontuur's daughters use the Eames table in the upstairs living room for craft activities; around it are Alexander Begge's Casalino chairs for Casala. • Im oberen Wohnzimmer nutzen die Töchter zum Basteln den Eames-Tisch. Casalino-Stühle von Alexander Begge für Casala. • Dans le séjour du haut, les filles bricolent sur la table Eames, assises sur des chaises Casalino dessinées par Alexander Begge pour Casala.

"The panoramic view of the North Sea Canal is the most important picture in the apartment." SYLVIA AVONTUUR

„Der Panoramablick über den Nordseekanal ist das wichtigste Kunstwerk in unserer Wohnung."
« La vue panoramique sur le canal de la mer du Nord est la plus grande œuvre d'art dans notre appartement. »

ATHENS
GREECE

Greek Chic

Impressed by its dignity, Penny Loukakou of Architectones02 bought this classical building in the district of Pangrati in 2005 and set about turning it into a new home for her family of four, transforming the severely neglected property with sensitivity and contemporary ideas. She also built an extension of three bedrooms and two bathrooms to the original 19th-century structure. Inside, the interplay of black and white is a key theme, most notably in the handcrafted cement-tile floors that dominate the living area—their pattern reminds the owner of the graphic art of M. C. Escher.

Die Würde des klassizistischen Wohnhauses im Stadtteil Pangrati verleitete die Architektin Penny Loukakou von Architectones02 dazu, es im Jahr 2005 zu kaufen. Sie nahm sich des stark vernachlässigten Gebäudes aus dem 19. Jahrhundert an und verwandelte es mit Feingefühl und modernen Ideen in das neue Zuhause ihrer vierköpfigen Familie. Ein Anbau mit drei Schlafzimmern und zwei Bädern komplettiert die Renovierung. Die Innenräume sind vom Spiel zwischen Schwarz und Weiß geprägt. Vor allem der Fußboden aus handgefertigten Zementfliesen definiert die Räume, sein Muster erinnert die Hausherrin an die Augen täuschenden Grafiken von M. C. Escher.

Fascinée par la noblesse du bâtiment néoclassique situé dans le quartier de Pangrati, l'architecte Penny Loukakou du cabinet Architectones02 l'a acheté en 2005. Prenant les choses en mains, avec beaucoup de sensibilité et des idées modernes, elle a transformé cette maison du 19ᵉ siècle laissée à l'abandon en nouveau domicile pour une famille de quatre personnes. Une extension abritant trois chambres à coucher et deux salles de bains complète le projet. Le jeu entre le noir et le blanc définit les espaces intérieurs. Le sol en carreaux de ciment faits à la main domine les pièces, ses motifs rappellent à la maîtresse de maison les dessins en trompe-l'œil de M. C. Escher.

P. 31 Cement tiles in black, white and gray lend a graphic note to the living area. • Die Zementfliesen in Schwarz, Weiß und Grau geben dem Wohnraum eine grafische Dynamik. • Les carreaux en ciment noirs, blancs et gris structurent graphiquement les espaces.

← The chairs and table are from Habitat, the lamp is a Bertjan Pot design for Moooi. • Stühle und Tisch der Essgruppe kommen von Habitat, die Lampe entwarf Bertjan Pot für Moooi. • Les chaises et la table viennent de chez Habitat, la lampe a été dessinée par Bertjan Pot pour Moooi.

↑ Keen travellers, the owners had a vinyl wall sticker depicting a map of the world placed behind the bed. • Die Hausbesitzer reisen gerne und so schmückt eine Weltkarte aus Vinylklebefolie die Wand hinter dem Bett. • Les propriétaires aimant voyager, un planisphère sur feuille de vinyle adhésive orne le mur au-dessus du lit.

↑ Crowning the stairwell is a steel-and-glass structure whose swing door leads out onto the roof terrace. • Eine Konstruktion aus Stahl und Glas schließt das Treppenhaus ab und führt durch die Schwingtür zur Dachterrasse. • Une construction en acier et verre ferme la cage d'escalier de la maison; une porte battante s'ouvre sur le toit-terrasse.

PP. 36–37 In the living room, the fireplace is set into the bottom of a white projector wall. • Die weiße Kaminwand im Wohnzimmer eignet sich gut als Projektionsfläche für den Beamer. • Au-dessus de la cheminée du séjour, un grand écran de projection pour le vidéo-projecteur.

↖ In the bathroom, the color scheme changes: the waterproof lime plaster is tinted light blue. • Im Bad verändert sich das Farbschema: Der wasserfeste Kalkgipsputz ist blau eingefärbt. • La salle de bains offre une autre palette : l'enduit en plâtre imperméable est teinté en bleu.

← The elegant wooden kitchen units were custom-made to a design by Architectones02. • Die elegante Holzeinbauküche ist eine Maßanfertigung nach Entwürfen von Architectones02. • L'élégante cuisine intégrée a été réalisée sur mesure d'après des dessins d'Architectones02.

BADALING
CHINA

Freedom in a Cage

China's Great Wall, constructed between the 5th century BC and the 16th century, was an architectural response to an ancient challenge—the threat of invasion. The Commune by the Great Wall, built in 2002, represents a more modern challenge. First, each of the 12 architects commissioned for the project had to design a modern house that could stand in the shadow of one of the world's most enduring landmarks. In addition, they had to build it for just one million dollars, using Chinese construction materials. The result? Some of the finest avant-garde Asian architecture around. Japanese architect Kengo Kuma's Bamboo Wall pays homage to Asia's most versatile and evocative building material. Bamboo's lightness makes a perfect counterpoint to the solidity of the Great Wall (the project is located some 43 miles north of Beijing). Movable bamboo walls line the facade, affording open views of the rugged countryside.

Die Chinesische Mauer wurde zwischen dem 5. Jahrhundert v. Chr. und dem 16. Jahrhundert erbaut. Sie diente als Schutzwall gegen nördliche Grenzvölker. 2002 erhielt das Weltwunder eine würdige Ergänzung: die Commune by the Great Wall an der Großen Mauer in Badaling, 70 Kilometer nördlich von Peking. Ein Dutzend Architekten, die in Asien bauen, erhielten den Auftrag, je ein Haus zu entwerfen, das visuell mit der Großen Mauer harmoniert, aus chinesischen Baumaterialien besteht und nicht mehr als eine Million Dollar kostet. Entstanden ist ein außergewöhnlicher Komplex asiatischer Avantgarde-Architektur. Das Bamboo Wall, ein Werk des japanischen Architekten Kengo Kuma, ist eine Hommage an den Bambus, dem wohl typischsten Baumaterial für Asien. Seine Leichtigkeit bildet einen Kontrast zur massiven Großen Mauer. So umzäunen das Haus mehrere Bambus-Schiebewände, die einen Blick auf die unberührte Landschaft erlauben.

La Grande Muraille de Chine fut la réponse architecturale à un vieux défi : les invasions mongoles. Inaugurée en 2002, la Commune by the Great Wall relève un défi plus moderne. 12 architectes furent chargés de construire une maison moderne capable de cohabiter avec l'un des monuments les plus célèbres du monde. Chacun disposait d'un budget d'un million de dollars et devait utiliser des matériaux chinois. Le résultat ? Un complexe d'habitations digne d'un musée des fleurons de l'architecture asiatique d'avant-garde. La réalisation du japonais Kengo Kuma rend hommage au matériau le plus polyvalent et évocateur d'Asie. La légèreté du bambou en fait le parfait contrepoint à la masse solide de la Grande Muraille (la maison se dresse près du tronçon de Badaling, à 70 km au nord de Pékin). Les cloisons amovibles de la façade offrent des vues dégagées sur la campagne. Bamboo Wall compte six chambres, deux passerelles intérieures en pierre et un salon de thé.

← Kuma balances "delicacy and rough-ness." Here dark stone floors contrast with the airy bamboo supports. • Kuma setzt auf Kontraste: Poliertes trifft auf Raues, wie hier beim Boden aus Natur-stein und den luftigen Bambusstützen. • Kuma équilibre la « délicatesse et la rugosité ». Ici, des dalles en pierre fon-cée contrastent avec les colonnes aériennes en bambou.

→ One of six bedrooms in Bamboo Wall. Each bedroom has a private bath. • Eines der sechs Schlafzimmer mit eigenem Badezimmer im Bamboo Wall. • Une des six chambres à coucher. Chacune a sa propre salle de bains.

↘ Like the nearby Great Wall, the Commune's architecture adapts to the contours of the landscape. • Nach dem Vorbild der Chinesischen Mauer passt sich die Architektur dem Landschafts-verlauf an. • Inspirée de la Grande Muraille, l'architecture suit les formes du paysage.

↓ The location in the remote "Walnut Valley", an hour's drive from Beijing, gua-rantees a meditative tranquillity. • Die Lage im abgeschiedenen „Walnusstal", eine Stunde von Peking entfernt, bietet meditative Ruhe. • Le site, dans la « val-lée des noix » isolée, à une heure de Pékin, offre un calme propice à la méditation.

P. 39 Sunshine streaming through tall bamboo lends serenity to all the interior spaces. • Meditatives Lichtspiel zwi-schen den Bambusstäben sorgt für eine friedliche Atmosphäre in allen Räumen. • Les rayons obliques du soleil entre les hauts bambous donnent aux pièces une atmosphère paisible et sereine.

PP. 42–43 Large plate-glass windows in the dining room link the exterior bam-boo walls to the ones within. • Große Wandfenster im Esszimmer machen aus den inneren und äußeren Bambuswän-den optisch eine Einheit. • Dans la salle à manger, les grandes baies vitrées unissent les cloisons en bambou de l'extérieur et celles de l'intérieur.

BARCELONA
SPAIN

Bohemian Splendor

After months of eyeing an unused terrace of the building next door to his apartment, Lázaro Rosa-Violán eventually asked if the flat to which it belongs was available. The answer was yes. The interior designer left its basic layout untouched, but introduced his own designs along with finds from elsewhere. Now the apartment is living space, furniture laboratory and gallery, all in one. Traces of its prior use as the premises of a textiles company still remain, however—such as in the former lobby, now a bathroom, where the wooden paneling of one of the walls conceals an old safe.

Monatelang schaute der Interiordesigner Lázaro Rosa-Violán von seinem Zuhause auf die ungenutzte Terrasse im Nachbarhaus. Als er schließlich nachfragte, ob die dazugehörige Wohnung frei sei, fiel die Antwort positiv aus. An der Grundstruktur änderte er nichts, stattdessen brachte er seine eigenen Entwürfe und Funde von anderen Orten hierher. So wurde das Apartment sein Lebensraum, Möbellabor und Ausstellungsort in einem. Dabei kann man die frühere Nutzung als Sitz einer Textilfirma immer noch erahnen – zum Beispiel in der ehemaligen Lobby, heute ein Bad mit holzvertäfelter Wand, hinter der sich ein alter Safe verbirgt.

Pendant des mois, l'architecte d'intérieur Lázaro Rosa Violán a contemplé de son appartement la terrasse inutilisée de la maison voisine. Il a fini par demander si le logement était inoccupé et la réponse a été positive. Il n'a pas modifié la structure de base, se contentant d'apporter ici ses projets pour d'autres endroits et ses trouvailles. L'appartement est ainsi devenu tout à la fois un espace de vie, un laboratoire de meubles et un lieu d'exposition. Ceci dit, on devine encore qu'il a abrité autrefois une usine textile, par exemple dans l'ancienne entrée devenue une salle de bains dont le mur lambrissé dissimule un vieux coffre-fort.

P. 45 The actual kitchen door was overlaid with a second door that Rosa-Violán liked better; above it is a horned bison skull. • Auf der eigentlichen Küchentür sitzt eine zweite, die Rosa-Violán schöner fand; darüber eine Bisontrophäe. • Rosa-Violán trouvait cette porte plus belle que la porte originale de la cuisine et l'a placée dessus. Au-dessus un crâne de bison avec ses cornes.

← The lights in the hall echo a Rosa-Violán design for a hotel, and an old nautical map leans against a mirror. • Die Flurlampen wiederholen Entwürfe des Besitzers für ein Hotel, am Spiegel lehnt eine Seekarte. • Les lampes du corridor ont été à l'origine dessinées pour un hôtel, une carte maritime encadrée est posée sur le miroir.

↓ The mirrored doors behind the four-poster bed were salvaged from an old jewelry store. • Aus einem alten Schmuckladen wurden die Spiegeltüren hinter dem Bett gerettet. • Les portes-miroirs derrière le lit ont été récupérées dans une vieille bijouterie.

→ Quite a few furniture items in the living room are the designer's own work. • Mehrere Möbel im Wohnzimmer sind Eigenentwürfe des Designers. • Le propriétaire a dessiné quelques-uns des meubles du séjour.

↑ A Japanese oil painting from the 19th century adorns the spacious kitchen. • Ein japanisches Ölgemälde aus dem 19. Jahrhundert dekoriert die Küche. • Une peinture à l'huile japonaise du 19ᵉ siècle décore la cuisine.

→ The doors in the background, now part of a cupboard, are from another of Rosa-Violán's apartments. • Die Tür im Hintergrund stammt aus einer anderen Wohnung Rosa-Violáns und dient nun als Schrankfront. • Les portes du fond viennent d'un autre appartement de Rosa-Violán et dissimulent maintenant un placard.

← The wall paneling conceals a safe from the time when the apartment was a business premises. • Hinter der Wandtäfelung verbirgt sich der Safe des ehemaligen Firmensitzes. • Derrière le lambris se cache le coffre-fort de l'ancienne entreprise.

↑ A roof of teak lattice was built as a sun shade for the terrace. • Das Sonnendach der Terrasse wurde aus Teak gefertigt. • La terrasse couverte a été réalisée en teck.

→ In the oak parquet-floored hall stands a replica Henry Moore sculpture. • Im Flur mit Eichenparkett steht die Replik einer Skulptur von Henry Moore. • Dans le couloir parqueté de chêne, la reproduction d'une sculpture d'Henry Moore.

BEIJING
CHINA

New Tradition

The artist Shao Fan, known for his radical deconstructions of traditional Chinese furniture, had always dreamed of building his own house. He bought a large tract of land in a suburban Beijing neighborhood. Dividing the property among himself and five friends, Shao Fan designed a complex that challenges the norms of Western-style housing, and updates the traditional Chinese approach to living space. Calling his building style "contemporary courtyard living"—in effect he has modernized the hutong and moved it to the suburbs. Shao's own house is the star of the complex, which is surrounded by a high wall made of blue brick. As in the traditional Beijing courtyard house, or si he yuan, the living area consists of a series of rooms arranged around two main courtyards—in this instance, one containing rare plum trees, a popular subject in Chinese poetry and painting. Inside, Shao's own chair sculptures seem to float in midair, alongside perfect ancient Buddha statues and an 8,000-year-old piece of jade. The decor is spare, but this house feels full, for it holds within its blue walls all the promise of contemporary China.

Der Künstler Shao Fan, bekannt für beeindruckende Dekonstruktionen traditioneller chinesischer Möbel, träumte schon immer davon, sein eigenes Haus zu bauen. Er erwarb ein großes Grundstück in einem Pekinger Vorort und teilte es zwischen sich und fünf Freunden auf. Der Gebäudekomplex, den er dafür entworfen hat, stellt die Prinzipien der westlichen Bauart auf den Kopf und revitalisiert gleichzeitig die Lebensweise im Hutong, den er in die Vorstadt gebracht hat. Shao Fans Haus ist das herausragendste auf dem Grundstück, das von hohen Mauern aus blauem Backstein umgeben wird. Wie in einem traditionellen Pekinger Innenhofhaus, einem si he yuan, sind die Wohnräume um zwei große Innenhöfe angelegt. In einem stehen seltene Pflaumenbäume, im alten China ein beliebtes Motiv in Dichtkunst und Malerei. Im Inneren des Hauses „schweben" Shaos Stuhl-Skulpturen neben antiken Buddha-Statuen und einem 8000 Jahre alten Stück Jade. Die Einrichtung ist spärlich, enthält aber alle Verheißungen des neuen China.

L'artiste Shao Fan, connu pour ses déconstructions radicales de mobilier traditionnel chinois, avait toujours rêvé de construire sa maison de bout en bout. Après avoir acquis un grand terrain dans une banlieue de Pékin, décrite par sa femme Anna comme «pleine d'étrangers», il l'a divisé avec cinq autres amis. Puis, il a bâti un complexe qui défie les normes occidentales du développement immobilier privé tout en rénovant le concept chinois de l'espace de vie. S'il a baptisé son style «vie moderne en cour», c'est qu'il s'agit d'une modernisation du hutong. Sa propre demeure est le joyau du complexe, ceint d'un haut mur en briques bleues. Comme dans la maison pékinoise traditionnelle, ou si he yuan, les pièces sont disposées autour de deux cours, dont l'une accueille des prunus mume, un motif apprécié dans la peinture et la poésie chinoise. À l'intérieur, ses sculptures chaises semblent flotter aux côtés de bouddhas anciens et d'un morceau de jade vieux de 8000 ans. En dépit de son décor dépouillé, la maison respire la plénitude, chargée de toutes les promesses de la Chine contemporaine.

P. 53 *The Cloud,* a Shao Fan oil painting, hangs above an ensemble of antique Chinese furniture. • Über antiken chinesischen Möbeln hängt *Die Wolke,* ein Ölgemälde von Shao Fan. • Au-dessus de meubles chinois anciens est suspendu *Le Nuage,* une peinture à l'huile de Shao Fan.

↑ The acrylic tabletop is a Shao Fan design. His wife Anna Liu Li found the antique Chinese Buddhas in a Hong Kong shop. • Der Tisch mit Acrylplatte ist ein Entwurf von Shao Fan. Die antiken chinesischen Buddhas hat seine Frau Anna Liu Li in einem Geschäft in Hongkong aufgestöbert. • La table en plateau acrylique a été conçu par Shao Fan. Son épouse Anna Liu Li a découvert les bouddhas antiques chinois dans une boutique de Hong Kong.

← A guest bedroom featuring a 200-year-old Ching Dynasty mahogany bed. • Ein Gästezimmer mit einem 200 Jahre alten Mahagonibett aus der Qing-Dynastie. • Dans une chambre d'amis, un lit en acajou de la dynastie Qing, vieux de 200 ans.

↓ In another living area, Shao Fan designed this wood table with two levels, to produce a "floating" effect. • Dieser Holztisch mit zwei „schwebenden" Ebenen wurde ebenfalls von Shao Fan entworfen. • Shao Fan a dessiné cette table en bois avec deux niveaux pour créer un effet de « flottement ».

↑ The square table is from Shanxi province; the Buddha statue is of Tibetan origin. • Aus der Provinz Shanxi stammt der quadratische Tisch, die Buddha-Statue ist tibetischen Ursprungs. • La table carrée vient de la province Shanxi, la statue de Bouddha est d'origine tibétaine.

↓ One of the house's several living areas with Chinese and Tibetan furniture. • Einer der vielen Wohnräume mit chinesischen und tibetischen Möbeln. • Une des nombreuses pièces de la maison abritant des meubles chinois et tibétains.

↑ A reception area, with two Shao Fan polished steel Ming chairs. The painting is also by Shao Fan. • Empfangsraum mit zwei „Ming"-Edelstahlstühlen, entworfen von Shao Fan. Auch das Gemälde stammt vom Künstler. • Dans une aire de réception, deux chaises « Ming » en acier poli de Shao Fan. Le tableau est également de lui.

↓ The artist in his studio, sitting at a table he made himself; its top was hewn from a single piece of wood. • Der Hausherr sitzt im Atelier an einem selbst gebauten Tisch, dessen Platte aus einem einzigen Stück Holz besteht. • Le maître de maison est assis dans l'atelier à une table qu'il a lui-même fabriquée, son plateau est fait d'un seul morceau de bois.

BEIJING
CHINA

Le Rouge et le Vert

North of Beijing's Forbidden City, in three restored 17th-century pavilions, Jehanne de Biolley and her husband, Harrison Liu, have created an eclectic and intimate home. Belgian-born de Biolley is a jewelry designer with a love for Chinese stones and Asian motifs; Liu is a Chinese artist and actor who paints and designs furniture. Together, they have turned this once dilapidated printing factory and school into a colorful jewel box of a house. The compound updates the traditional Beijing courtyard house to accommodate the needs of a work-at-home family. One building is for living, another combines a kitchen and guest room, while the third houses de Biolley's workshop. In the center of the complex, there is a large and homey courtyard where the couple's son Chang Ji can play among trees. The bold reds and greens of the window panes and the living room's tall lacquered columns echo the colors of de Biolley's bright necklaces and bracelets. The interior features furniture and paintings by Liu, and lovely found objects, like a gramophone and a stack of 1950s Chinese opera records that the couple discovered on the streets of Beijing.

Jehanne de Biolley und ihr Ehemann Harrison Liu haben nördlich der Verbotenen Stadt in Peking aus einer ehemaligen Druckerei und Schule ein behagliches Zuhause geschaffen. Es besteht aus drei Pavillons aus dem 17. Jahrhundert und reflektiert die Vorlieben des Paares. De Biolley – die gebürtige Belgierin ist Schmuckdesignerin – liebt chinesische Steine und asiatische Motive. Und der Künstler und Schauspieler Liu entwirft Möbel, die er bemalt. De Biolley und Liu machten aus dem traditionellen Innenhofhaus ein modernes Wohn- und Arbeitsmodell: Einer der Pavillons ist Wohnzimmer, im zweiten befinden sich Küche und Gästezimmer, im dritten ist de Biolleys Werkstatt untergebracht. Den lauschigen Hof – an den Bäumen baumeln traditionelle Draht- und Papierlaternen – hat Chang Ji, der Sohn des Paares, zu einer Spielwiese gemacht. Grellrot und -grün bemalte Fensterrahmen, rot lackierte Säulen im Wohnraum, ein altes Grammofon, ein Stapel Platten aus den 1950er Jahren mit chinesischen Opern – in den Straßen Pekings aufgestöbert – und die Möbel und Gemälde von Liu ergeben einen wundervoll eklektischen Mix.

Au nord de la Cité Interdite, trois pavillons du 17e siècle ont été reconvertis par la Belge Jehanne de Biolley et son mari Harrison Liu en une demeure intime qui reflète leur personnalité. Créatrice de bijoux, de Biolley aime les gemmes chinois et les motifs asiatiques ; Liu, artiste et acteur, crée et peint des meubles. Ils ont uni leur inspiration pour transformer cette imprimerie et cette école délabrées en écrin de couleurs. Les bâtiments ont été reliés en une version moderne de la maison pékinoise traditionnelle selon les besoins du couple qui travaille chez lui. Le premier sert pour vivre ; le second abrite la cuisine et une chambre d'amis ; le troisième est l'atelier de Jehanne. Dans la cour centrale, leur fils Chang Ji joue parmi les arbres ornés de lanternes en papier et fil de fer. Les rouges et verts des fenêtres et les colonnes laquées du séjour rappellent les créations colorées de la maîtresse de maison. Le décor éclectique est agrémenté de toiles de Liu et de jolis objets chinés dans les rues de Pékin, comme un gramophone et des piles de disques d'opéras chinois des années 1950.

P. 59 The living room has tall, red-lacquered columns, green leather sofas that date from the 1970s, and a rug from Xinjiang. • Die grünen Ledersofas im Wohnzimmer mit den rot lackierten Säulen sind aus den 1970ern. Der Wollteppich stammt aus Xinjiang. • Dans le salon, des colonnes en laque rouge, des canapés en cuir vert des années 1970 et un tapis de Xinjiang.

↖ A dark shelf unit provides a striking backdrop for the collection of vases and books. • Eine dunkle Regalwand hebt die Vasen- und Büchersammlung wirkungsvoll hervor. • Une étagère murale sombre met en valeur la collection de vases et de livres.

↑ The brass four-poster bed was designed by Harrison Liu. It is covered with silk velvet, gold brocade, and satin cushions. • Das Messingbett mit Kissen aus Samt, Satin und Brokat ist ein Entwurf von Harrison Liu. • Le lit en laiton avec des coussins de velours, brocart et satin a été dessiné par Harrison Liu.

↘ Red Buddhist prayer beads dangle above a porcelain jar that bears the inscription "double happiness" in Chinese. • Eine rote buddhistische Gebetskette über einem Porzellangefäß mit der chinesischen Inschrift „Doppeltes Glück". • Un chapelet bouddhique rouge au-dessus d'une jarre en porcelaine où est écrit « double bonheur ».

← Opaque skylights soften the daylight entering the rustic bathroom. • Durch milchige Oberlichter fällt das Tageslicht weich ins rustikale Badezimmer. • Filtrée par le verre laiteux des lanterneaux, la lumière tombe doucement dans la salle de bains rustique.

↑ The intricate openwork of this wooden screen is accentuated by a red-and-gold silk brocade lining. • Rotgoldener Seidenbrokat betont die aufwändigen Schnitzereien der Trennwand. • Les motifs de ce paravent sont mis en valeur par une doublure en brocart de soie rouge et or.

BERLIN
GERMANY

Communist Vintage

Until artist Erik Schmidt rented his studio flat, he knew nothing about former East Germany's massive prefab blocks, and "United Nations Square" was an address that had no connotations for him. Schmidt, needless to say, is a Wessi. Every citizen of the GDR was familiar with the the "Snake" and the "Boomerang," developments totaling 1,280 apartments in the heart of the city, built from 1968 by Hermann Henselmann. In those days, only East Germans who toed the Party line were allowed to move into these flats; now it is Schmidt who is privileged, not because of his political views but because in the entire block there are only six flats of the type he wanted, with a studio and roof garden. His new home has even influenced his art: he has painted the view from the window, made a video, and devised a fictional home story as an art project. He sent photos from this project to advertising agencies—the dreary concrete legacy of Socialist architecture happens to be hip at present, so Schmidt's apartment is often used as a backdrop for TV ads or pop videos.

Bevor der Künstler Erik Schmidt seine 130 Quadratmeter große Atelierwohnung mietete, wusste er nichts über Plattenbauten, und der Platz der Vereinten Nationen war für ihn Berliner Niemandsland. Natürlich ist Schmidt Wessi, denn jeder DDR-Bürger kannte die „Schlange" und den „Bumerang" mit 1280 Wohnungen mitten in der Stadt, ab 1968 gebaut vom sozialistischen Chefarchitekten Hermann Henselmann. Damals durften dort nur linientreue DDR-Bürger einziehen, heute hat Schmidt das Vergnügen. Nicht wegen seiner Gesinnung, sondern weil es seinen Wohnungstyp mit Atelier und Dachgarten nur sechsmal in dem Block gibt. Das neue Zuhause hat sogar seine Kunst beeinflusst: Er malte den Blick aus seinem Fenster, drehte ein Video und dachte sich als Kunstprojekt eine fiktive Homestory aus. Davon schickte er Fotos an Werbeagenturen. Und weil die sozialistische Betontristesse gerade hip ist, dient Schmidts Wohnung oft als Kulisse für Werbespots oder Pop-Videos.

Avant de louer son atelier de 130 mètres carrés, le créateur Erik Schmidt ne savait rien des cités ni de la Place des Nations-Unies. Forcément, il est un Wessi, un Allemand de l'Ouest. Les citoyens de l'Est, eux, connaissaient le «Serpent» et le «Boomerang», construits à partir de 1968 par le chef architecte socialiste Hermann Henselmann. À l'époque, ces 1280 appartements du centre-ville étaient réservés à ceux qui étaient fidèles à la ligne politique du parti. Aujourd'hui Schmidt est un privilégié, pas à cause de ses idées mais parce que le type d'appartement qu'il habite, avec atelier et jardin suspendu, n'existe que six fois dans le bloc. Son nouveau logis a même influencé son art : il a peint ce qu'il voit de sa fenêtre, tourné un film vidéo et imaginé une homestory destinée à un projet artistique. Il en a envoyé des photos à des agences de publicité. Et comme le béton triste est branché en ce moment, son appartement sert souvent de décor à des spots publicitaires et des vidéos pop.

64

P. 65 The spiral staircase leads to the rooftop studio. • Die Wendeltreppe führt zum Dachatelier. • Un escalier en colimaçon mène à l'atelier.

↑ Number 28 is part of the curving 330-yard-long apartment building known as the "Snake." • Das Haus Nummer 28 ist Teil der sogenannten Schlange, eines geschwungenen Blocks von dreihundert Meter Länge. • La maison numéro 28 fait partie du « serpent », une barre ondulée de troiscent mètres de long.

↓ When Schmidt stripped the wallpaper, he was left with bare concrete. In some rooms, he preserved the walls in their raw state; in others, he left samples of wallpaper, like pictures, as a souvenir. • Als Schmidt die Tapeten abnahm, kam der blanke Plattenbeton hervor, den er in einigen Räumen so beließ, mitunter kleben als Reminiszenz die alten Muster noch an der Wand, wie Bilder. • Sous les papiers peints, il n'y avait que le béton nu. Dans quelques pièces, Schmidt a laissé les murs tels quels, dans d'autres les vieux motifs sont restés collés au mur comme des tableaux.

→ Simple metal tracks allow for the shelves by the desk to be arranged as required. • Schlichte Regalschienen machen eine freie Fächerkombination am Arbeitsplatz möglich. • De sobres étagères peuvent être librement combinées.

↘ Much of the furniture dates from East German times; much else is from junk sales. The Ikea table goes with anything. • Viele Möbel stammen aus DDR-Zeiten, andere sind vom Trödel. Der Tisch von Ikea passt zu allem. • De nombreux meubles viennent de l'ex-RDA, d'autres de la brocante de l'Ouest. La table d'Ikea va avec tout.

P. 68 The bedside light echoes the classic Arco lamp designed by Achille Castiglioni for Flos in the 1960s. • Eine Stehlampe im Stil der Arco, die Achille Castiglioni in den 1960er Jahren für Flos entworfen hat, dient als Nachtlicht. • Un lampadaire dans le style d'Arco, dessiné par Achille Castiglioni pour Flos dans les années 1960, sert de lampe de chevet.

P. 69 In the dining room, the artist stripped the walls of his prefab concrete apartment. • Im Esszimmer legte Schmidt die Betonwände des Plattenbaus frei. • Dans la salle à manger, le propriétaire a mis les murs de béton à nu.

BERLIN
GERMANY

Concrete Art

When media entrepreneur Christian Boros saw the above-ground air-raid bunker in Berlin-Mitte, he was instantly captivated. For years, he had been looking for somewhere to put his growing art collection and this World War II colossus seemed an eminently suitable, if somewhat unusual, candidate. On top of the four-story structure, Boros had architect Jens Casper install a penthouse for himself, his wife, Karen and their young son. The concrete of its broad roof and load-bearing internal walls echoes the bunker below; the glass shell, on the other hand, offers a contrasting sense of lightness. Inside, the furnishings are elegantly Modernist with humorous touches, while shell limestone floors add a feeling of patinated permanence.

Als der Medienunternehmer Christian Boros den Bunker in Berlin-Mitte zum ersten Mal sah, war er begeistert. Schon seit Jahren suchte er einen Ort für seine wachsende Kunstsammlung, und der vierstöckige Koloss aus dem Zweiten Weltkrieg schien dafür der ideale, wenn auch ungewöhnliche Kandidat. Für ihn, seine Frau Karen und den kleinen Sohn setzte der Architekt Jens Casper ein Penthouse oben auf den Bunker. Das breite Betondach und die tragenden Innenwände übernehmen das Material der vorgefundenen Architektur, eine gläserne Hülle suggeriert dagegen Leichtigkeit . Im Inneren herrscht eleganter Modernismus mit Augenzwinkern, während Böden aus Muschelkalkstein ein Gefühl von patinierter Beständigkeit erzeugen.

Ce bunker au centre de Berlin a rempli propriétaire d'une entreprise de médias Christian Boros d'enthousiame la première fois qu'il l'a vu. Il cherchait depuis des années un endroit susceptible d'abriter sa collection d'œuvres d'art et le colosse de quatre étages datant de la Seconde Guerre mondiale avait le potentiel adéquat quoiqu'insolite. Pour lui, son épouse Karen et leur petit garçon, l'architecte Jens Casper a posé un penthouse tout en haut du bunker. Le large toit de béton et les murs intérieurs porteurs ont repris le matériau de l'architecture d'origine tandis qu'une enveloppe de verre suggère la légèreté. À l'intérieur règne un modernisme élégant agrémenté de clins d'œil, les sols en calcaire coquillier génèrent une impression de permanence patinée.

P. 71 The bookshelf behind the group of Martin Eisler chairs was integrated into Jens Casper's architecture. • Eine Sitzgruppe von Martin Eisler steht vor dem Buchregal, das in die Architektur von Jens Casper integriert wurde. • Un canapé et des fauteuils de Martin Eisler devant une bibliothèque intégrée dans l'architecture par Jens Casper.

↑ The custom-built kitchen features 500-year-old oak and Gaggenau appliances. • Für die maßgefertigte Küche mit Geräten von Gaggenau wurde 500 Jahre alte Eiche verwendet. • La cuisine sur mesure est faite de chêne âgé de cinq siècles, les appareils sont de Gaggenau.

↗ From the entrance hall visitors can spot Olafur Eliasson's light sculpture *Eye see you*. • Von der Eingangshalle fällt der Blick auf das Lichtobjekt *Eye see you* von Olafur Eliasson. • Du hall d'entrée, on aperçoit la sculpture lumineuse *Eye see you* d'Olafur Eliasson.

→ Curtains by Eiting Räume create soft walls in the master bedroom. The Murano glass chandelier was made by Fratelli Barovier. • Eine weiche Schlafzimmerwand bilden die Vorhänge, angefertigt von Eiting Räume. Der Muranoglas-Lüster stammt von Fratelli Barovier. • Les rideaux confectionnés par Eiting Räume forment un mur souple et moelleux pour la chambre à coucher. Le lustre en verre de Murano est de Fratelli Barovier.

PP. 74–75 To the left of the de Sede leather cubes is a painting by Franz Ackermann, to the right a Damien Hirst. • Auf Lederwürfeln von de Sede sitzend, kann man links ein Werk von Franz Ackermann und rechts eine Arbeit von Damien Hirst betrachten. • Assis sur les cubes en cuir de de Sede, on peut contempler à gauche une œuvre de Franz Ackermann, à droite un travail de Damien Hirst.

← The couple's son sleeps in an oak bed from the Bergisches Land region. • Im Kinderzimmer schläft der Sohn in einem Eichenbett aus dem Bergischen Land. • Dans sa chambre à coucher, le fils de la maison dort dans un lit de chêne du Bergisches Land.

→ Shell limestone was used both for the bathroom furniture and for all the apartment's floors. • Für die Badeinbauten wie auch die Böden im gesamten Penthouse wurde Muschelkalk verwendet. • Du calcaire coquillier a été utilisé pour les meubles encastrés de la salle de bains ainsi que pour tous les sols du penthouse.

"Only art has the power to turn a bunker into
something that is relevant to us today." CHRISTIAN BOROS

„Nur die Kunst hat die Kraft, aus einem Bunker etwas
für uns heute Relevantes zu machen."
« Seul l'art a le pouvoir de transformer un bunker en un
espace qui nous parle aujourd'hui. »

BEVERLY HILLS
USA

Mid-century Elegance

In 1957, architect Wayne McAllister built a chic Modernist bungalow with pool. Half a century later, it was discovered by Eugenio López Alonso, founder of the Colección Jumex, which is the largest private Latin American collection of contemporary art. In their restoration, he and the architects at Marmol Radziner were careful to respect the integrity of this mid-century gem. In addition to fitting glazed sliding doors that allow more sunlight into the rooms, they chose furnishings that reflect the residence's style and period—and whose neutral tones ensure the displayed works from the collection are given due prominence. The result, says López Alonso with satisfaction, is "clean, uncluttered and Californian"— which is just how he likes it.

1957 baute der Architekt Wayne McAllister einen mondänen Bungalow mit Pool. Eugenio López Alonso, Gründer der Colección Jumex, der größten lateinamerikanische Privatsammlung zeitgenössischer Kunst, entdeckte ihn ein halbes Jahrhundert später für sich. Beim Umbau achtete er mit den Architekten von Marmol Radziner darauf, die Integrität dieses Mid-Century-Juwels zu bewahren. Um mehr Sonnenlicht in die Räume zu lassen, wurden gläserne Schiebetüren eingefügt. Die Möblierung orientiert sich an der Erbauungszeit und bleibt farblich zurückhaltend – was ausgewählten Werken der Kunstsammlung den ihnen gebührenden Auftritt verschafft. Das Ergebnis, erklärt López Alonso zufrieden, sei genau so, wie er es mag: „Klar, kalifornisch und aufgeräumt."

L'architecte Wayne McAllister avait construit en 1957 à Beverly Hills un bungalow représentatif avec piscine. Eugenio López Alonso, le fondateur de la Colección Jumex, la plus importante collection privée d'art contemporain d'Amérique Latine, l'a redécouvert un demi-siècle plus tard. Durant les travaux, il a veillé avec les architectes de Marmol Radziner à préserver l'intégrité de ce bijou des années 1950. Des portes coulissantes en verre laissent aujourd'hui passer plus de lumière dans les pièces. Le mobilier, orienté sur l'époque de construction du bungalow, reste sobre sur le plan des couleurs, ce qui fait ressortir comme elles le méritent des œuvres choisies de la collection du propriétaire. Le résultat, explique López Alonso avec satisfaction, est exactement ce qu'il aime : « Clair, ordonné et californien. »

P. 79 A Claes Oldenburg sculpture stands behind a Kagan sofa and a Nakashima table in the master bedroom. • Im Hauptschlafzimmer: eine Skulptur von Claes Oldenburg hinter Sofa von Vladimir Kagan und Tisch von Nakashima. • Dans la chambre principale, une sculpture de Claes Oldenburg se dresse derrière un canapé Kagan et une table basse de Nakashima.

← In the entrance stands *Love Lasts Forever*, a sculpture of stacked skeletons by Maurizio Cattelan. • Am Eingang steht Maurizio Cattelans Skulptur *Love Lasts Forever* aus gestapelten Tierskeletten. • Dans l'entrée se dresse *Love Lasts Forever*, une sculpture composée de squelettes empilés réalisée par Maurizio Cattelan.

↑ Jean Prouvé stools line the kitchen counter. • An der Kücheninsel paradieren Hocker von Jean Prouvé. • Des tabourets de Jean Prouvé devant l'îlot de cuisine.

↓ The library is furnished with a Jean Royère sofa, a Carlo Scarpa chair, and a George Nakashima table. • Die Bibliothek ist mit einem Sofa von Jean Royère, einem Sessel von Carlo Scarpa und einem Tisch von George Nakashima eingerichtet. • Dans la bibliothèque, un canapé de Jean Royère, un fauteuil de Carlo Scarpa et une table basse de George Nakashima.

PP. 82–83 In the living room, the sofa was inspired by an Isamu Noguchi design of the 1940s. The cream-colored armchair is one of only three surviving examples of a model created by Carlo Graffi, a disciple of Carlo Mollino. • Das Sofa im Wohnzimmer entstand nach einem Entwurf von Isamu Noguchi aus den 1940ern. Der helle Sessel ist eines von nur drei noch erhaltenen Exemplaren eines Modells, das Carlo Graffi, ein Schüler von Carlo Mollino, designt hat. • Dans le séjour, le canapé a été inspiré par un design d'Isamu Noguchi des années 1940. Le fauteuil en crème est l'un des trois derniers exemplaires d'un modèle créé par Carlo Graffi, un disciple de Carlo Mollino.

← The tub provides a spectacular view over the swimming pool. • Die Badewanne bietet einen fantastischen Blick auf den Swimmingpool. • De la baignoire, on a une vue spectaculaire sur la piscine.

↑ The artwork behind the master bed is a 1973 Ed Ruscha oil painting titled *Virtue*. • Über dem Bett hängt das Ölgemälde *Virtue* von Ed Ruscha aus dem Jahr 1973. • Au-dessus du lit de la chambre principale, une peinture à l'huile d'Ed Ruscha datant de 1973 et intitulée *Virtue*.

BIARRITZ
FRANCE

Cabanon de Charme

The guesthouse of Isabel López-Quesada's holiday residence was once part of a pheasant farm. Built around 1950 with rudimentary concrete walls, it is, essentially, a simple, functional timber-frame structure. "But I liked the shape of it," the interior designer says. "I decided to retain the basic structure and clad the walls with hand-finished pine boards." The windows, doors, and furniture are an eclectic mix of pieces left over from her interior projects, market finds, and gifts from friends. López-Quesada's clarity of vision ensured there was great harmony to the overall composition: "I envisioned a mountain-hut or chalet ambience, something very rustic and simple."

Das Gästehaus der Ferienresidenz von Isabel López-Quesada gehörte früher zu einer Fasanenzucht. Es wurde etwa 1950 erbaut und mit simplen Betonwänden ausgestattet; im Kern ist es ein schlicht-funktionaler Holzständerbau. „Aber die Form gefiel mir", so die Interiordesignerin. „Also beschloss ich, die Grundkonstruktion zu erhalten und mit handbearbeiteten Pinienbohlen zu verkleiden." Fenster, Türen und Möbel sind eine eklektische Sammlung – Überbleibsel von ihren Einrichtungsprojekten, dazu Marktfunde und Geschenke von Freunden. Dennoch wird die Komposition durch López-Quesadas klare Vision zusammengehalten: „Mir schwebte eine Atmosphäre wie in einer Berghütte vor, ganz rustikal und einfach."

La maison d'amis de la résidence de vacances d'Isabel López-Quesada faisait autrefois partie d'un élevage de faisans. Réalisée vers 1950 avec des murs de béton, c'est une construction à ossature de bois simple et fonctionnelle. « Mais sa forme me plaisait », dit la décoratrice, « j'ai donc décidé de garder la structure de base et de la revêtir de madriers de pin travaillés à la main. » Les fenêtres, les portes et les meubles sont une collection éclectique de vestiges de projets de décoration, d'objets découverts au marché et de cadeaux d'amis. Mais la vision claire de López-Quesada donne de la cohérence à la composition : « J'avais en vue une atmosphère de chalet, totalement rustique et simple. »

P. 87 The original timber-frame structure is now clad in pine boards; former ventilation shafts allow light into the space. • Pinienbretter verkleiden die alte Balkenkonstruktion, ehemalige Lüftungsluken lassen Tageslicht herein. • Des planches de pin habillent les poutres d'origine, les anciennes lucarnes d'aération laissent passer la lumière du jour.

PP. 88–89 The large living room is laid out as a loft-like space. Badly damaged, this part of the building had to be torn down and was subsequently rebuilt using recycled corrugated metal sheets. • Das Wohnzimmer ist als großer Loftraum angelegt. Dieser Teil des Gebäudes war zu stark zerstört und wurde daher abgerissen und mit dem recycelten Wellblech rekonstruiert. • Le séjour est conçu comme un vaste loft. Trop endommagée, cette partie du bâtiment a été démolie et remplacée par de la tôle recyclée.

→ Untreated wood was used for new kitchen furniture, while the sink was donated by a client who'd just got a new one. • Neue Küchenmöbel sind aus unbehandeltem Holz, das Waschbecken stiftete ein Klient, als er selbst ein neues bekam. • Les nouveaux meubles de cuisine sont en bois non traité, l'évier a été laissé à la maîtresse de maison par un client quand il en a eu un autre.

↑ Belgian linen adorns the comfy bed in this children's bedroom. • Im Kinderschlafzimmer steht ein mit belgischem Leinen bezogenes einladendes Bett. • Dans la chambre d'enfants, un lit confortable revêtu de toile de lin belge.

→ A snail-shaped shower cubicle is made of black fibre cement. • Aus schwarzem Faserzement besteht die schneckenförmige Duschkabine. • La douche en colimaçon est en fibrociment noir.

→ → The wooden mirror was a gift from López-Quesada's sister-in-law; the bathtub is clad in pine. • Der Holzspiegel ist ein Geschenk von López-Quesadas Schwägerin, die Wanne wurde mit Pinie verkleidet. • Le miroir en bois est un cadeau de la belle-sœur de López-Quesada, la baignoire est habillée de pin.

BRUSSELS
BELGIUM

The Luxury of Space

When architects build their own homes, you expect the results to be of a piece. That's certainly the case with the penthouse of one of the partners in the practice M. & J.-M. Jaspers & J. Eyers. Perched on top of the former premises of coffee roasters Jacqmotte near the Palais de Justice, the apartment boasts expansive interiors and an ambience of masculine luxury, in which the guiding principle was restraint. Its strengths are unmistakably obvious: panoramic views of the city escape, top-class furniture by the likes of Eames and Citterio, and 7,000 square feet of space.

Wenn Architekten für sich selbst bauen, ist das Resultat idealerweise wie aus einem Guss. So auch das Penthouse, das einer der Büroeigentümer von M. & J.-M. Jaspers & J. Eyers in direkter Nähe zum Palais de Justice bewohnt. Auf dem früheren Gelände der Kaffeerösterei Jacqmotte entstand dieses Loftgebäude mit weitläufigen Räumen. Bei der Konzeption der luxuriösen maskulinen Atmosphäre galt Zurückhaltung als Maxime. Der wahre Rang der Immobilie ist dennoch offensichtlich: ein Panoramablick über Brüssels Dächer, hochwertige Möbel von Eames bis Citterio und vor allem viel Platz auf 650 Quadratmetern.

Quand des architectes construisent pour eux, le résultat devrait être parfaitement cohérent. C'est le cas dans le penthouse qu'habite l'un des propriétaires du bureau M. & J.-M. Jaspers & J. Eyers à proximité du Palais de Justice. Ce loft aux espaces généreux a vu le jour sur l'ancien site de l'usine de torréfaction Jacqmotte. Pour concevoir l'atmosphère masculine luxueuse, la règle d'or a été la retenue. Mais la qualité du bâtiment n'en est pas moins manifeste : une vue panoramique sur la ville, des meubles de grande qualité d'Eames à Citterio et surtout beaucoup de place sur 650 mètres carrés.

P. 93 With its Flexform chairs, the hall invites visitors to take a seat. In the background is the door to the pool. • Die Halle lädt dazu ein, auf Polsterstühlen von Flexform Platz zu nehmen. Im Hintergrund der Durchgang zum Pool. • Le hall invite avec des chaises de Flexform. Au fond, la porte qui donne sur la piscine.

← *Brno* cantilever chairs by Mies van der Rohe, now made by Knoll, are grouped around the conference table, beyond which is a partial map of Brussels showing the firm's built projects. • Vor einem Plan von Brüssel mit realisierten Bauprojekten stehen im Konferenzraum die Freischwinger *Brno* von Mies van der Rohe, die heute von Knoll produziert werden. • Dans la salle de conférences, devant un plan de Bruxelles montrant les projets de construction réalisés par les architectes, les fauteuils luges *Brno* de Mies van der Rohe, diffusés aujourd'hui par Knoll.

↑ The head of the oak bed doubles as a desk, the Tolomeo lamps are from Artemide. • Das Kopfende des Eichenbetts geht in einen Schreibtisch über, die Tolomeo-Leuchten sind von Artemide. • La tête du lit de chêne se prolonge en bureau, les lampes Tolomeo sont d'Artemide.

PP. 96–97 A black shelf unit contrasts
with deeply cushioned Flexform sofas by
Antonio Citterio. • Die üppigen Sofas
von Antonio Citterio für Flexform werden durch das Schrankelement kontrastiert. • Les canapés confortables dessinés par Antonio Citterio pour Flexform
contrastent avec le noir de l'armoire
murale.

↑ The floor and walls in the bath are in
white Portuguese limestone. • Für
Boden und Wände im Bad wurde ein
weißer Kalkstein aus Portugal verarbei-
tet. • Pour le sol et les murs de la salle de
bains, on a utilisé de la pierre calcaire
blanche du Portugal.

→ The corridor to the rear of the shelf
unit links the kitchen and the bedroom. •
Auf der Rückseite der Schrankwand verbindet ein Flur Küche und Schlafzimmer.
• Derrière l'armoire murale, un couloir
relie la cuisine et la chambre à coucher.

BUDAPEST
HUNGARY

Racy Grace

In 1940, gynecologist István Mark had a Modernist villa built on Gellért Hill, in which he pursued an extravagant lifestyle and indulged his passion for Bauhaus and Art Deco designs, furnishing his home accordingly. After being divided up into apartments and a kindergarten under the communist regime, the house captured the heart of real-estate agent and interior designer Adam Ilkovits in 2001. There followed four years of restoration work, in which Ilkovits aimed to recapture the spirit of Budapest high-society life in the 1930s: "I wanted to retain the soul of these glamorous spaces while also bringing them into the 21st century."

1940 ließ der Gynäkologe István Mark auf dem Gellértberg eine modernistische Villa bauen und nutzte sie als Bühne für seinen rasanten Lebensstil. Mark bewunderte Bauhausdesign und Art déco und richtete sein Zuhause entsprechend ein. 2001 fand die Immobilie im Makler und Interiordesigner Adam Ilkovits einen neuen Liebhaber. In kommunistischer Zeit war das Haus in einzelne Wohnungen aufgeteilt und teils zu einem Kindergarten umfunktioniert worden. Während des vier Jahre dauernden Umbaus restaurierte Ilkovits alles im Geist eines Budapester Großbürgerhauses der 1930er: „Ich wollte die Seele dieser glamourösen Räume erhalten, sie aber gleichzeitig ins 21. Jahrhundert überführen."

En 1940, le gynécologue István Mark a fait construire sur le mont Gellért une villa moderniste et y a profité des douceurs de la vie. Ayant une prédilection pour le design Bauhaus et l'Art Déco, il a décoré les pièces à l'avenant. En 2001 l'immeuble a trouvé un nouvel amateur en la personne d'Adam Ilkovits, agent immobilier et architecte d'intérieur. À l'époque communiste, la maison était divisée en appartements et abritait aussi un jardin d'enfants. Pendant les travaux de rénovation qui ont duré quatre ans, Ilkovits a tout restauré en ayant en tête une maison de maître bourgeoise des années 1930 à Budapest : « Je voulais préserver l'âme des pièces glamoureuses tout en les transposant au 21ᵉ siècle. »

P. 101 In the foyer beyond the main
entrance is a Riley Brooklands racing car
from 1930. • Hinter dem Haupteingang
liegt ein Foyer, in dem ein Riley-Brook-
lands-Rennwagen von 1930 steht. •
Dans le hall de l'entrée principale se
trouve une Riley Brooklands de 1930.

↑ A portrait of Ladislas I, also known as
Saint Ladislas, stands on a plinth next to
the bathroom door. Siena marble covers
the wall behind the bath. • Eine Büste
von Ladislaus I., auch der heilige Ladislaus genannt, flankiert die Tür zum Bad.
Die Wand hinter der Badewanne ist mit
Marmor aus Sienna verkleidet. • Une
tête sculptée de Ladislas Ier, appelé aussi
saint Ladislas, à côté de la porte de la
salle de bains. Le mur derrière la baignoire est revêtu de marbre de Sienne.

→ The table is an antique from the
Marché aux Puces in Paris, the wooden
chairs with the parallel bars are by Josef
Hoffmann. • Der Tisch ist eine Antiquität
vom Pariser Marché aux Puces, die
Holz-Fauteuils entwarf Josef Hoffmann.
• La table est une antiquité chinée aux
Puces de Paris, Josef Hoffmann a conçu
les fauteuils en bois à barreaux.

← The mint-green conservatory furniture was designed in the style of Otto Prutscher and upholstered in black leather. • Die zartgrünen Wintergartenmöbel im Stil Otto Prutschers tragen schwarze Lederpolster. • Couleur menthe à l'eau, les meubles du jardin d'hiver dans le style d'Otto Prutscher sont capitonnés de cuir noir.

↖ The glass cabinet contains Hungarian porcelain by Herend. • Ungarisches Porzellan von Herend fand in der Ausstellungsvitrine seinen Platz. • La porcelaine hongroise de Herend a trouvé sa place dans l'armoire vitrée.

↓ Custom-made wooden blinds provide shade in the living room, which features a desk by Ludwig Kozma. • Maßgefertigte Holzjalousien verdunkeln das Wohnzimmer, in dem ein Schreibtisch von Ludwig Kozma steht. • Des stores vénitiens en bois faits sur mesure assombrissent la pièce dans laquelle se trouve un bureau de Ludwig Kozma.

← The white-finish kitchen counter was designed by owner Adam Ilkovits. • Der weiß lackierte Küchentresen folgt einem Entwurf des Eigentümers Adam Ilkovits. • Le comptoir de la cuisine laqué de blanc a été réalisé d'après un dessin du propriétaire Adam Ilkovit.

→ Macassar ebony lines the walls and doors of the lobby to the living area. • Wände und Türen in der Vorhalle zum Wohnbereich sind mit Makassar-Eben-holz verkleidet. • Les murs et les portes du hall qui donne sur le séjour ont été revêtus d'ébène de Macassar.

↓ Hungarian architect and designer Ludwig Kozma also designed the pine-wood and oak veneer bed. • Das Bett aus Kiefer mit Eichenfurnier entwarf ebenfalls der ungarische Architekt und Designer Ludwig Kozma. • Le lit en pin plaqué chêne a également été conçu par l'architecte et designer hongrois Ludwig Kozma.

↙ Above the washbasin is a hand-carved mirror from the 18th century. • Über dem Waschbecken hängt ein handgeschnitzter Spiegel aus dem 18. Jahrhundert. • Au-dessus du lavabo, un miroir du 18e siècle sculpté à la main.

BUENOS AIRES
ARGENTINA

The Perfect Bachelor Pad

After many years abroad, cult art director Juan Gatti has rediscovered Buenos Aires. As a graphic designer, he brought a new aesthetic style to Pedro Almodóvar's movie posters and has worked as an artistic director and photographer for luxury brands such as Sybilla, Chloé, Karl Lagerfeld, Loewe, and many others. "I fell in love with the city," he tells us from his 1930s apartment in Plaza San Martín in Buenos Aires. At his home, where picture windows provide postcard-style views of iconic city features such as the Kavanagh Building, the church of the Holy Sacrament, the port, and the jacaranda trees in Plaza San Martín, Gatti welcomes friends from all over the world. For the reconstruction of his apartment, he engaged the architects Carlos Rivadulla and Claudia Conde Grand, who gave the rooms a distinctive clarity and a modern, classical feel. Gatti's extensive trawling of flea markets and a neutral palette have done the rest. "I like American and Scandinavian furniture of the 1950s. My dream has always been to have a playboy-style apartment like those envisioned by legendary Argentinian cartoonist Guillermo Divito," he confides with his trademark sophisticated humor.

Der Artdirector und Fotograf mit Kultstatus, der die Filmplakate für Pedro Almodóvar entwirft und für Luxusmarken wie Sybilla, Chloé, Karl Lagerfeld oder Loewe tätig war, feierte nach Jahren der Trennung ein Wiedersehen mit Buenos Aires. „Ich liebe diese Stadt", bekennt er bei unserem Anruf in seinem Apartment aus den 1930er Jahren an der Plaza San Martín. Aus den Fenstern seines Zuhauses, wo Gatti seine Freunde aus aller Welt empfängt, hat man eine herrliche Aussicht auf einige Sehenswürdigkeiten, etwa das Kavanagh-Gebäude, die Basilica del Santísimo Sacramento, den Hafen oder die Jacarandas der Plaza San Martín. Für den Umbau seiner Wohnung engagierte Gatti die Architekten Carlos Rivadulla und Claudia Conde Grand, die für eine moderne klassische Note und für die Klarheit der Räume sorgten. Seine Streifzüge durch die Flohmärkte und eine neutrale Palette taten das Übrige. „Mir gefallen die amerikanischen und skandinavischen Möbel der 1950er Jahre. Eigentlich habe ich mir immer ein Apartment im Playboy-Stil gewünscht, wie vom argentinischen Comic-Maestro Guillermo Divito gezeichnet", sagt Gatti verschmitzt.

Créateur de l'esthétique graphique des films de Pedro Almodóvar, directeur artistique, graphiste et photographe de couturiers et de marques prestigieuses tels que Sybilla, Chloé, Karl Lagerfeld ou Loewe, Juan Gatti a retrouvé Buenos Aires après des années d'absence. « J'en suis tombé amoureux », déclare-t-il depuis son appartement situé dans un édifice des années 1930 où il reçoit ses amis du monde entier. Il a confié sa restructuration aux architectes Carlos Rivadulla et Claudia Conde Grand qui ont rendu les pièces plus claires et leur ont apporté une touche à la fois classique et moderne. Les fenêtres donnent sur l'immeuble Kavanagh, l'église du Santísimo Sacramento, le port et les jacarandas de la place San Martín en contrebas. Pour le décor, Gatti a opté pour une palette neutre et ses trouvailles dans les marchés aux puces. « J'aime les meubles américains et scandinaves des années 1950 », confie-t-il, ajoutant avec humour : « J'ai toujours rêvé d'avoir une garçonnière de playboy dans le style de celles des bandes dessinées de Guillermo Divito, le légendaire illustrateur argentin. »

P. 109 Living room with staircase leading to Juan Gatti's bedroom. • Das
Wohnzimmer mit der zum Schlafzimmer
führenden Treppe. • Le séjour, avec l'escalier qui monte à la chambre.

↑ Gatti found the trio of 1950s nest
tables at a Buenos Aires antique market.
• Die drei Satztische aus den 1950er
Jahren fand Gatti auf einem Antikmarkt
in Buenos Aires. • Gatti a trouvé la table
gigogne des années 1950 sur un marché
d'antiquités de Buenos Aires.

→ Illustrations by Guillermo Divito hang
above the kitchen's Eames DCM chairs.
• In der Küche hängen über den DCM-
Stühlen von Eames Illustrationen von
Guillermo Divito. • Dans la cuisine, des
illustrations de Guillermo Divito au-
dessus des chaises DCM d'Eames.

PP. 112–113 Seen through the window is
the Kavanagh Building, constructed in
1934. On the foal-hide rug, two armchairs
from the 1960s. • Durch das Wohnzim-
merfenster sieht man das 1934 errichtete
Kavanagh-Gebäude. Auf dem Boden ein
Teppich aus Fohlenfell, darauf Armsessel
aus den 1960er Jahren. • Par la fenêtre
du séjour, on aperçoit le Kavanagh,
construit en 1934. Deux fauteuils des
années 1960 sur un tapis en poulain.

← In the study, a 1960s armchair in the style of Finn Juhl. • Im Arbeitszimmer steht ein Sessel aus den 1960er Jahren im Stil Finn Juhls. • Dans le bureau, un fauteuil des années 1960, dans le style Finn Juhl.

↑ Gatti's bedroom is situated in a gallery overlooking the living room. On the bed, an otter-skin throw and on the wall, photos from his collection of 1930s nudes. • Gattis Schlafzimmer auf der Galerie über dem Wohnzimmer. Eine Decke aus Otterfell liegt auf dem Bett. An der Wand lehnen Aktaufnahmen der 1930er, die er seit Jahren sammelt.

• La chambre est située sur une mezzanine donnant sur le séjour. Plaid en loutre sur le lit et, au mur, des nus des années 1930.

CAPE TOWN
SOUTH AFRICA

Contemporary Colonial

When apartheid was still the rule in South Africa, the heart of Cape Town was pretty much out of bounds. Today, all that's changed. The area around Long Street, Bree Street, and up to Kloof Street is full of galleries and crowded bars. Craig Port's loft is in the middle of all this. Like its forerunners in New York, London, and Paris, the space preserves its original shape as a warehouse, though the ambience is softened by subtle decoration. At all times of day, sunshine floods across the pale wood floors. There are windows everywhere, looking out towards Table Mountain and the town. The walls are of brick, covered in white: they exemplify the approach of Port, which has been to preserve the authenticity of the place and to give it only the thinnest veneer of covering. There's no veranda, no walkway, and no unnecessary effects: this is relentless industrial chic. All the purchases for the loft were made in Long Street, at auctions, or in Cape Town second-hand shops. There's nothing ostentatious, only the occasional small luxury, such as the Art Deco table picked up at Groote-Schuur Hospital, once the HQ of the celebrated Dr. Christiaan Barnard. Well chosen.

Zu Zeiten der Apartheid wollte niemand so recht in die Innenstadt – das ist heute anders. In der Umgebung der Long Street, der Bree Street und weiter oben zur Kloof Street hin sind Galerien und Bars stets gut besucht. Das Loft liegt mittendrin. Wie in New York, London oder Paris wahrt es seine Lageratmosphäre, die jedoch mithilfe einer wohlüberlegten Dekoration wohnlich gestaltet wurde. Den ganzen Tag lang wirft die Sonne ein Streifenmuster auf das helle Parkett. Es gibt überall Fenster zum Tafelberg oder zum Stadtzentrum. Die weiß getünchten Ziegelwände verraten viel über Craig Ports Methode, die Ursprünglichkeit eines Ortes zu wahren, indem er seine eigenen Vorstellungen kaum wahrnehmbar einbringt. Veranden, platzraubende Kunstsammlungen oder überflüssige Effekte sucht man hier vergebens. Der Hausherr setzt auf Industrie-Chic, auf karge, eher nüchterne Akzente. Die Einrichtung stammt aus der Umgebung der Long Street, von Auktionen, Versteigerungen oder aus Trödelläden. Angeberei ist verpönt, aber ein wenig Luxus darf sein, wie bei dem Art-déco-Tisch, den Port in der Groote-Schuur-Klinik aufgetrieben hat, wo der berühmte Professor Christiaan Barnard einst operierte. Keine schlechte Wahl.

Au temps de l'apartheid, le cœur de la cité était un lieu infréquentable. Aujourd'hui, tout a changé. C'est autour de Long Street, Bree Street et en remontant sur Kloof Street, que la ville étale sa liberté avec ses galeries et ses bars. Ce loft est au milieu de la centrifugeuse. Comme ses modèles de New York, Londres ou de Paris, il préserve sa forme d'entrepôt et adoucit l'ambiance à l'aide d'une décoration pointue. À tout instant de la journée, les rayons du soleil strient le parquet en bois clair. La luminosité est d'ailleurs un élément essentiel: partout des fenêtres sont percées en direction de la Montagne de la Table ou du centre-ville. Les murs de briques recouverts de blanc témoignent de la démarche de Craig Port: préserver l'authenticité du lieu, ne revêtir l'ensemble que d'une fine pellicule. Point de véranda, de passerelles, d'encombrantes collections ou d'effets superfétatoires: on la joue industriel chic, dans la sobriété assumée. Le shopping a été réalisé autour de Long Street, aux enchères ou chez les quelques brocanteurs de la ville. Rien d'ostentatoire, juste de petits luxes, comme cette table Art Déco chinée au Groote-Schuur Hospital où officiait le célèbre professeur Christiaan Barnard. Un bon choix.

P. 117 The teal-colored mirror frames resemble portholes; together with 1950s armchairs in the same shade, they lend the room a maritime feel. • Die petrolfarben gerahmten Spiegelteller wirken wie Bullaugen und geben dem Raum in Kombination mit den Sesseln aus den 1950ern ein maritimes Flair. • Les assiettes-miroirs au bord bleu pétrole ressemblent à des hublots ; avec les fauteuils de la même couleur qui datent des années 1950, elles donnent à la pièce une touche maritime.

↑ The metal-frame bed once belonged to the Groote-Schuur Hospital. • Das Krankenhausbett kommt aus alten Beständen der Groote-Schuur-Klinik. • Le lit d'hôpital vient des anciens stocks de la clinique Groote-Schuur.

→ Craig Port's fondness for symmetry becomes clear on and around this vanity. • Craig Ports Hang zur Symmetrie zeigt sich in dem Ensemble um den Schminktisch. • La table à maquillage et ce qui l'entoure montrent le penchant de Craig Port pour la symétrie.

↖ In the thoroughly functional kitchen, metal is the dominant material. The 1950s stools came from a Cape Town milk bar. • Die Küche ist funktionell eingerichtet, hier dominiert Metall. Die Barhocker aus den 1950er Jahren stammen aus einer Milchbar in Kapstadt. • Fonctionnelle avant tout, dans la cuisine domine le métal. Les tabourets des années 1950 proviennent d'un milk-bar de Cape Town.

← Under a collection of mirrors, the owner's study—with an Art Deco table from Groote Schuur Hospital and an ostrich egg lamp designed by Trevor Dykman. • Viele Spiegel dekorieren eine Wand im Arbeitszimmer. Der Artdéco-Tisch stammt aus der Groote-Schuur-Klinik, die Straußeneier-Lampe entwarf Trevor Dykman. • Sous une collection de miroirs, le bureau du propriétaire, avec sa table Art Déco chinée au Groote Schuur Hospital, et sa lampe méduse en œufs d'autruche signée Trevor Dykman.

↑ The wardrobe was once a cake trolley. • Als Kleiderschrank dient ein ehemals für den Transport von Backwaren benutztes Rollregal. • En guise de penderie, un trolley utilisé autrefois pour les pâtisseries.

PP. 122–123 The square living room with its re-upholstered sofas and club chairs purchased in the city. The sculptures on the walls are by Brett Murray, an artist from the Cape. • Der Wohnraum mit neu bezogenen Sofas und Klubsesseln, die Craig Port in Kapstadt kaufte. An den Wänden Skulpturen von Brett Murray, einem lokalen Künstler. • Le salon carré avec ses canapés rehoussés et ses clubs chinés en ville. Aux murs, les sculptures sont de Brett Murray, un artiste de Cape Town.

CAPE TOWN
SOUTH AFRICA

The Power of Color

It used to be a "whites only" suburb – a sinister label if ever there was one. When the mixed-race artist Willie Bester arrived, color arrived in his slipstream. His house is a promising blue on the outside. Around it, a decor typical of a Karoo desert farm (the Karoo is close by) flirts with mosaics and objects salvaged and cast in new roles. Willie Bester himself drew up the plans for his circular home, with no corner crannies where bad thoughts could lurk. The first thing you see inside it is a steel structure strongly resembling a hot water boiler, and setting the tone for the whole house. Actually, it's a column, supporting the staircase. A gigantic portrait of Nelson Mandela overlooks the living room. The kitchen and dining room are one; the bedrooms are on the second floor, with a wing for the three children; and the studio is adjacent. Willie Bester's work has won considerable recognition in Europe, and he has now embarked on a series of new experiments. As the months go by, his "industrial park" steadily fills with fresh creations. Viewed as life sources, his factory pipes and tubes are like so many arteries attached to an imaginary pumping heart. The organism is alive. It quivers with inspiration. One day, it's a house; the next, it's a museum.

Dies war einmal ein „whites only"-Vorort – was für eine finstere Bezeichnung. Als sich der Künstler Willie Bester hier einkaufte, brachte er die Farbe gleich mit. Schon die bläuliche Fassade ist ein gutes Zeichen. Das Dekor wie von einer Farm in der nahe gelegenen Wüste Karoo harmoniert mit Mosaiken und neu zusammengesetzten Objekten vom Trödel. Bester selbst zeichnete die Pläne für den runden Bau, wo sich böse Gedanken gar nicht erst einnisten können. Zunächst fällt der Blick auf eine Stahlkonstruktion, die einem Heizkessel ähnelt. Tatsächlich dient sie als Stützpfeiler für die Treppe. Im Salon hängt als Ausdruck der Verehrung ein Porträt Nelson Mandelas. Wie in einem Loft gehen Küche und Esszimmer ineinander über. Die Zimmer liegen im ersten Stock, ein separater Flügel ist den Kindern vorbehalten. Im Atelier nebenan widmet sich Willie Bester, der inzwischen auch in Europa bekannt ist, neuen Experimenten. Nach und nach füllt sich sein „Industriepark" mit neuen Kreationen. Als eine Quelle der Energie führen die Fabrikrohre wie Arterien zu einem imaginären Herzen: Der Organismus lebt, die Inspiration fliesst. Heute ist dies ein Haus, morgen vielleicht schon ein Museum.

C'était une banlieue « whites only » – sinistre appellation s'il en est. Quand l'artiste métis Willie Bester a investi les lieux, la couleur se devait d'être au rendez-vous. C'est un extérieur bleuté de bon augure qui accueille le visiteur. Autour, un décor de ferme du Karoo (le désert voisin) flirte avec les mosaïques et des objets de récupération réinventés. Bester a lui-même dessiné les plans d'une maison circulaire, sans recoins pour les mauvaises pensées. On tombe alors sur une structure en acier semblable à une chaudière. Le ton est donné. C'est en vérité un pilier qui soutient l'escalier. Révérence oblige, un grand portrait de Nelson Mandela, fait face au salon. À la manière d'un loft, cuisine et salle à manger se relayent ; les chambres sont à l'étage, avec une aile pour les trois enfants ; l'atelier est contigu. Reconnu désormais en Europe, Willie Bester s'y livre à de nouvelles expérimentations. Mois après mois, ce « parc industriel » s'enrichit de nouvelles créations. Source de vie, les tuyaux d'usine sont des artères reliées à un cœur imaginaire. L'organisme est vivant. Il bat au gré des inspirations. Un jour, c'est une maison, un autre, c'est un musée.

↑ The boiler recycled as a column for the staircase is emblematic of the work of this artist, who places industrial society at the center of his creative work. • Ein als Treppenpfeiler zweckentfremdeter recycelter Heizkessel ist sinnbildlich für das große Thema des Künstlers: die moderne Industriegesellschaft. • La chaudière recyclée en pilier pour l'escalier est emblématique du travail de l'artiste qui place la société industrielle au centre de sa création.

→ The chairs at the bar are recycled drains; in general, Bester's raw materials are pieces of wood, tin cans, squashed paint tubes, and other objects picked up on the streets of the townships. • Ausrangierte Wasserrohre bilden die Beine der Barhocker. Ausgangsmaterial für Besters Werke sind oft Holzstücke, Konservendosen, ausgedrückte Farbtuben und verschiedene andere Dinge, die er auf den Straßen der Elendsviertel sammelt. • Les fauteuils du bar sont des

conduites d'eau revisitées ; de manière générale, les matières premières de Bester sont des bouts de bois, des conserves, des tubes de peinture écrasés et divers objets ramassés dans les rues des bidonvilles.

← and P. 125 The two-story atrium forms the heart of the house. A Nelson Mandela portrait by the owner adorns the wall facing the upper level. • Das Atrium erstreckt sich über zwei Stockwerke und bildet das Zentrum des Hauses. Im Obergeschoss schmückt ein vom Besitzer gemaltes Porträt Nelson Mandelas die Wand. • L'atrium couvre deux étages et forme le cœur de la maison. Au premier étage, un portrait de Nelson Mandela peint par le propriétaire.

↑ Willie Bester grew up during the prohibition of blacks taking any part in the creative arts. He has represented his country in many foreign exhibitions. • Willie Bester erlebte noch mit, dass Schwarze vom Kunstbetrieb ausgeschlossen waren. Heute vertritt er sein Land auf zahlreichen Ausstellungen. • Willie Bester a grandi avec l'interdiction faite aux Noirs de toucher aux arts. Il a représenté son pays dans de nombreuses expositions.

CARVALHAL
PORTUGAL

Sophisticated Simplicity

For most of the year, star decorator Jacques Grange's life is full of refinement. He lives in writer Colette's former apartment in Paris's Palais-Royal and has a client list that includes Caroline of Monaco and Francis Ford Coppola. In August, however, he and his antique-dealer partner Pierre Passebon escape to a beach residence in the Alentejo region, which is striking in its simplicity. Tucked behind lofty dunes, it consists of three cabanas, accessed via a dirt road. One houses the kitchen and dining room, another a guestroom, and a third the master suite. The living room, meanwhile, is located in an old livestock barn. The interiors are deliberately down-to-earth. There are local Portuguese touches, African fabrics, and a handful of signed pieces. "My dream was always to have a house on a quiet, untouched beach," explains Grange. "For me, it's a kind of paradise on Earth."

Der weltberühmte Interiordesigner Jacques Grange bewegt sich die meiste Zeit des Jahres in äußerst eleganter Umgebung. Er bewohnt das ehemalige Apartment der Schriftstellerin Colette im Pariser Palais-Royal, und in seiner Kundenkartei finden sich Namen wie Caroline von Monaco und Francis Ford Coppola. Doch im August fliehen er und sein Lebensgefährte, der Antiquitätenhändler Pierre Passebon, in ein erstaunlich einfaches Strandrefugium im portugiesischen Alentejo. Es besteht aus drei Cabanas hinter hohen Dünen, zu denen ein Sandweg führt. Eine enthält die Küche und das Esszimmer, die andere das Gästezimmer und eine dritte das Schlafzimmer. Der Wohnbereich ist in einem alten Stall untergebracht. Die Inneneinrichtung wurde bewusst schlicht gehalten – portugiesische Akzente, afrikanische Stoffe und eine Handvoll Designobjekte. „Mein Traum war es stets, ein Haus an einem ruhigen, unberührten Strand zu besitzen", erklärt Grange. „Für mich ist dies das Paradies auf Erden."

Pendant l'année, le célèbre décorateur mondialement connu Jacques Grange mène grand train. Habitant à Paris dans l'ancien appartement de Colette au Palais-Royal, ses clients incluent Caroline de Monaco et Francis Ford Coppola. Mais quand vient le mois d'août, son compagnon l'antiquaire Pierre Passebon et lui s'échappent dans leur retraite d'une étonnante simplicité dans la région d'Alentejo. Cachée derrière des dunes, on y accède par une piste en terre. Elle est composée de trois cabanes abritant la cuisine/salle à manger, une chambre d'amis et la suite des maîtres. Le séjour est situé dans une vieille étable. Le décor est volontairement sobre, avec quelques touches portugaises, des textiles africains et plusieurs meubles signés. « J'ai toujours rêvé d'une maison sur une plage intacte et tranquille », explique Grange. « Pour moi, c'est un peu le paradis sur terre. »

P. 131 In one corner of the master bedroom, collages by Yves Saint Laurent sit on a 19th-century "cartonnier." The chair comes from the Villa Taylor, a famous Art Deco residence in Marrakech. • In einer Ecke des Schlafzimmers stehen Collagen von Yves Saint Laurent auf einer Kommode aus dem 19. Jahrhundert. Der Stuhl entstammt der Villa Taylor, einer berühmten Art-déco-Residenz in Marrakesch. • Dans un coin de la chambre des maîtres, des collages d'Yves Saint Laurent sur un cartonnier du 19ᵉ siècle. Le fauteuil provient de la Villa Taylor, une célèbre résidence Art Déco de Marrakech.

↑ Jean Royère chairs and a table designed by Carlo Pessina grace the kitchen. The ceramics are Portuguese. • Jean-Royère-Stühle und ein von Carlo Pessina entworfener Tisch in der Küche. Die Keramiken sind portugiesischer Herkunft. • Dans la cuisine, des chaises de Jean Royère autour d'une table de Carlo Pessina. Les céramiques sont portugaises.

↗ At one end of the living room, a buffalo's skull surveys a Roger Capron coffee table and a copy of a 1930s sofa in rope by Audoux-Minet. • Am einen Ende des Wohnzimmers blickt der Schädel eines Büffels auf einen Sofatisch von Roger Capron und den Nachbau eines Flechtsofas aus den 1930er Jahren von Audoux-Minet. • À l'extrémité du séjour, un crâne de buffle domine une table basse de Roger Capron et la copie d'un canapé en corde des années 1930 d'Audoux-Minet.

→ A panel of ceramic tiles created by Jean Mayodon in the 1930s hangs above the rustic master bed. The two lamps are early 20th-century French. • Eine Platte aus Keramikkacheln, von Jean Mayodon in den 1930ern geschaffen, hängt über dem rustikalen Bett. Die beiden französischen Lampen sind frühes 20. Jahrhundert. • Au-dessus du grand lit rustique, un panneau en carreaux de céramique créé par Jean Mayodon dans les années 1930. Les deux lampes françaises datent du début du 20ᵉ siècle.

← Grange adapted a "less is more" approach for the master bathroom. • Im Bad hat sich Grange für das Prinzip „Weniger ist mehr" entschieden. • Dans la salle de bains, Grange a adopté une démarche minimaliste.

↑ The teak table and benches at the other end of the living room are from Bali. There are also cushions made from African fabrics, a straw and leather rug from Morocco, and a coffee table from Amazonia. • Der Tisch und die Bänke aus Teakholz im hinteren Teil des Wohnzimmers kommen aus Bali. Dazu Kissen aus afrikanischen Stoffen, ein marokka-

nischer Teppich aus Stroh und Leder sowie und ein geschweiftes Tischchen aus dem Amazonasgebiet. • La table et les bancs en teck au fond du séjour viennent de Bali. Les coussins du canapé sont en tissus africains, le tapis en paille et cuir vient du Maroc, la petite table basse aux formes arrondies d'Amazonie.

CHIANG MAI
THAILAND

Jungle Cool

It was through friends that artist Rirkrit Tiravanija and photographer Antoinette Aurell came across this jungle-like plot in the north of the country some years ago. "We made a spontaneous decision to build our new house here. We could instantly picture the way it would open up to its tropical surroundings," Aurell explains. In addition to New York-based architects Solveig Fernlund and Neil Logan and their Thai colleague Aroon Puritat, a feng shui master was also involved in the planning of this concrete-frame residence. It comprises three separate pavilions raised up on low stilts and linked by covered courtyard walkways. Large expanses of glass and terrazzo flooring define the interiors, which blend American and Asian influences.

Durch Freunde stießen der Künstler Rirkrit Tiravanija und die Fotografin Antoinette Aurell vor einigen Jahren auf die dschungelartige Parzelle im Norden des Landes. „Die Entscheidung, hier unser neues Zuhause zu bauen, fiel spontan. Wir konnten uns sofort vorstellen, wie sich das Haus später zur tropischen Umgebung öffnen würde", erklärt Aurell. Neben den New Yorker Architekten Solveig Fernlund und Neil Logan sowie ihrem thailändischen Kollegen Aroon Puritat war auch ein Feng-Shui-Meister in die Planung der Betonständerkonstruktion involviert. Drei Pavillons auf niedrigen Stützen werden durch einen überdachten Umgang im Innenhof miteinander verbunden. Große Fensterfronten und Terrazzoböden prägen die Interieurs, in denen amerikanische und asiatische Einflüsse aufeinandertreffen.

Il y a quelques années, des amis ont fait découvrir à l'artiste Rirkrit Tiravanija et la photographe Antoinette Aurelle ce terrain aux airs de jungle, au nord du pays. «Nous nous sommes spontanément décidés à installer ici notre nouveau foyer. Tout de suite nous avons imaginé comment la maison s'ouvrirait plus tard sur l'environnement tropical.» À côté des architectes new-yorkais Solveig Fernlund et Neil Logan ainsi que leur collègue thaïlandais Aroon Puritat, un maître du feng-shui était impliqué dans le planning de la construction dotée de pieds en béton. Trois pavillons posés sur des supports bas sont reliés entre eux par une galerie circulaire couverte dans la cour intérieure. De vastes baies vitrées et des sols en terrazzo caractérisent les intérieurs où se marient les influences américaines et asiatiques.

P. 137   A local artist made the concrete tiles with bamboo imprints. The desk and lamp are both by George Nelson. • Ein lokaler Künstler fertigte die Betonfliesen mit Bambusabdruck. Schreibtisch und Lampe sind Entwürfe von George Nelson. • Un artiste local a fabriqué les carreaux en béton avec impression bambou. Le bureau et la lampe sont de George Nelson.

←   One of the three pavilions contains the studio, opposite of which is the kitchen area. • Einer der drei Pavillons ist das Atelier, gegenüber befindet sich die Küche. • Un des trois pavillons sert d'atelier, la cuisine se trouve en face.

↑   The kitchen was planned by New York architects Solveig Fernlund and Neil Logan. • Die Küche planten die New Yorker Architekten Solveig Fernlund und Neil Logan. • La cuisine a été conçue par les architectes new-yorkais Solveig Fernlund et Neil Logan.

↑ In the lower-level living area, cushions were placed on a broad step to make a sofa. • Für das Sofa im tiefer gelegenen Wohnraum wurden Sitzkissen auf einer breiten Stufe ausgelegt. • Pour réaliser le canapé en contrebas, des coussins ont été disposés sur une large marche.

→ A raised roof with strips of windows enables daylight to enter the bedroom area, which has a tatami bed. • Durch eine Dacherhöhung mit Fensterbändern erhält der Schlafbereich mit dem Tatami-Bett Tageslicht. • Un toit rehaussé équipé d'une rangée de fenêtres laisse passer la lumière dans la pièce tatami.

CIPICONG
INDONESIA

Eurasian Elegance

A learned European friend who once visited Cipicong (pronounced *chippy-chong*)—Jaya Ibrahim's homage to his Javanese roots—came back gasping: "It is like Venice of the East". As the crescent moon rises over the lush rice bowl in the shadow of Mount Salak, Cipicong acquires an operatic dimension, with no boundaries or fencing, just an infinity of surrounding hills and valleys. An hour and a half's drive south of Jakarta, Cipicong is sited near a palace where Sir Raffles, and later the Dutch and Sukarno, stayed. Ibrahim, who worked in London for many years before returning home, built a house with many references—a Venetian window, colonnaded verandas, Palladian arches—but resolved the styles into a seamless synthesis. The details are quintessentially Eastern: banana leaves replace acanthus leaves in the decorative capitals and jasmine buds, borrowed from a 10th-century Javanese palace, crown the loggia. Like many creative artists, Jaya Ibrahim carries numerous styles in his head. In Cipicong, he has triumphantly reinterpreted them to create something uniquely his own.

Als ein gebildeter Europäer in Cipicong (tschippitschong ausgesprochen) – Jaya Ibrahims Hommage an seine javanischen Wurzeln – zu Besuch war, staunte er: „Ein Venedig des Ostens!" Wenn die Mondsichel über den Reisfeldern im Schatten des Berges Salak aufgeht, bekommt Cipicong etwas Opernhaftes, Grenzenloses in einer Unendlichkeit von Hügeln und Tälern. Von Jakarta aus mit dem Auto in anderthalb Stunden zu erreichen, liegt das Anwesen in der Nähe eines Palastes, in dem der britische Kolonialbeamte Sir Raffles, später die Holländer und Indonesiens erster Staatspräsident Sukarno residierten. Ibrahim, der vor seiner Rückkehr in die Heimat lange in London gearbeite hatte, baute sich ein Haus voller Anspielungen – hier ein venezianisches Fenster, dort säulengeschmückte Veranden, Bögen wie bei Palladio. Dabei ist es ihm gelungen, die verschiedenen Stile zu einer Synthese zu führen. Im Detail ist alles grundsätzlich asiatisch: Bananenblätter statt Akanthus zieren die Kapitele, Jasminknospen die Loggia. Wie viele andere Künstler lässt sich auch Jaya Ibrahim von den verschiedensten Stilrichtungen inspirieren, die er in Cipicong neu interpretiert und zu einer gelungenen Eigenkreation zusammengefügt hat.

Un éminent confrère européen qui s'était un jour rendu à Cipicong (à prononcer tchipitchong, l'hommage rendu par Jaya Ibrahim à ses racines javanaises, a déclaré à son retour, ravi : « C'est la Venise de l'Orient ! » Lorsque le croissant de lune s'élève au-dessus des luxuriantes rizières à l'ombre du mont Salak, Cipicong atteint une dimension lyrique : ni limites ni clôtures, juste des collines et vallées à perte de vue. À une heure et demie de route de Jakarta, Cipicong est situé à proximité du palais dans lequel ont vécu Sir Raffles et, plus tard, les Hollandais et Sukarno. Ibrahim, qui a travaillé de longues années à Londres, s'est construit une maison aux références nombreuses – fenêtre vénitienne, vérandas à péristyle, arcs palladiens –, tout en fondant ces styles en une synthèse parfaite. Les détails sont par essence orientaux : des feuilles de bananier remplacent les feuilles d'acanthe dans les chapiteaux et des boutons de jasmin, motif emprunté à un palais javanais du 10e siècle, surmontent la loggia. Comme bien d'autres artistes, Jaya Ibrahim s'est frotté à de nombreux styles. Cipicong en est une brillante réinterprétation toute personnelle.

P. 143 A pair of rattan chairs designed by Jaya Ibrahim are placed on either side of a door leading to a bedroom. • Die beiden von Jaya Ibrahim entworfenen Rattanstühle stehen neben einer Tür, die zu einem der Schlafzimmer führt. • Deux chaises en rotin signées Jaya Ibrahim flanquent la porte de la chambre.

← A 14th-century urn now forms part of the courtyard fountain. The terracotta bowls are used as candleholders during festivities. • Eine Urne aus dem 14. Jahr-hundert ist heute Bestandteil des Brun-nens im Innenhof, die Terrakottatöpfe werden bei Festen als Kerzenbehälter genutzt. • Dans la cour intérieure, une urne du 14e siècle fait aujourd'hui partie du puits, les coupes en terre cuite se transfor-ment en chandeliers pendant les fêtes.

↑ The antique cupboard contains crockery and the door leads to the adja-cent bedroom. • Ein antiker Schrank dient zur Geschirraufbewahrung, durch die offene Tür schaut man in ein weiteres Schlafzimmer. • Une armoire ancienne abrite la vaisselle, la porte mène à la chambre à coucher voisine.

↓ Engravings depicting ancient vases flank the living-room mirror. • Kupfer-stiche antiker Vasen umrahmen den Spiegel im Wohnzimmer. • Des gravu-res sur cuivre encadrent le miroir dans le séjour.

↑ A mirror from Sumatra and a pair of 18th-century doors break up the wall behind the bed. The cut crystal hanging lamp is also from Sumatra. • Die Rückwand des Bettes beleben ein Spiegel aus Sumatra und zwei Türen aus dem 18. Jahrhundert. Die Lampe aus geschliffenem Kristallglas stammt ebenfalls aus Sumatra. • Un miroir de Sumatra et deux portes du 18ᵉ siècle égaient le mur derrière le lit. Le lustre en cristal taillé est aussi de Sumatra.

→ Even the bathroom stays true to the stylistic theme of light walls and dark wood. • Die Gestaltung der Räume mit hellen Wänden und dunklem Holz ist auch im Bad konsequent umgesetzt. • Le principe de décoration des pièces, murs clairs et bois sombres, est aussi mis en pratique dans la salle de bains.

COJÍMAR
CUBA

Fishing for Colors

Cojímar is a nice, quiet fishing town 30 minutes east of Havana, with a colonial fortress built around 1645 to protect the bay from pirates. A bronze statue of the giant of American literature, Ernest Hemingway, is across from the fort since the writer used to go for lunch at the nearby La Terraza restaurant in the 1950s. A few meters away from the restaurant, on a steep site on the bank of the Rio Cojímar river, Cuban architect Arquímedes Poveda designed a modern house in 1958 with a complex floor plan resulting from the clever use of the slope of the reinforced-concrete roofs. This allowed for a dynamic interior space where the street-level entrance forks into two floors connected by a wooden staircase—one located some steps downwards and containing the living room and a pier-like deck, the other a mezzanine for the command-bridge-like dining room that both overlooks the entrance and benefits from an outside view. Naval references are further displayed in the whale-shaped dining table, the porthole windows, and the mariner's compass at the entrance.

Cojímar ist ein ruhiges Fischerdorf 30 Minuten östlich von Havanna. Seine Festung wurde 1645 errichtet, um die Bucht vor Piraten zu schützen. Gegenüber der Festung steht ein Pavillon mit einer Bronzestatue von Ernest Hemingway. Der amerikanische Schriftsteller pflegte im nahe gelegenen Restaurant La Terraza zu Mittag zu essen. Ein paar Meter vom Restaurant entfernt, direkt am Ufer des Flusses Rio Cojímar, liegt ein Haus des kubanischen Architekten Arquímedes Poveda, Baujahr 1958. Der komplexe Grundriss nutzt die Hanglage geschickt aus und vermittelt dem Inneren räumliche Dynamik. Das ebenerdige Foyer verzweigt sich auf zwei Ebenen, die durch eine Treppe aus Holz miteinander verbunden sind. Auf der ein paar Stufen tiefer gelegenen Ebene befindet sich der Wohnraum und eine Terrasse, die einem Landungssteg nachempfunden ist. Die andere Ebene bildet ein Zwischengeschoss mit dem Esszimmer. Wie von einer Kommandobrücke aus sieht man von hier auf den Eingang und nach draußen. Und überall findet sich maritime Motivik: Der Tisch hat die Form eines Walfischs und die Eingangshalle einen Seefahrerkompass und Bullaugen.

Cojímar est un joli et paisible port de pêche à trente minutes à l'est de La Havane, doté d'une forteresse coloniale bâtie vers 1645 pour protéger la baie des pirates. Juste en face, un kiosque abrite une statue en bronze d'Ernest Hemingway car, dans les années 1950, ce géant de la littérature américaine avait l'habitude d'aller déjeuner au restaurant voisin de « La Terraza ». Quelques mètres plus loin, sur la berge du fleuve Rio Cojímar, l'architecte cubain Arquímedes Poveda a conçu en 1958 une maison moderne avec un plan complexe et dynamique qui tire le meilleur profit du terrain escarpé et des appuis nautiques des toits en béton armé. Côté rue, l'entrée donne sur un escalier en bois qui descend vers le séjour et la terrasse embarcadère, ou monte vers une mezzanine accueillant la salle à manger / passerelle de commandement qui jouit d'une belle vue. Les références navales et marines se retrouvent dans la table en forme de baleine, les fenêtres en hublots et le compas de l'entrée.

P.149 The entrance is located on a level halfway between the living and dining room. Above the entrance is a cabinet with a design inspired by the works of Piet Mondrian. • Der Eingang befindet sich auf halber Höhe zwischen Wohn- und Esszimmer. Über der Tür ist ein Schrank zu sehen, dessen Front von Werken Piet Mondrians inspiriert wurde. • L'entrée est située à mi-hauteur, entre le séjour et la salle à manger. Au-dessus de la porte, on voit un placard inspiré d'œuvres de Mondrian.

← A row of portholes leads up to the front door, above which a naked light bulb provides illumination at night. • Bullaugen säumen den Weg zur Haustür, über der eine einfache Glühbirne als Nachtlicht dient. • Des hublots

bordent le chemin qui mène à la porte de la maison, au-dessus de laquelle une simple ampoule électrique sert de veilleuse.

↑ The dining room, located on the house's upper floor, has the most privileged location for enjoying the views of the Cojímar River. The whale-shaped table is yet another allusion to the maritime theme. • Das Esszimmer im Obergeschoss hat die beste Lage, um die Aussicht auf den Cojímar-Fluss zu genießen. Der Tisch in Walform ist eine weitere Anspielung auf die Meereswelt. • C'est de la salle à manger, située à un niveau supérieur, que l'on a la plus belle vue sur le Cojímar. La table en forme de baleine est une autre référence marine.

P.152 From the house's entrance, one can see its spatial layout, with the mezzanine-type dining room on top and the living room below. • Dank der doppelten Deckenhöhe des Eingangsbereichs kann man die räumliche Aufteilung erkennen – oben das Esszimmer, unten der Wohnbereich. • Depuis la haute entrée, on peut apprécier la distribution spatiale très dynamique de la maison, avec sa salle à manger en mezzanine et son séjour en contrebas.

P.153 Turquoise bathroom tiles further emphasize the interior's lively color scheme. • Das Hellblau der Innenräume wird im Bad durch türkisfarbene Fliesen intensiviert. • Le bleu ciel des pièces est intensifié dans la salle de bains par des carreaux turquoise.

COPENHAGEN
DENMARK

Classicism with a Twist

Not many people can claim to have lived in the family home of Tania (Karen) Blixen's father. Alexander Kølpin, however, is one of them. The house was built in 1760, and when the interior designer and artistic director of the Copenhagen International Ballet Festival bought it in 2005, its elegance still shone through the layers of neglect. "I was able to use my stage design training," he says. "After all, both in dance and in interiors, the aim is to tell a story." Kølpin breathed new life into the classical plasterwork, floors, and doors, which had thankfully remained intact, and applied a painstakingly researched color scheme. In 2011, he moved with his wife, Sarah Zobel Kølpin, to Los Angeles and left the house in the hands of a prominent Danish family.

Wer kann schon behaupten, im Elternhaus von Tania (Karen) Blixens Vater gelebt zu haben? Wohl nur wenige außer Alexander Kølpin, dem künstlerischen Leiter des Copenhagen International Ballet Festival und Interiordesigner. Als er 2005 das Anwesen von 1760 kaufte, war die einstige Grazie trotz des Verfalls noch zu erahnen. „Hier konnte ich meine Bühnenausbildung nutzen", erklärt er. „Denn im Tanz wie auch bei Räumen geht es darum, eine Geschichte zu erzählen." Zum Glück waren noch die klassizistischen Stuckelemente, Böden und Türen erhalten. Kølpin belebte sie neu, unter anderem mit einem sorgfältig recherchierten Farbprogramm. 2011 zog er mit seiner Ehefrau Sarah Zobel Kølpin nach Los Angeles und übergab die Schlüssel an eine einflussreiche dänische Familie.

Ils sont rares ceux qui peuvent prétendre avoir vécu dans la maison familiale du père de Tania (Karen) Blixen, mais c'est le cas d'Alexander Kølpin, directeur artistique du Copenhagen International Ballet Festival et architecte d'intérieur. En 2005, lorsqu'il a acheté la propriété datant de 1760, on pouvait encore en deviner la grâce malgré son délabrement. « Ici j'ai pu utiliser ma formation scénique », dit-il, « en effet, qu'il s'agisse de danse ou d'espaces, on veut raconter une histoire. » Heureusement les stucs néoclassiques, les sols et les portes étaient encore intacts. Kølpin leur a rendu la vie, en mettant, entre autres, soigneusement au point la palette de couleurs. En 2011, il s'est installé avec son épouse Zarah Zobel Kølpin à Los Angeleset a remis la clé de la maison ressuscitée à une influente famille danoise.

P.155 Arne Jacobsen Series 7 chairs are grouped around the dining table, the patterned wallpaper is by Farrow & Ball. • Am Esstisch sitzt man auf Arne Jacobsen Stühlen der Serie 7, die Tapete ist von Farrow & Ball. • D'anciennes chaises Série 7 d'Arne Jacobsen autour de la table, le papier peint à motifs est de Farrow & Ball.

← The kitchen lamp was bought at auction, the table is in the Spanish colonial style. • Die Küchenleuchte stammt von einer Auktion, der Tisch ist spanischer Kolonialstil. • Le plafonnier de la cuisine a été acquis dans une vente aux enchères, la table est de style colonial espagnol.

↑ In the living room is a bust of one of Alexander Kølpin's ancestors, after whom he was named. • Im Wohnzimmer steht die Büste eines Vorfahren von Alexander Kølpin, nach dem er benannt wurde. • Dans le séjour, le buste d'un aïeul, à qui Alexander Kolpin doit son nom.

↑ In the bedroom, striped wallpaper by Farrow & Ball creates a soothing atmosphere. • Im Schlafzimmer schafft eine Streifentapete von Farrow & Ball eine Stimmung der Ausgeglichenheit. • Un papier peint rayé de Farrow & Ball donne une atmosphère du calme à coucher.

↗ A flea-market vase stands next to a TASCHEN book of Helmut Newton photographs. • Neben dem TASCHEN-Bildband zu Helmut Newton steht eine skulpturale Vase vom Flohmarkt. • À côté de l'album d'Helmut Newton de TASCHEN, un vase à pied baroque chiné aux Puces.

→ The wood floor in the dressing room was handpainted by a Danish specialist for historic parquet. The mirror and antique center table were bought at auction. The decorative wall coverings by Greeff were made by F. Schumacher & Co. • Ein dänischer Spezialist für Schlossparkett gab dem Dielenboden im Ankleidezimmer ein Schachbrettmuster. Die Greeff-Tapete stammt von F. Schumacher & Co., Standspiegel und Tisch wurden auf Auktionen ersteigert. • Le plancher du dressing a été peint en damier par un spécialiste danois des parquets historiques. Le miroir et la table ancienne ont été achetés aux enchères. Les papiers peints de Greeff ont été réalisés par F. Schumacher & Co.

PP. 160–161 Kølpin took the paintings above the doors as the starting point for the room's color scheme. • Als Grundlage für das Farbschema des Raums dienten Kølpin die Gemälde über den Türen. • Kølpin s'est inspiré des couleurs du tableaux suspendus au-dessus des portes pour choisir celles de la pièce.

COROMANDEL
NEW ZEALAND

Living in a Box

"I grew up on a farm and wanted to get back to nature and give my kids something like the lifestyle I'd enjoyed in child-hood," declares architect Ken Crosson. The site he chose for the family's vacation home is certainly remote (the nearest town is some 12 miles away). He also eschewed many mod cons. There is no dishwasher, TV, or computer. Crosson's in-tent was to create something "gutsy" and "regional." He took inspiration from local wooden "trip" dams built by 19th-century loggers and clad the structure in Lawson's cypress. He also fitted it with two decks, which can be raised to shut up the house when the family is not there. The most unusual element, however, is the bathtub on wheels, which can be filled inside and then pushed around. "You can have a bath in front of the fire or under the stars," enthuses Crosson. How's that for getting back to nature?

„Ich bin auf einer Farm aufgewachsen und wollte zurück zur Natur und meinen Kindern ähnliche Erfahrungen bieten, wie ich sie als Kind erleben durfte", erklärt der Architekt Ken Crosson. Das Grundstück, das er für das Ferienhaus der Familie auswählte, ist auf jeden Fall sehr abgelegen, die nächste Stadt liegt 20 Kilometer entfernt. Außerdem verzich-tete er auf viel modernen Komfort. Es gibt keine Geschirrspülmaschine, keinen Fernseher oder Computer. Crosson wollte etwas „Uriges" und „Landestypisches" schaffen. Er ließ sich von den Dammwegen der Holzfäller des 19. Jahrhunderts inspirieren und verkleidete die Struktur mit dem Holz von Lawson-Zypressen. Auch mit zwei hölzernen Plattformen stattete er es aus, die hochgezogen werden können und das Haus verschließen, wenn die Familie abwe-send ist. Das ungewöhnlichste Element ist jedoch die Badewanne auf Rädern. „Man kann vor dem Kamin oder unter dem Sternenhimmel baden", schwärmt Crosson. Wenn das kein Zurück zur Natur ist!

« Ayant grandi dans une ferme, j'ai voulu me rapprocher de la nature et offrir à mes enfants la même vie saine », explique l'architecte Ken Crosson. Il a conçu sa maison de vacances, bâtie sur un site isolé (à 20 km de la ville la plus proche), sobre et « régionale », renonçant à la plupart des commodités modernes : pas de lave-vaisselle, de télé ni d'ordinateur. S'inspirant des barrages à bascule construits par les bûcherons au 19e siècle, il a tapissé la structure de bardeaux en cyprès de Lawson et l'a équipée de terrasses qui se relèvent pour fermer la maison quand la famille n'est pas là. Toutefois, le plus original, c'est la baignoire sur roulettes que l'on remplit à l'intérieur puis que l'on pousse où l'on veut. « On peut prendre son bain devant la cheminée ou sous les étoiles. » Ça, c'est ce qui s'appelle un vrai retour à la nature.

P. 163 The Crosson-designed master bed from Lawson's cypress. • Das von Crosson entworfene Doppelbett aus dem Holz von Lawson-Zypressen. • Le lit de la chambre principale, dessiné par Crosson, en cyprès de Lawson.

↑ Warm pinewood defines the interiors. The narrow corridor leads from the bedroom to the living room. • Warmes Pinienholz bestimmt die Architektur. Durch einen schmalen Flur gelangt man vom Schlaf- ins Wohnzimmer. • Du bois de pin aux teintes chaudes caractérise l'architecture. Un couloir étroit relie la chambre à coucher au séjour.

↗ On the oak veranda, which boasts views of the Coromandel peninsula's coastline, are Butterfly chairs by Jorge Ferrari-Hardoy. • Butterfly-Stühle von Jorge Ferrari-Hardoy warten auf der

Eichenveranda mit Ausblick über die Küste der Coromandel-Halbinsel. • Des chaises Butterfly de Jorge Ferrari-Hardoy se dressent sur la terrasse de chêne avec vue sur la côte de la presqu'île de Coromandel.

→ Riccardo Blumer's Laleggera chairs flank an oak dining table designed by Crosson. • Riccardo Blumers Laleggera-Stühle flankieren einen von Crosson entworfenen Esstisch aus Eichenholz. • Autour d'une table en chêne dessinée par Crosson, des chaises Laleggera de Riccardo Blumer.

← Hoop pine plywood was used for the kitchen cabinets. • Die Küchenschränke sind aus Schuppentannen-Sperrholz. • Les placards de la cuisine sont en contreplaqué de pin de Hoop.

↑ The terrace can be raised like a drawbridge when the owners leave the house. • Wenn die Bewohner das Haus verlassen, können sie die Terrasse wie eine Zugbrücke einziehen. • Lorsque les habitants quittent la maison, ils peuvent lever la terrasse comme un pont-levis.

DRESDEN
GERMANY

From Bauhaus to Our House

For their own home, architect Jens Zander and lawyer Stefan Heinemann selected a truly fabulous location: it boasts direct access to the Elbe River. Completed in 2006, the building offers a Modernist counterpoint to the neo-Renaissance villas of Dresden's Prussian Quarter and, despite being large enough to house Zander's office, a legal practice, and three other apartments as well, it feels not bulky but, in fact, agreeably lean. Inside, the architecture acts primarily as a backdrop for a well-judged collection of contemporary art. Even the pieces of furniture are positioned like works of art, with every shade and material combination chosen with judicious care.

Der Architekt Jens Zander und Anwalt Stefan Heinemann haben ihr eigenes Haus in fabelhafter Lage mit direktem Elbzugang platziert. Das 2006 errichtete Gebäude setzt unter den Neorenaissance-Villen des Preußischen Viertels einen Akzent im Geist der Moderne. Obwohl neben Zanders eigener Wohnung auch sein Büro, eine Anwaltskanzlei und drei weitere Wohnungen darin untergebracht sind, wirkt die Architektur nicht massiv, sondern angenehm schlank. Im Inneren bildet sie vor allem die Bühne für eine wohltemperierte Sammlung zeitgenössischer Kunst. Selbst die Möbel sind hier wie Kunstwerke im Raum platziert, jede Farbnuance und jede Materialkombination wurde mit Bedacht gesetzt.

L'architecte Jens Zander et l'avocat Stefan Heinemann ont construit sur un site fabuleux, avec accès direct à l'Elbe. Le bâtiment qui date de 2006 pose un accent moderne parmi les villas néo-Renaissance du Quartier Prussien. Bien qu'il abrite aussi le bureau de Zander, un cabinet d'avocat et trois autres appartements, ses lignes ne semblent pas massives mais agréablement élancées. À l'intérieur, l'architecture sert surtout de décor à une collection bien équilibrée d'objets de l'art contemporain. Même les meubles ont été disposés dans les pièces comme des œuvres d'art, l'utilisation de chaque nuance de couleur et de chaque matériau a été longuement soupesée.

P. 169 Industrial flooring in epoxy resin accentuates the entrance hall and stairs. • Ein Industrieboden aus Epoxidharz definiert den Eingangsbereich und die Treppen. • Un sol industriel en résine Epoxy dans l'entrée et les escaliers.

← The red wall above the kitchen units, designed by the architect himself, feels like a work of art in its own right. • Die rote Wand oberhalb der vom Architekten entworfenen Küchenzeile wirkt intensiv wie Kunst. • Au-dessus des éléments de cuisine dessinés par l'architecte, le mur rouge a des airs d'œuvre d'art.

↑ The only contrast in the white bedroom comes courtesy of the bipartite painting by Frank Nitsche. • Den einzigen Akzent im weißen Schlafzimmer setzt das zweiteilige Gemälde von Frank Nitsche. • Le tableau en deux parties de Frank Nitsche est le seul accent sombre dans la chambre à coucher blanche.

PP. 172–173 The library's chairs—all heirloom pieces—form an ensemble in Bauhaus colors. • In der Wohnbibliothek bilden die Polstermöbel (allesamt Erbstücke) ein Ensemble in Bauhausfarben. • Dans le séjour/bibliothèque, les fauteuils rembourrés, tous hérités, forment un ensemble aux couleurs du Bauhaus.

← This expansive space featuring oak parquet and a Moroccan rug leads out onto the riverside terrace. • Von dem großzügigen Raum mit marokkanischem Teppich auf Eichenparkett gelangt man auf die Terrasse mit Elbblick. • La vaste pièce dont le parquet de chêne est recouvert d'un tapis marocain s'ouvre sur une terrasse qui offre un accès à l'Elbe.

↓ Clad in Marazzi tiles, the washbasin unit also acts as seating and storage space. • Der mit Marazzi-Fliesen verkleidete Waschtisch dient zugleich als Sitzbank und Stauraum. • Le lavabo encastré habillé de carreaux Marazzi sert aussi de banc et d'espace de rangement.

ESSAOUIRA
MOROCCO

Relaxed Tradition

Orson Welles's playground when he was filming *Othello* and a hippie rendezvous in the early 1970s, Essaouira has long attracted artists, writers, and fashion designers. Without directly belonging to this tribe, Geneviève Canet and Joël Martial discovered the region in the early 1990s. They were enchanted by the hospitality of the local people and the magnificent countryside, and a year later, they bought a village house nearby. It was a ruin, and anyway much too small, everybody said. But what a surprise for the begrudgers! The place has metamorphosed into a charming retreat. Ever since the beaten earth of the patio gave way to checkerboard slabs and the terrace walls were covered in pinkish lime wash to go with its cement tiles, the visitors have stopped sneering. In essence, the house has lost nothing of its original structure. Facing the patio, a kitchen-living room leads through to a bedroom. Upstairs, the terrace opens onto two small rooms. The argan wood furniture, designed by Joël Martial, is the work of a local carpenter.

Essaouira, Anfang der 1970er Jahre ein berühmter Hippie-Ort, wo sich bereits Orson Welles zur Zeit seines Othello-Erfolges vergnügte, zieht seit vielen Jahren Künstler, Schriftsteller und Modemacher an. Geneviève Canet und Joël Martial gehören zwar nicht direkt zu dieser Szene, als sie die Gegend jedoch Anfang der 1990er Jahre entdeckten, waren sie von der Gastfreundschaft der Einheimischen und der großartigen Landschaft so begeistert, dass sie ein Jahr später in der Umgebung ein Haus kauften. Mit seiner bescheidenen Fassade in einem kleinen Dorf war es zunächst kein Prunkstück. Doch Zweifler wurden spätestens dann eines Besseren belehrt, als der schlichte Lehmboden im Patio sich in ein schwarz-weißes Schachbrett verwandelt hatte. Die gekalkten Mauern, die auf der Terrasse rosa getüncht sind, überzeugen ebenso wie die Zementfliesen. Trotzdem blieb die ursprüngliche Struktur erhalten: Am Patio liegt ein großes Wohnzimmer, eine Kombination aus Salon und Küche, die in einen weiteren Raum führt. Im ersten Stock führt eine Terrasse in zwei kleine Zimmer. Die Möbel aus Arganholz wurden nach einem Entwurf von Joël Martial in einer Schreinerei vor Ort angefertigt.

Cité hippie au début des années 1970, terrain de jeu d'Orson Welles à l'époque de son Othello, Essaouira attire depuis longtemps artistes, écrivains et gens de mode. Sans directement appartenir à la tribu, Geneviève Canet et Joël Martial découvrent la région au début des années 1990. Séduits par l'hospitalité du cru et la magnificence des paysages, ils achètent une maison des environs. À l'origine modeste façade au cœur d'un humble village, l'endroit se mue en refuge de charme. Quelle surprise pour ses contempteurs ! Depuis que la terre battue qui couvrait le patio a été reléguée aux oubliettes, qu'à la place un damier noir et blanc joue à la marelle, que les murs passés à la chaux, teintés en rose sur la terrasse, amusent des carrelages de ciment, eh bien, les visiteurs ne badinent plus. Fondamentalement, la maison n'a pas perdu sa structure originelle. Devant le patio, une salle de séjour à la fois salon et cuisine borde une chambre ; à l'étage, la terrasse s'ouvre sur deux petites pièces. Le mobilier en bois d'argan, dessiné par Joël Martial, est l'œuvre d'un menuisier local.

P. 177 The door on the left in the upstairs guest room leads out onto the roof terrace. • Aus dem Gästezimmer im Obergeschoss führt links eine Tür auf die Dachterrasse. • Dans cette chambre du premier étage, une porte, à gauche, mène au toit-terrasse.

← The kitchen is organized in the regional style. • Die Küche ist nach einheimischer Art eingerichtet. • La cuisine est aménagée dans le style de la région.

↖ Beyond the arch is the kitchen, which has a floor of terra-cotta tiles. • Durch einen Rundbogen im Erdgeschoss gelangt man in die mit Terrakottafliesen ausgelegte Küche. • Au rez-de-chaussée, un arc en plein cintre s'ouvre sur la cuisine carrelée de terre cuite.

↓ The bed stands on a plinth and a linen curtain blocks the sun's rays. Light and shade make subtle play in this soberly decorated space. • Das Bett liegt etwas erhöht, ein Leinenvorhang schützt vor Sonnenstrahlen. Licht und Schatten beleben den schlicht dekorierten Raum. • Le lit est placé sur une estrade voilée par un rideau en lin. Ombre et lumière jouent à cache-cache dans cet espace sobre.

↑ The earthen-colored staircase lead-
ing to the upper floor. • Die rosafarbene
Treppe führt in den ersten Stock. •
L'escalier rose mène à l'étage.

↗ In the corridor, the blue of the walls
and ceiling echoes that of the tiles. • Die
Farbe der Fliesen im Korridor wird im
Blau der Decke und Wände aufgenommen. • On retrouve la couleur des carreaux du couloir dans le bleu du plafond
et des murs.

→ The fireplace designed by Joël Martial, with its Moorish arch. • Der von Joël
Martial entworfene Kamin erinnert an
die geschwungenen Formen der mauri-
schen Architektur. • La cheminée
dessinée par Joël Martial évoque les
courbes mauresques.

← A tiled fountain adds a touch of bold color to the terrace. • Ein gekachelter Brunnen setzt farbige Akzente auf der Terrasse. • Un puits carrelé égaie la terrasse avec ses accents de couleur.

↓ The masonry banquettes *(doukana)* of the ground-floor living room are covered with Indian cushions. The furniture, like the sconces and coffee table, was made by a local craftsman after sketches by Joël Martial. • Auf den gemauerten Bänken *(doukana)* im Salon des Erdgeschosses liegen indische Kissen. Die Möbel, wie die Appliken und der Couchtisch, wurden nach Entwürfen von Joël Martial vor Ort produziert. • Les banquettes en maçonnerie *(doukana)* du salon du rez-de-chaussée sont recouvertes de coussins indiens. Le mobilier, comme les appliques et la table ronde, a été fabriqué par un artisan local d'après les croquis de Joël Martial.

↑ In the rest area on the top floor, shades of pink and green form a harmonious combination. • Im Ruheraum unter dem Dach wurden Rosa- und Grüntöne harmonisch kombiniert. • Une harmonieuse combinaison de rose et de vert dans la salle de repos sous le toit.

↓ Behind a narrow doorway is a round shower in a bathroom pared down to essentials. • Hinter einer schmalen Tür liegt ein einfaches Bad mit runder Dusche. • Derrière une porte étroite, la douche ronde d'une salle de bains dépouillée.

FARO JOSÉ IGNACIO
URUGUAY

Luxe, Calme et Simplicité

For Argentine architect Azul García Uriburu, the tiny fishing village of Faro José Ignacio is all about the family. Her father, Nicolás (a famous artist), lives nearby and her mother runs a local guesthouse. She and her husband, Marcos Pereda, own a house directly on the windswept beach, where they spend vacations with their four children. Ask García Uriburu why she likes the locality and she'll mention the safe beach, the seals and dolphins frolicking in the ocean, and the fact that you can walk everywhere. She designed the symmetrical house herself, with the goal of integrating it into the natural setting. The façade is clad with pine and the interior painted a sand color. "The look is very monochromatic here," she says. "It's people who add color." And how is life on the beach? "It's incredible," she admits. "When we're there, it feels as if we were alone on Earth."

Für die argentinische Architektin Azul García Uriburu ist das winzige Fischerdorf Faro José Ignacio ein wichtiger Dreh- und Angelpunkt ihres Familienlebens: Ihr Vater Nicolás (ein berühmter Künstler) lebt ganz in der Nähe, ihre Mutter führt am Ort ein Gästehaus. Azul und ihr Ehemann Marcos Pereda besitzen unmittelbar am windgepeitschten Strand ein Haus, wo sie mit ihren vier Kindern die Ferien verbringen. Sobald man Azul García Uriburu fragt, warum sie diesen Platz so mag, wird sie den sicheren Strand, die Seehunde und Delfine im Meer anführen sowie die Tatsache, dass man überallhin zu Fuß gehen kann. Sie selbst hat das symmetrische Haus mit der Absicht entworfen, dass es sich harmonisch in seine natürliche Umgebung integriert. Die Fassade ist mit Kiefernholz verkleidet, die Innenwände wurden sandfarben gestrichen. „Alles wirkt sehr monochrom hier", räumt sie ein, „es sind die Menschen, die Farbe hinzufügen." Und sie sagt: „Es ist unglaublich: Wenn wir uns hier aufhalten, haben wir das Gefühl, allein auf der Erde zu sein."

Pour l'architecte argentine Azul García Uriburu, le minuscule village de pêcheurs de Faro José Ignacio est une affaire de famille. Sa mère y dirige une guest-house et son père Nicolás (un artiste célèbre) vit non loin. Son mari Marcos Pereda et elle y passent leurs vacances avec leurs quatre enfants, appréciant la plage tranquille, les phoques, les dauphins et le fait de pouvoir se rendre à pied n'importe où. La maison qu'elle a construite sur la plage venteuse est symétrique et conçue pour s'intégrer dans le paysage. La façade est tapissée de bardeaux en pin et les intérieurs sont peints couleur sable. « L'effet est très monochrome », explique-t-elle. « Ce sont les gens qui apportent de la couleur. » Quant au fait de vivre au bord de la mer : « C'est merveilleux. Ici, on a vraiment l'impression d'être seuls sur terre. »

P.185 The quarrystone chimney in the living area extends up through the roof. • Das Bruchsteinmauerwerk des Wohnzimmerkamins setzt sich auf dem Dach als Schornstein fort. • On retrouve sur le toit la pierre de taille de la cheminée du séjour.

← The table on the back terrace is used for serving lunch and dinner. All the furniture was designed by Isabelle Firmin Dido. • Alle Möbel auf der hinteren Terrasse wurden von Isabelle Firmin Didot entworfen. • Les meubles sur la terrasse à l'arrière de la maison ont été créés par Isabelle Firmin Didot.

→ Sandy hues dominate the kitchen, where the glass door to the terrace has bamboo blinds for shade. • Sandige Farbtöne prägen die Küche, in der Bambusrollos die Glastür zur Terrasse verdunkeln. • Des tons de sable caractérisent la cuisine, des stores en bambou s'enroulent sur la porte en verre menant à la terrasse.

P.188 The bedroom's French doors afford direct access to the beach. • Das Schlafzimmer hat über Flügeltüren direkten Zugang zum Strand. • La chambre a un accès direct à la plage grâce à des portes à battants.

P.189 At the rear of the chimney is a second fireplace; in front of it is a wooden bed that serves as a sofa. • Der Kamin heizt hinten ein weiteres Zimmer, in dem ein Holzbett als Sofa dient. • La cheminée chauffe une autre pièce dans laquelle un lit en bois sert de canapé.

"The look is very monochromatic. It's the people who add color." AZUL GARCÍA URIBURU

„Alles wirkt sehr monochrom hier. Es sind die Menschen, die Farbe hinzufügen."
« L'effet est très monochrome ici. Ce sont les gens qui apportent de la couleur. »

FIRE ISLAND
USA

Surfing in Style

New York-based architect Alan Wanzenberg has not one but two houses on Fire Island. The four-bedroom Ocean House used to belong to fashion designer Perry Ellis. The smaller Bay House was built on the site of an almost identical structure, which burned down in a 1992 fire. Linked by a cedar boardwalk, they are wonderfully remote. The land on either side belongs to the National Parks Service, which means no neighbors. According to Wanzenberg, the Ocean House "is extroverted, lighter, brighter." The Bay House, meanwhile, is "darker, a bit moodier." Both are decorated with a refined mix of postwar French furniture, Swedish Neoclassical pieces, and a number of built-in elements. Life there is apparently wonderfully laid-back. "The options for doing things are quite limited," the lucky owner rejoices. "What I've come to enjoy are the long periods of unstructured time."

Der New Yorker Architekt Alan Wanzenberg besitzt nicht nur ein, sondern zwei Häuser auf Fire Island. Das sogenannte Ocean House mit vier Schlafzimmern gehörte zuvor dem Modeschöpfer Perry Ellis. Das kleinere Bay House entstand auf dem Grundriss eines nahezu identischen, 1992 abgebrannten Bauwerks. Beide sind mit einem Holzsteg aus Zedernholz verbunden und wunderbar einsam gelegen. Das Land zu beiden Seiten gehört der Nationalen Parkverwaltung – es gibt also keine Nachbarn. Laut Wanzenberg ist das Ocean House „extrovertierter, leichter, heller", das Bay House dagegen „düsterer, ein wenig melancholisch". Beide hat er mit einer raffinierten Mischung aus französischen Möbeln der Nachkriegszeit, schwedischem Klassizismus und Einbauelementen eingerichtet. Das Leben scheint dort auf wundersame Weise entspannt abzulaufen. „Die Möglichkeiten zur Beschäftigung sind hier ziemlich begrenzt", strahlt der glückliche Besitzer. „Ich genieße einfach die langen Phasen unverplanter Zeit."

L'architecte Alan Wanzenberg, basé à New York, n'a pas une mais deux maisons sur Fire Island. Ocean House, qui compte quatre chambres, appartenait autrefois au créateur Perry Ellis. Bay House, plus petite, a été construite sur le site d'une structure quasiment identique détruite par un incendie en 1992. Reliées par une promenade en cèdre, elles sont merveilleusement isolées, le terrain tout autour appartenant aux parcs nationaux. Donc, pas de voisins. Selon Wanzenberg, Ocean House est «extravertie, claire, légère, tandis que Bay House est plus sombre, mélancolique». Toutes deux sont aménagées avec des éléments encastrés et un assortiment raffiné de meubles français des années 1950 et néoclassiques suédois. Il y règne une atmosphère décontractée. «Il n'y a pas grand-chose à faire ici. J'ai pris goût à ces longues périodes de temps déstructuré.»

P. 191 A Mathieu Matégot light fixture hangs above a seating area in the Bay House bedroom. • Eine Deckenlampe von Mathieu Matégot hängt im Bay House über der Sitzgruppe des Schlafzimmers. • Un luminaire de Mathieu Matégot est suspendu au-dessus du coin salon de la chambre de Bay House.

← Steps lead down from the house to a cedarwood sun deck located right on the bay. • Über ein paar Stufen gelangt man vom Haus auf das Sonnendeck aus Zedernplanken, das direkt an der Bucht liegt. • Quelques marches mènent de la maison à la terrasse en cèdre ensoleillée, située sur la baie.

↑ Two armchairs from Dominique stand in front of the fireplace in the Ocean House living room. The other chairs are by Charlotte Perriand and the two blue lamps from Fantoni. • Im Ocean House stehen zwei Lehnstühle von Dominique

vor dem Kamin im Wohnzimmer. Die übrigen Stühle sind von Charlotte Perriand, die beiden blauen Glaslampen von Fantoni. • Dans le séjour d'Ocean House, deux fauteuils de Dominique devant la cheminée. Les autres sièges sont de Charlotte Perriand, et les deux lampes bleues viennent de chez Fantoni.

PP. 194–195 Wanzenberg designed the bed in the Bay House from fir. • Wanzenberg entwarf das Bett aus Kiefernholz im Bay House. • Wanzenberg a dessiné le lit en sapin de la chambre de Bay House.

← A French 1950s chair stands in front of an antique Swedish chest in the master bedroom of the Ocean House. The checkered woolen blanket dates from the early 20th century. • Im Ocean House steht im Schlafzimmer ein französischer Stuhl aus den 1950ern vor einer antiken schwedischen Kommode. Die karierte Wolldecke stammt aus dem frühen 20. Jahrhundert. • Dans la chambre principale d'Ocean House, une chaise française des années 1950 devant un vieux secrétaire suédois. La couverture à carreaux en laine date du début du 20ᵉ siècle.

↓ Two Paul László chairs face an Edward Durell Stone sofa in the Bay House sitting room. The rug is Moroccan. • Im Bay House stehen im Wohnzimmer zwei Stühle von Paul László einem Sofa von Edward Durell Stone gegenüber. Der Teppich kommt aus Marokko. • Dans le salon de Bay House, une paire de fauteuils de Paul László face à un canapé d'Edward Durell Stone. Le tapis est marocain.

→ A surfboard is propped up against the wall in one of the Ocean House bathrooms. • Ein Surfbrett lehnt an der Wand eines der Badezimmer im Ocean House. • Dans l'une des salles de bains d'Ocean House, une planche de surf est posée contre un mur.

GEGGIANO
ITALY

When Walls Speak Volumes

The Villa di Geggiano rises from its lush surrounding landscape like a dignified old lady covered in jewels and swathed in sumptuous green silk. The avenue of cypresses, elegant façade, *teatrino all'aperto* (open-air theater), porticoes festooned with cherubs, and, finally, the chapel remind one that this is no ordinary place: The Bianchi Bandinellis, who built the house on much older foundations at the end of the 18th century, have a family tree that includes Pope Alexander III and a world-class archeologist-cum–art historian. The owners of the Villa di Geggiano, Ruggiero Boscu and his wife Alessandra Bianchi Bandinelli, are passionate about the property and its vineyards, and have passed on their enthusiasm to their sons Andrea and Alessandro. Today, the two brothers and their families have turned their backs on the stresses of life in Rome and settled at Geggiano among the frescoes by Ignazio Moder and furniture by Agostino Fantastici to look after their vines and preserve their incomparable inheritance.

Wie sich die Villa di Geggiano in der Landschaft erhebt, gleicht sie einer würdevollen alten Dame mit Juwelen und grüner Seidenstola. Die zypressengesäumte Allee, die elegante Fassade, das kleine Freilichttheater (teatrino all'aperto), die Kapelle, und die Putti über den Portalen – all dies lässt auf einen außergewöhnlichen Ort schließen. Die Familie Bianchi Bandinelli, zu deren Stammbaum auch Papst Alexander III. und ein weltberühmter Archäologe und Kunsthistoriker gehören, ließ die Villa Ende des 18. Jahrhunderts auf den Grundmauern eines früheren Gebäudes errichten und hat sie seitdem hingebungsvoll instand gehalten. Die Liebe zu Haus und Weinbergen hat sich von den heutigen Besitzern Ruggiero Boscu und seiner Frau Alessandra Bianchi Bandinelli längst auf ihre Söhne Andrea und Alessandro übertragen. Inzwischen haben die beiden Brüder samt ihren Familien dem Stress von Rom den Rücken gekehrt, um in Geggiano zu leben, umgeben von Fresken Ignazio Moders und den Möbeln von Agostino Fantastici. Sie verwalten ihr Weingut und die Ländereien und kümmern sich um ihr unvergleichliches Anwesen.

Telle une vieille dame très digne parée de ses bijoux et portant un sompteux boa de plumes, la villa di Geggiano émerge du paysage luxuriant qui l'entoure. Son allée bordée de cyprès, sa façade élégante, son **teatrino all'aperto** (petit théâtre en plein air) ses portiques ornés de chérubins et sa chapelle nous révèlent son caractère exceptionnel. La maison a été édifiée sur des vestiges plus anciens vers la fin du 18ᵉ siècle par la famille Bianchi Bandinelli dont l'arbre généalogique peut s'enorgueillir d'un pape, Alexandre III, et d'un archéologue et historien d'art, dont la réputation internationale n'est plus à faire. La famille s'occupe toujours avec le même dévouement de la demeure ancestrale, et les actuels propriétaires, Ruggiero Boscu et son épouse Alessandra Bianchi Bandinelli, éprouvent une telle passion pour la villa et ses vignobles qu'ils ont réussi à transmettre leur enthousiasme à leurs fils Andrea et Alessandro. Aujourd'hui, les deux frères et leurs familles ont tourné le dos à la vie stressante en Rome et sont venus vivre à Geggiano entre les fresques d'Ignazio Moder et les meubles d'Agostino Fantastici, pour veiller sur les vignobles et, surtout, pour préserver un héritage incomparable.

P. 199 Towards the end of the 18th century, the Duke of Lorraine presented the Bianchi Bandinelli children with this superb wooden horse. • Gegen Ende des 18. Jahrhunderts schenkte der Herzog von Lothringen den Kindern der Familie Bianchi Bandinelli dieses wunderbare Holzpferd. • Ce superbe cheval en bois sculpté polychrome a été offert par le duc de Lorraine aux enfants des Bianchi Bandinelli vers la fin du 18ᵉ siècle.

← In the private chapel, the decor shows the Bianchi Bandinellis' taste for luxury and elegance. • In der Privatkapelle zeugt die prächtige Ausgestaltung vom erlesenen Geschmack der Familie Bianchi Bandinelli. • Dans la chapelle privée, le décor témoigne du goût des Bianchi Bandinelli pour le faste élégant.

↑ From this window one has a fine view of the *teatrino all'aperto*. • Von diesem Fenster aus hat man einen guten Blick auf das *teatrino all'aperto*. • Sur cette fenêtre on peut admirer le *teatrino all'aperto*.

↗ Sienese cabinetmakers of the late 18th century decorated the furniture in the Blue Salon like porcelain, in blue and white. The fan and the small electric lamp both date from the early 20th century. • Kunstschreiner aus Siena verzierten gegen Ende des 18. Jahrhunderts die Möbel im Blauen Salon mit blau-weißem Dekor, der an Porzellan denken lässt. Der Fächer und die kleine Lampe stammen vom Anfang des 20. Jahrhunderts. • Des ébénistes siennois de la fin du 18ᵉ siècle décorèrent le mobilier dans le Salon bleu en imitant la porcelaine bleue et blanche. L'éventail et

la petite lampe électrique datent du début du 20ᵉ siècle.

PP. 202–203 In the Blue Salon, the walls are covered with wallpaper from the former Paris store Au Grand Balcon. • Die Tapete im Blauen Salon stammt aus dem damaligen Pariser Geschäft Au Grand Balcon. • Dans le Salon bleu, le papier peint des murs provient de l'ancien magasin parisien Au Grand Balcon.

← The visitor is greeted by the late 18th-century frescoes of Ignazio Moder. • Schon am Eingang erwarten den Besucher die Fresken Ignazio Moders vom Ende des 18. Jahrhunderts. • Le visiteur est accueilli dès l'entrée par les fresques peintes vers la fin du 18ᵉ siècle par Ignazio Moder.

↓ The tapestry rooms contain magnificent painted furniture made in about 1790, though the "tapestries" in question are no more than large canvases. • Im Gobelin-Salon stehen herrlich bemalte Möbel von 1790. Die „Gobelins" entpuppen sich allerdings bei näherem Hinsehen als auf Leinwand gemalt. • Le salon des Tapisseries abrite un magnifique mobilier peint exécuté vers 1790, mais les tapisseries ne sont en réalité que de grandes toiles peintes.

↑ The gallery is adorned with frescoes in the style of Pompeian wall paintings with Rococo decor. • Fresken im Stil von pompejanischen Wandmalereien mit Rokoko-Verzierung schmücken die Wände der Galerie. • Des fresques de style pompéien à décor rococo couvrent les murs de la galerie.

↓ The gold-hued ornamentation of the door inlays blends harmoniously with the Brunswick green of the walls. • Die goldfarbenen Ornamente der Türfüllungen harmonieren mit der Wandfarbe in Braunschweiger Grün. • Les dorures des panneaux de porte s'harmonisent à la couleur des murs, un vert Brunswick.

↓ In this bedroom, the playwright Vittorio Alfieri (1749–1803)—who was a frequent house guest—spent many nights in the superb silk-hung four-poster bed. • In diesem Zimmer schlief der Dramatiker Vittorio Alfieri (1749–1803), der häufig zu Gast war, unter einem seidenen Betthimmel. • L'auteur dramatique Vittorio Alfieri (1749–1803) passa souvent la nuit dans ce superbe lit à baldaquin drapé de soie.

HAMWOOD
IRELAND

My Home Is My Museum

When they arrived at Hamwood in 1961, Charles Hamilton and his wife, Anne, were deeply disappointed by the house that Charles was to inherit from his father the following year. For one thing, the façade of the great horseshoe-shaped building was hidden under a cloak of ivy, and for another the window frames were covered in dismal dark paint. Anne remembers how at the time, her dream was to own a large, light-filled, welcoming home. She decided to tear off all the ivy and the exterior stucco, which revealed some frighteningly uneven surfaces. Thereafter, it was an uphill struggle to restore the house's original façade. Hamwood was built in 1764 by Sir Charles Hamilton, the ancestor of the present owner, in the purest Neoclassical style. Today, though the presence of two curved wings may take you by surprise, you will find yourself seduced immediately after by the Central European style of the front hall, with its Russian pine panelling. Charles and Anne made a deliberate decision not to touch the interior decoration, leaving the furniture, the pictures, and the bibelots as they found them. This, in retrospect, is why Hamwood remains one of the most authentic houses of its kind to be found anywhere in Ireland.

Als Charles Hamilton und seine Frau Anne 1961 in Hamwood eintrafen, waren sie recht enttäuscht vom Anblick des Hauses, das Charles im Jahr darauf nach dem Tod seines Vaters erben sollte. Die Fassade des hufeisenförmigen Baus verschwand unter dem Efeu, und die Fensterlaibungen waren in düsteren Farben gestrichen. Anne erinnert sich, dass sie damals von einem großen, lichten, freundlichen Zuhause träumte und deshalb beschloss, Efeu und Verputz zu entfernen. Mit dem Resultat, dass schrecklich unebene Außenmauern zum Vorschein kamen. Es bedurfte einiger Anstrengungen, bis das 1764 von Sir Charles Hamilton, einem Vorfahren des heutigen Besitzers, in schnörkellosem Klassizismus erbaute Haus wieder präsentabel aussah. Mögen heute die beiden gekrümmten Flügel die Besucher erstaunen, so bezaubert sie die im mitteleuropäischen Stil mit russischer Kiefer getäfelte Eingangshalle ganz gewiss. Charles und Anne haben die Innenausstattung nicht angetastet: Möbel, Bilder und Nippes blieben, wie und wo sie waren. So zählt Hamwood zu den authentischsten Landsitzen der Grünen Insel.

En arrivant à Hamwood, en 1961, Charles Hamilton et son épouse Anne furent assez déçus en voyant la maison dont Charles hérita l'année suivante, après le décès de son père. La façade de cette grande demeure en forme de fer à cheval était dissimulée sous le lierre et les encadrements des fenêtres étaient recouverts de peinture sombre. Anne se souvient qu'elle rêvait alors d'une grande maison claire et accueillante. Elle décida donc d'ôter le lierre et le stuc, ce qui lui valut de devoir affronter des murs extérieurs d'une inégalité effrayante. Ensuite, de nombreux efforts furent nécessaires pour que la maison retrouve sa façade d'époque. Hamwood a été construit en 1764 par Sir Charles Hamilton, un ancêtre du propriétaire actuel, dans un style néoclassique dépouillé. Et si aujourd'hui la présence de deux ailes en arrondi peut étonner les visiteurs, ceux-ci sont charmés par l'entrée – style Europe centrale – lambrissée de pin provenant de Russie. Charles et Anne ont décidé de ne pas toucher à la décoration intérieure, laissant intacts le mobilier, les tableaux et les bibelots. Voilà pourquoi Hamwood compte parmi les demeures les plus authentiques de Île Verte.

P. 207 The wood used in the construction of Hamwood came from Russia. Curving corridors were designed to reduce drafts and keep the rooms in the central part of the building as far as possible from the entrance in one of the wings. • Das Holz, das beim Bau von Hamwood verwendet wurde, stammte aus Russland. Die gekurvten Korridore sollen den Durchzug brechen und die Salons des Haupttrakts so weit wie möglich von der Eingangstür in einem der Flügel trennen. • Le bois utilisé pour construire Hamwood vient de Russie. Les corridors courbes doivent couper les courants d'air et éloigner au maximum les salons du corps central de la porte d'entrée dans l'une des ailes.

↑ In traditional Anglo-Saxon fashion, the mantelpiece is decorated with souvenirs and heirloom items. Above, are tastefully framed portrait miniatures. • Nach angelsächsischer Tradition ist der Kaminsims mit Erbstücken und Souvenirs dekoriert. Darüber hängen Miniaturporträts in edler Rahmung. • Comme le veut la tradition anglo-saxonne, la tablette de cheminée est décorée de souvenirs et d'objets hérités. Au-dessus, des portraits miniatures.

↗ The house bears a passing resemblance to a Russian *dacha*, and when one knows where the wood in the corridors came from, this is hardly surprising. On the other hand the stag's antlers, the prints, and walking sticks are quintessential Irish gentry. • Das Haus ähnelt ein wenig einer russischen Datscha.

Kennt man die Herkunft des für die Korridore verwendeten Holzes, erstaunt dies nicht. Die Hirschgeweihe, Stiche und Wanderstöcke gehören dagegen unbestreitbar zum Alltag der irischen Gentry. • La maison ressemble un peu à une « datcha ». Quand on connaît l'origine du bois utilisé pour les corridors, cela ne surprend pas. En revanche, les bois de cerf, les gravures, les cannes font incontestablement partie du quotidien de la « gentry » irlandaise.

→ In one of the bedrooms is a four-poster bed hung with apricot-colored fabric. • In einem Schlafzimmer steht ein Himmelbett mit apricotfarbenen Stoffbahnen. • Dans une chambre à coucher, un lit à baldaquin drapé d'étoffe abricot.

↑ Under the mirror-backed shelves leans a simple Victorian silhouette. • Unter einem Regal mit verspiegelter Rückwand lehnt ein viktorianischer Scherenschnitt. • Sous une étagère à fond de miroir, un cadre avec une petite silhouette victorienne.

PP. 210–211 The main drawing room at Hamwood is at once cozy and formal. The gilded frames of the "rocaille" mirror, the paintings, and the miniatures harmonize wonderfully with the wallpaper, which was hung several years ago by David Skinner, the "archeologist of Irish wallpaper." • Der große Salon von Hamwood zeigt sich „cozy" und förmlich zugleich. Die vergoldeten Rahmen des Rocaille-Spiegels und der Gemälde und Miniaturen sind abgestimmt auf die Tapete, die vor einigen Jahren David Skinner anbrachte, der „Archäologe der irischen Tapetenkunst". • Le grand salon de Hamwood, à la fois « cozy » et formel. L'encadrement doré du miroir rocaille et des tableaux et des miniatures s'harmonise avec le papier peint posé il y a quelques années, par David Skinner, « l'archéologue du papier peint irlandais ».

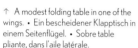

↑ A modest folding table in one of the wings. • Ein bescheidener Klapptisch in einem Seitenflügel. • Sobre table pliante, dans l'aile latérale.

↑ On a small 18th-century table, a porcelain lamp—representing a cherub with a basin on his head—is topped by a Montgolfière lampshade. • Auf einem Beistelltisch aus dem 18. Jahrhundert wird eine Porzellanlampe – ein Cherub, der eine Schale trägt – von einer Montgolfiere beschirmt. • Sur une petite table d'appoint 18e, une lampe en porcelaine – un chérubin portant une vasque –, est coiffée d'un abat-jour style « montgolfière ».

↓ Anne Hamilton has happily combined shades of pink, fuchsia, vanilla, and caramel with the period furniture, which includes several fine four-poster beds. • Anne Hamilton hat es verstanden, Rosa-, Fuchsien-, Vanille- und Karmeltöne mit Stilmöbeln zu kombinieren, darunter einige Himmelbetten. • Anne Hamilton a su combiner des tons roses, fuchsia, vanille et caramel et les meubles d'époque, dont quelques beaux lits à baldaquin.

HAVANA
CUBA

Wonderful Wood

Patios, porticoes, and persiennes are the three major features of Cuba's architectural legacy. And the most suitable means of dealing with its tropical climate and extroverted way of life. In the 1950s, these elements were reinterpreted by Cuban architects. Among them, Frank Martínez achieved a synthesis between the international avant-garde and Cuban tradition in creating an original architectural language: his 1955 design for the Pérez Farfante family in Nuevo Vedado successfully combined Corbusian syntax with traditional Cuban architecture. The clever layout separates the prismatic structure on stilts into two separate housing blocks by means of a central soaring space. The open ground floor becomes an extended porch set upon a clifftop. The floor-to-ceiling carpentry, which includes both louvers and panes of glass, reasserts the lines of the windows, which provide cross-ventilation as well as natural light. The two apartments are identical, with terrazzo floors, exposed-concrete blocks, and wood paneling to display works of art by Cuban artists. Martínez's approach to segregating the living spaces from the bedrooms by using traditional features proves that form can follow function while also reaffirming cultural identity.

Die wichtigsten Merkmale der traditionellen kubanischen Architektur sind Innenhöfe, Säulengänge und Jalousien. Sie passen zum tropischen Klima und extrovertierten Lebensstil der Kubaner. In den 1950ern interpretieren Architekten wie Frank Martínez diese Elemente neu. Seine Synthese zwischen internationaler Avantgarde und kubanischen Usus brachte eine originelle Architektursprache hervor. Sein Entwurf für das Haus der Familie Pérez Farfante in Nuevo Vedado von 1955 ist eine gelungene Kreuzung der Formenwelt Le Corbusiers und traditioneller kubanischer Architektur. Das prismatische Gebäude steht auf Stützen und wird von einem hohen Raum in der Mitte in zwei separate Funktionsblöcke getrennt. Das offene Erdgeschoss wiederum erweitert sich zu einer Veranda, die auf einem Felsen liegt. Deckenhohe Holzverkleidungen und Fenster mit integrierten Lamellenjalousien verleihen den Räumen Struktur. Beide Wohnbereiche sind identisch: Böden aus Terrazzofliesen, Wände aus Betonblöcken und Holzvertäfelung für die Werke kubanischer Künstler. Martínez' Villa zeigt, dass Form der Funktion folgen und dabei zugleich die kulturelle Identität stärken kann.

Patios, portiques et persiennes sont les trois grandes caractéristiques des vieilles maisons cubaines, étant parfaitement adaptées à son climat tropical et à son style de vie extraverti. Dans les années 1950, ces éléments ont été réinterprétés par des architectes cubains. Frank Martínez a synthétisé l'avant-garde internationale et la tradition cubaine en créant un langage original et contemporain : la demeure qu'il a conçue pour les Pérez Farfante à Nuevo Vedado en 1955 marie avec succès la syntaxe le-corbusienne et l'architecture cubaine traditionnelle. Son plan ingénieux divise la structure sur pilotis en deux corps de bâtiments à l'aide d'un puits central. La charpenterie s'étend du sol au plafond, les persiennes et les baies vitrées soulignant la ligne de fenêtres tout en laissant passer l'air et la lumière naturelle. Les deux appartements jumeaux ont des sols en mosaïque, des murs de béton brut et des boiseries où sont accrochées des œuvres d'artistes cubains. La séparation des espaces de séjour des chambres à coucher à l'aide d'éléments traditionnels prouve que la forme peut épouser la fonction tout en réaffirmant l'identité culturelle.

P. 215 A large floor-to-ceiling window illuminates the study. • Das Arbeitszimmer erhält sein Licht durch ein Fenster, das sich vom Boden bis zur Decke erstreckt. • Le bureau, éclairé par un grande fenêtre qui va du sol au plafond.

↑ The combination of wood-paneled walls and furniture in warm hues tempers the severity of the concrete architecture. • Holzvertäfelte Wände und Möbel in warmen Tönen nehmen der Betonkonstruktion ihre Härte. • Des murs lambrissés et des meubles aux teintes chaudes adoucissent la rigueur du béton.

↑ The mahogany chairs and table are in keeping with the Modernist Corbusian ambience. • Stilecht fügt sich die Mahagoni-Sitzgruppe in das moderne Ambiente im Stil Le Corbusiers ein. • La table et les chaises en acajou s'intègrent avec élégance dans l'ambiance moderne de style Le Corbusier.

→ Features such as the rectangular bar block in wood combine rigor and sensuality. • Einbauten wie dieser Barblock in Edelholz verbinden Strenge und Sinnlichkeit. • Dans ce bloc-bar prismatique en bois précieux, la rigueur se mêle à la sensualité.

↖ One of the terraces with a gallery-type ceiling over the central entrance space that divides the building's two functional blocks. • Eine der überdachten, galerieähnlichen Terrassen über dem zentralen Eingangsbereich, der die Funktionsblöcke des Gebäudes unterteilt. • Une des terrasses couvertes, telle une galerie au-dessus de l'entrée centrale qui divise les blocs fonctionnels du bâtiment.

← The spatial fluidity and integration of the different rooms, which may be opened and closed at will, are some of the most outstanding features of this modern villa. • Der Raumfluss und das Ineinanderübergehen unterschiedlicher Wohnbereiche, die ganz nach Belieben geöffnet oder abgetrennt werden können, zeichnen dieses moderne Haus aus. • La fluidité spatiale et l'intégration des différents espaces qui peuvent s'ouvrir et se fermer à volonté font partie des caractéristiques les plus frappantes de cette architecture moderne.

↑ A folding partition enables this open space to be divided into separate living and dining rooms. • Mit einer faltbaren Trennwand lässt sich der große Raum in Wohn- und Esszimmer unterteilen. • Une cloison dépliante transforme la pièce spacieuse en séjour et en salle à manger.

HONG KONG
CHINA

The Bolder the Better

Some say a man's home is his castle, but David Tang's eclectic, eccentric house is more like a playground—for the mind as well as the senses. Hong Kong's most famous bon vivant businessman and art collector lives with his wife in one of the city's rare historic houses, located on a winding road in the hills above the skyscraper-mad city. Unusually for Hong Kong, the rooms have rather generous proportions and high ceilings. "I have lived here for years and I would never want to leave," Tang declares. Every space is filled with a profusion of the things Tang loves best in life—plush chairs (each one flanked by a reading lamp), fine contemporary and old paintings, his nine-foot-long Steinway grand piano, and piles upon piles of books. The sitting room with its intense greens and reds and vibrant fuschias reflects the aesthetic of his Hong Kong boutique Shanghai Tang. "I hate minimalism," he opines. "Rooms look their best when they are covered with colors and objects." By contrast, the bedroom—where Tang retires early to read voraciously—is a muted haven of pale hues, presided over by Chinese scrolls that read: "A palace of quietude and calm discussions; with poets reading poems in serenity."

David Tang, Geschäftsmann, Bonvivant und Kunstsammler, lebt zusammen mit seiner Frau in einem historischen Haus, wie es in Hongkong nicht mehr viele gibt. Die Villa liegt in den Hügeln über der Wolkenkratzer-närrischen Stadt und hat ungewöhnlich hohe Räume. „In all den Jahren, in denen ich hier lebe, wollte ich noch nie wegziehen", erklärt Tang, der Opulenz liebt. Die Räume sind gefüllt mit üppig gepolsterten, von Lampen flankierten Sesseln, wertvollen Bildern, einem großen Steinway-Flügel und Büchern. Die Farben im Wohnzimmer – Grün, Rot und ein leuchtendes Fuchsia – sind auch die Hausfarben seiner Boutique Shanghai Tang: „Minimalismus ist nicht mein Ding. In allen großartigen Palästen der Welt findet man eine Kombination von unterschiedlichen Dingen und kräftigen Tönen." Einzig sein Schlafzimmer ist in zurückhaltenden Nuancen gehalten. Hier zieht er sich oft früh am Abend zurück, um zu lesen. Auf den chinesischen Hängerollen an der Wand steht: „Ein Palast des Friedens und der ruhigen Gespräche; mit Dichtern, die Gedichte in klarem Geist vortragen."

Si la demeure d'un homme est son château, celle de David Tang serait plutôt un terrain de jeux. L'homme d'affaires et collectionneur, le plus célèbre bon vivant de Hong Kong, vit avec son épouse dans l'une des dernières maisons historiques de la ville, dans une rue sinueuse qui domine les gratte-ciels. Les pièces sont hautes sous plafond, détail inhabituel à Hong-Kong. « J'habite ici depuis des années et ne voudrais vivre nulle part ailleurs », déclare Tang. L'intérieur est rempli d'une profusion de tout ce qui fait son bonheur : profonds fauteuils (flanqués d'une lampe), tableaux contemporains et anciens, son Steinway et des piles de livres. Le salon vert, rouge et fuchsia reflète l'esthétique de sa boutique Shanghai Tang. « Je hais le minimalisme. J'ai remarqué que, dans tous les palaces et les grandes demeures, les pièces sont remplies de couleurs et d'objets. » En revanche, la chambre, où il se retire tôt pour dévorer des livres, est un havre de tons pâles dominé par un rouleau chinois proclamant : « Un palais de quiétude et de discussions calmes ; où les poètes lisent des poèmes dans la sérénité. »

P. 221 In the foyer, blue silk draperies and a blue antique rug from Tibet. • Die Eingangshalle mit blauen Seidenvorhängen und einem antiken Tibet-Teppich. • Dans le vestibule, la note bleue des draperies en soie et d'un tapis tibétain ancien.

← The acid-green armchair and embroidered pink velvet curtains in the sitting room display Tang's preference for bold, intense colors and his love of rich detail. • Der giftgrüne Sessel und die bestickten Samtvorhänge in Pink im Wohnzimmer offenbaren Tangs Vorliebe für kräftige, intensive Farben und seinen Hang zu opulenten Details. • Le salon. Le fauteuil vert acidulé et les rideaux brodés en velours rose fuchsia

témoignent du goût de Tang pour les couleurs fortes et intenses, ainsi que de son amour des détails raffinés.

↓ Another view of the sitting room—note that every chair or sofa corner has its own reading lamp. • Jede Sitzgelegenheit im Wohnzimmer hat ihre eigene Leselampe. • Une autre vue du salon; chaque siège a sa propre lampe de lecture.

↑ Brightly colored walls set off Tang's
collection of paintings by Jack Vettriano,
Augustus John, and Douglas Gray. •
Auf den farbigen Wänden kommen die
Werke von Jack Vettriano, Augustus
John und Douglas Gray aus Tangs Kunstsammlung besonders gut zur Geltung. •
Les couleurs vives des murs mettent en
valeur la collection d'œuvres d'art
signées Jack Vettriano, Augustus John
et Douglas Gray.

→ Tang's huge collection of books spills
over to his dining room. The setting is
completed by two large paintings in
unusual, oval-shaped wooden frames. •
Im Esszimmer stapeln sich Bücher aus
David Tangs umfangreicher Sammlung.
Davor lehnen zwei große Gemälde in
ungewöhnlichen ovalen Holzrahmen. •
L'impressionnante collection de livres
déborde dans la salle à manger. Le décor
est complété par deux grands tableaux
dans d'originaux cadres en bois ovales.

↑ Tang's serene, neutral-toned bedroom with traditional Chinese scrolls that read: "A palace of quietude and calm discussions; with poets reading poems in serenity." • Tangs Schlafzimmer in neutralen Tönen und mit traditionellen Hängerollen. Ihr Text: „Ein Palast des Friedens und der ruhigen Gespräche, mit Dichtern, die Gedichte in klarem Geist vortragen." • La chambre à coucher de Tang, avec ses tons neutres et ses rouleaux traditionnels chinois où il est écrit: « Un palais de quiétude et de discussions calmes; où les poètes lisent des poèmes dans la sérénité. »

→ The sitting room has a red velvet lounger Tang rescued from a Paris hotel. • Im Wohnzimmer steht ein rotes Rundsofa, das Tang aus einem Pariser Hotel gerettet hat, das umdekoriert wurde. • Dans le salon, une banquette ronde en velours rouge provenant d'un hôtel parisien.

HYDRA
GREECE

Rhapsody in Blue and White

Even if you know nothing of its splendid past, the fine white façade and graceful loggia of the Paouris Palace overlooking the port of Hydra is not a sight you will easily forget. Built after the 1821 revolution by Lazaros Kondouriotis for his sister, the palace was purchased on the eve of World War II by Katherina Paouris, a woman of legendary brilliance and beauty, who went on to restore it to its former glory. With its antique treasures, opalines, Venetian mirrors, china, paintings, and religious icons, the house that Ms. Paouris decorated in such luxurious good taste reflects an era that is long gone. Her innate romanticism didn't prevent this remarkable woman—who liked acid tones just as well as she liked Baroque and Modern art—from being the intimate friend of some of the greatest artists of her time. She once told her daughter Maria: "You and this house are the two great loves of my life"; and today her presence is as strong as ever in the building that is her most vivid memorial.

Selbst wenn Sie nichts von seiner glanzvollen Vergangenheit wissen, werden Sie den Paouris-Palast über dem Hafen von Hydra schon allein wegen seiner weißen Fassade mit der anmutigen Loggia nicht so schnell vergessen. Lazaros Kondouriotis hat den Palast nach der Revolution von 1821 für seine Schwester erbauen lassen. Kurz vor dem Zweiten Weltkrieg erwarb ihn die legendär schöne und kluge Katherina Paouris und verhalf dem Ensemble wieder zu seiner früheren Würde. Mit unverkennbar luxuriösem Geschmack eingerichtet, spiegelt das Gebäude mit seinen Antiquitäten, venezianischen Spiegeln, Opalgläsern, Porzellanen, Gemälden und Ikonen eine Epoche wider, die lange der Vergangenheit angehört. Diese großartige Frau, die sehr kräftige Farbtöne ebenso liebte wie Barock und die moderne Kunst, war eng mit den größten Künstlern ihrer Zeit befreundet. Zu ihrer Tochter Maria sagte sie: „Du und mein Haus, ihr seid die beiden großen Lieben meines Lebens!" Der Paouris-Palast hält ihr Gedenken in Ehren.

Il domine le port de Hydra et, même si on ignore son passé prestigieux, le majestueux Palais Paouris reste gravé dans la mémoire de tous ceux qui ont contemplé sa belle façade blanche ornée d'une grande loggia. Édifié après la révolution de 1821 par Lazaros Kondouriotis pour sa sœur, le palais fut acheté à la veille de la Seconde Guerre mondiale par Katherina Paouris, une femme d'une beauté et d'une intelligence légendaires, qui sut restituer à cet ensemble architectural imposant, sa gloire et sa beauté d'antan. Avec ses antiquités, ses miroirs vénitiens, ses opalines, ses porcelaines, ses tableaux et ses icônes, la demeure que Madame Paouris sut meubler avec un goût évident pour le faste, reflète une époque qui nous semble déjà lointaine. Une époque teintée de romantisme, ce qui n'empêcha pas cette femme formidable, qui aimait autant les tons acidulés que le baroque et l'art moderne, d'être l'amie intime des plus grands artistes. Celle qui disait à sa fille Maria : « J'ai vécu deux grandes histoires d'amour dans ma vie : ma maison et toi ! » demeure plus vivante que jamais dans ce palais qui continue d'honorer sa mémoire.

P. 229 When open, the blue painted shutters enliven the dining room. • Wenn geöffnet, beleben die Fensterläden in landestypischem Blau das Esszimmer. • Lorsqu'ils sont ouverts, les volets peints en bleu, ce qui est typique dans le pays, égaient la pièce.

← The bathroom, once decorated like an intimate salon by Katherina Paouris. • Die verstorbene Hausherrin dekorierte das Badezimmer so, als handelte es sich um einen intimen kleinen Salon. • Feu la maîtresse de maison a eu l'audace de décorer la salle de bains comme s'il s'agissait d'un petit salon intime.

↑ The dining room is filled with early 19th-century furniture. The period English china offsets the oval table and the white walls. • Das Esszimmer ist mit Mobiliar vom Beginn des 19. Jahrhunderts ausgestattet. Ein englisches Fayence-Tafelservice schmückt Tisch und Wände. • La salle à manger accueille un mobilier du début du 19e siècle. Un service en faïence anglais fait ressortir la table ovale et les murs blancs.

↓ The spacious kitchen, with its collection of saucepans and copper coffee pots. The English stove dates from the early 20th century. • Die geräumige Küche mit ihrer Sammlung von Kasserollen und kupfernen Kaffeekannen sowie einem englischen Herd vom Anfang des 20. Jahrhunderts. • La cuisine spacieuse avec sa collection de casseroles, de cafetières en cuivre et sa cuisinière anglaise qui date du début du 20e siècle.

↑ The loggia, with a 19th-century table and a Corinthian capital in carved wood. • Die Loggia mit einem Tisch aus dem 19. Jahrhundert und einem korinthischen Kapitell aus Holz. • La loggia abrite une table 19e et un chapiteau corinthien en bois sculpté.

↗ A portrait of Katherina Paouris dating from the 1930s. • Das Portät von Katherina Paouris stammt aus den 1930er Jahren. • Le portrait de Madame Katherina Paouris date des années 1930.

→ A collection of elaborately framed objects surrounds the washbasin. • Über dem Waschbecken sind Rahmen aller Art dekoriert. • Une collection de cadres tarabiscotés entoure le lavabo.

IBIZA
SPAIN

Sensationally Simple

"The old finca was a virtual ruin when my wife and I discovered it," recalls its owner, a retired French art and antique dealer. Together with the architect Pascal Cheikh-Djavadi, the couple restored the building, taking care to preserve as much of the original structure as possible and adding a modern wing that blends subtly with the existing architecture. Pristinely white rooms reflect the new occupants' key requirement: "We wanted the entire house to be bathed in light." Now daylight enters through black-framed windows, illuminating stylish interiors filled with notable 20th-century designer pieces—a field in which the former furniture dealer still excels.

„Die alte Finca war fast eine Ruine, als meine Frau und ich sie entdeckten", erzählt ihr Besitzer, ein französischer Antiquitäten- und Kunsthändler im Ruhestand. Gemeinsam mit dem Architekten Pascal Cheikh-Djavadi achtete das Paar bei der Restaurierung darauf, die alte Struktur möglichst umfassend zu erhalten. Ein neu angebauter Flügel fügt sich dezent in die vorhandene Bausubstanz ein. Weiße Innenräume tragen dem wichtigsten Wunsch der neuen Bewohner Rechnung: „Licht sollte das gesamte Haus durchfluten." Nun fällt es durch schwarze Fensterrahmen auf stilvolle Interieurs mit prominenten Designerstücken aus dem 20. Jahrhundert – nach wie vor ein Spezialgebiet des Hausherrn.

« La finca était pratiquement en ruine lorsque ma femme et moi l'avons découverte », raconte son propriétaire, un antiquaire et marchand d'art français en retraite. Pendant la restauration, effectuée avec l'architecte Pascal Cheikh-Djavadi, le couple a veillé à préserver le plus possible l'ancienne structure. Une aile nouvelle s'intègre discrètement dans la construction. Des pièces intérieures blanches répondent au souhait essentiel des nouveaux habitants : « La lumière devait inonder toute la maison. » Elle passe maintenant à travers les cadres de fenêtres noirs et éclaire des espaces élégants qui abritent des pièces réalisées par les plus grands designers du 20e siècle – une spécialité du maître de maison.

P. 235 Eero Saarinen's Tulip table and chair grace one corner of the kitchen, the chandelier is by Verner Panton. • Die Tulip-Sitzgruppe in einer Ecke der Küche stammt von Eero Saarinen, Verner Panton entwarf den Lüster. • Les chaises et la table Tulip dans un coin de la cuisine sont signées Eero Saarinen, Verner Panton a conçu le lustre.

↑ Two antique shamanic drums perch on the sideboard, above which is a mixed media painting by Linde Bialas. • Zwei antike Schamanentrommeln aus Tibet stehen auf dem Sideboard. Das Gemälde in Mischtechnik stammt von Linde Bialas. • Deux anciens tambours chamaniques du Tibet décorent le buffet. Le tableau en technique mixte est de Linde Bialas.

↗ Steps lead down to the living room, which features Harry Bertoia's Diamond chair, designed for Knoll in 1952. • Die Stufen führen ins Wohnzimmer, wo ein Exemplar von Harry Bertoias Diamond-Stuhl steht, ein Entwurf von 1952 für Knoll. • Les marches descendent dans le séjour où se dresse un exemplaire de la chaise Diamond d'Harry Bertoia, dessinée en 1952 pour Knoll.

→ The dining room lamp came from India; the table was created by the house's architect to go with Arne Jacobsen's 3107 chairs, part of his Series 7 range for Fritz Hansen. • Aus Indien stammt die Esszimmerlampe; den Tisch entwarf der Hausarchitekt passend zu Arne Jacobsens Stühlen Modell 3107 aus seiner Serie 7 für Fritz Hansen. • La lampe de la salle à manger vient d'Inde ; la table a été dessinée par l'architecte de la maison pour aller avec les chaises 3107 de la série 7 d'Arne Jacobsen, créée pour Fritz Hansen.

← The white marble kitchen island was built after a design by Pascal Cheikh-Djavadi. • Der Küchenblock wurde nach Entwürfen von Pascal Cheikh-Djavadi aus weißem Marmor gefertigt. • Le bloc-cuisine a été fabriqué en marbre blanc d'après des plans de Pascal Cheikh-Djavadi.

↑ Ghanaian stools are placed in front of the Zanotta sofa. • Zum Sofa von Zanotta gesellen sich Hocker aus Ghana. • Des tabourets du Ghana se joignent au canapé de Zanotta.

↓ At the Saturday flea market in Sant Jordi, the house's owners found this lamp in the style of Isamu Noguchi's Akari lanterns. • Auf dem Samstagsflohmarkt von Sant Jordi fanden die Besitzer diese Leuchte im Stil der Akari-Lampen von Isamu Noguchi. • Ce lampadaire qui évoque les lampes Akari d'Isamu Noguchi a été chiné aux Puces de Sant Jordi.

↓ Stones found on the property were used for repairing the walls. The steps lead to the garden. • Zur Reparatur der Mauern wurden Steine vom Grundstück verwendet. Eine Treppe führt in den Garten. • Les pierres on été trouvées sur le terrain. Un escalier mène au jardin.

← The washstand has a shallow-ended basin and is made of light concrete. • Der Waschtisch mit flach auslaufendem Beckenrand ist aus hellem Beton gegossen. • Le lavabo, avec sa cuvette à fond incliné, est en béton clair.

→ The three-legged chair in the bedroom was designed by Hans J. Wegner. A fireplace directly opposite the bed lends a rustic yet luxurious touch. • Der dreibeinige Stuhl im Schlafzimmer ist ein Entwurf von Hans J. Wegner. Sinnlicher Luxus: ein Kamin direkt gegenüber dem Bett. • La chaise à trois pieds de la chambre à coucher est signée Hans J. Wegner. Un luxe à la fois primitif et sensuel, la cheminée face au lit.

"Although the finca was almost in ruins, we immediately fell in love with it and the surrounding countryside." THE OWNER

„Obwohl die Finca kaum mehr als eine Ruine war, haben wir uns sofort in dieses Haus und die umliegende Landschaft verliebt."
« Bien que la finca ait été quasiment en ruine, nous sommes immédiatement tombés amoureux d'elle et du paysage environnant. »

ISTANBUL
TURKEY

A Strong Woman's Place

Since launching the design studio Autoban with Sefer Çağlar in 2003, Seyhan Özdemir has been a busy woman. As a result, she usually doesn't see her ground-floor apartment, which is situated in a 19th-century building on the European side of Istanbul, until the evening. It goes without saying that this trained architect furnished the flat herself—a host of creative ideas from the Autoban repertoire have turned the 2,700-square-foot apartment into something of a case study for the firm. The interiors are a highly organic blend of historic architecture and contemporary pieces by Özdemir herself and by people whose work she admires. Exposed brickwork provides the finishing touch to this artful composition and brings loft atmosphere to the historic shell.

Seyhan Özdemir hat viel zu tun, seit sie 2003 mit Sefer Çağlar das Designstudio Autoban lancierte. Deshalb verbringt sie meist nur die Abende in ihrer Wohnung, die im Erdgeschoss eines Gebäudes aus dem 19. Jahrhundert im europäischen Teil von Istanbul liegt. Natürlich richtete die studierte Architektin das Apartment selbst ein – mit zahlreichen Designideen aus dem Autoban-Repertoire ist die 250 Quadratmeter große Wohnung so ein „Case Study" ihres Labels geworden. Ganz organisch verbinden sich die historischen Formen nun mit zeitgenössischen Entwürfen, eigenen oder denen geschätzter Designerkollegen. Unverputztes Ziegelmauerwerk macht die Kombinationskunst komplett: Aus dem Flair der Vergangenheit wird Loftatmosphäre.

Depuis qu'elle a lancé en 2003 avec Sefer Çağlar le studio de design Autoban, Seyhan Özdemir est très occupée. Le plus souvent, elle ne passe que la soirée dans son appartement situé au rez-de-chaussée d'un bâtiment du 19ᵉ siècle, dans la partie européenne d'Istanbul. Architecte de formation, elle a évidemment décoré elle-même son chez-soi – avec de nombreux modèles du répertoire Autoban, l'appartement de 250 m² est une expérience d'«étude de cas» de sa marque. Les formes historiques se marient de manière parfaitement organique aux créations contemporaines, les siennes ou celles d'autres designers. Des murs en briques apparentes complètent l'ensemble, et l'ambiance du passé se transforme en atmosphère de loft.

P. 243 The flamboyant lamp is by Autoban, the shelves and table were custom-
made. • Der extravagante Lüster
stammt von Autoban, Regal und Tisch
sind maßgeschreinert. • Le lustre extravagant vient du studio Autoban, l'étagère
et la table ont été fabriquées sur mesure.

↑ "As the kitchen is the most important
place in a home, I planned and chose
everything myself," says Özdemir. The
aluminum chairs were designed by Philippe Starck for Emeco. • „Weil die
Küche der wichtigste Ort ist, habe ich sie
von A bis Z selbst geplant und bestückt",
sagt Özdemir. Die Alustühle entwarf Philippe Starck für Emeco. • «La cuisine
étant l'endroit le plus important, j'en ai fait
moi-même les plans de A à Z et je l'ai
équipée», dit Özdemir. Philippe Starck a
dessiné les chaises en aluminium pour
Emeco.

→ Chevron parquet flooring empha-
sizes the 65-foot-long hallway. • Die
fast 20 Meter Länge ihres Flurs betonte
die Designerin mit pfeilartig verlegtem
Fischgrätparkett. • La décoratrice a
accentué la longueur du couloir, près de
vingt mètres, avec un parquet à chevrons
posé «en flèche».

← Above the bed, which has a curving headboard with vertical bars, hangs the Double Octopus lamp; both are by Autoban. • Über dem Bett mit gekurvtem Sprossenhaupt hängt die Leuchte Double Octopus, beides von Autoban. • Au-dessus du lit, dont la tête à barreaux est arrondie, est suspendue la lampe Double Octopus, les deux sont signés Autoban.

↑ On the living room's white-painted brick wall is a black-and-white picture by the renowned Magnum photographer Ara Güler. • An der weiß getünchten Ziegelmauer des Wohnzimmers hängt eine Schwarz-Weiß-Aufnahme des berühmten Magnum-Fotografen Ara Güler. • Sur le mur badigeonné de blanc du séjour, une photo en noir et blanc d'Ara Güler, célèbre photographe de Magnum.

↓ Set against floor tiles from the Turkish firm Vitra, Jasper Morrison's Thinking Man's Chair brings a splash of red to the bathroom. • Im Bad setzt Jasper Morrisons Thinking Man's Chair einen roten Akzent auf den Fliesen der türkischen Marke Vitra. • Dans la salle de bains, la Thinking Man's Chair de Jasper Morrison pose un accent rouge sur le carrelage de la marque turque Vitra.

ITO-SHI
JAPAN

Temple of Everyday Life

The name of the house, "Hijiri," means holy—and there is indeed something almost spiritual about the lighting design in its interiors. Situated close to Ito-shi on the east coast of Japan, it was built by architect Eizo Shiina as a compact home for an interior designer and the head of a construction firm, both of whom are in their 60s. "When I saw the mountainous landscape, I thought the building would need to stay low to the ground in order to work," explains Shiina. Thanks to the wall of rock bordering the plot, he was able to radically open the façade on two sides without comprising to the occupants' privacy. Inside, travertine flooring and minimalist wooden fixtures complement the architecture's exposed concrete and glass.

„Hijiri", der Name des Hauses, bedeutet „heilig" – und entsprechend sakral wirkt die Lichtführung innerhalb der Räume. An der Ostküste bei Ito-shi baute Architekt Eizo Shiina ein kompaktes Zuhause für den Leiter einer Bau- und Ausstattungsfirma sowie eine Interiordesignerin, beide in ihren Sechzigern. „Beim Anblick der bergigen Landschaft hatte ich den Gedanken, das Gebäude müsse sich hocken, um zu funktionieren", erläutert Shiina. Dank der Lage direkt an einer Felswand konnte er die Fassade auf zwei Seiten radikal öffnen, ohne damit die Privatsphäre der Bewohner zu gefährden. Im Inneren ergänzen Böden aus Travertin und minimalistische Holzeinbauten die Architektur aus Sichtbeton und Glas.

Le nom de la maison, « Higiri », signifie « saint », et l'éclairage des pièces donne vraiment une impression de sacré. Sur la côte est, près d'Ito-shi, l'architecte Eizo Shiina a construit une maison compacte pour le directeur d'une entreprise de construction et d'ameublement et sa compagne, architecte d'intérieur, la soixantaine tous les deux. « En contemplant le paysage montagneux, je me suis dit que le bâtiment devrait être accroupi pour fonctionner », explique Shiina. La maison étant collée à un rocher, il a pu ouvrir radicalement deux de ses côtés sans compromettre l'intimité des habitants. À l'intérieur, des sols en travertin et des constructions de bois minimalistes complètent l'architecture en béton apparent et verre.

P. 249 Steps join the bench seat to the kitchen units, and around the dining table are Superleggera chairs by Gio Ponti. • Treppenstufen verbinden eine Sitzbank mit der Einbauküche, am Esstisch stehen Superleggera-Stühle von Gio Ponti. • Des marches relient la banquette à la cuisine intégrée, autour de la table de repas des chaises Superleggera de Gio Ponti.

← Shielded from view by a wall of rock, the kitchen's glass façade can open up to embrace the surroundings. • Durch eine Felswand vor Blicken geschützt, kann sich die Küchenfassade zur Umgebung öffnen. • Dissimulée des regards par une paroi rocheuse, la cuisine peut s'ouvrir sur le monde extérieur.

↓ Two identical bedrooms allow for undisturbed nights. • Zwei identische Schlafzimmer machen eine ungestörte Nachtruhe möglich. • Deux chambres à coucher identiques assurent le repos nocturne.

↑ The steep slope outside prevents prying eyes from peering into the bathroom, which has a toilet by Toto. • Ein steiler Hang verhindert neugierige Blicke ins Badezimmer mit der Toilette von Toto. • Une pente abrupte empêche les regards curieux d'entrer dans la salle de bains avec W.-C. de Toto.

↗ The window is some 13 feet wide; at night, illumination comes from light panels that run the length of the room. • Über vier Meter ist das Fenster breit – nach Einbruch der Dunkelheit beleuchten raumbreite Deckenpaneele das Bad. • La fenêtre fait plus de quatre mètres de large – lorsque la nuit tombe, la pièce est éclairée par des panneaux lumineux sur toute sa longueur.

→ Beyond the etched glass is the street, the back of the fireplace contains storage space. • Hinter den Ätzglasfenstern verbirgt sich die Straße, die Rückseite des Kamins bietet Stauraum. • La rue se cache derrière les fenêtres en verre dépoli à l'acide, le dos de la cheminée offre des espaces de rangement.

KAMAKURA
JAPAN

Checks and Balance

In the hands of architect Kengo Kuma, wood, bamboo, glass, stone, plastic, and metal lend themselves to unexpected uses. At the Lotus House, constructed in 2005 for businessman Yoichiro Ushioda (owner of neighboring Chizanso Villa), Kuma arranged narrow travertine blocks in a lattice pattern, hanging the rectangles from a thin and almost invisible steel framework. The effect is a stone screen, suspended effortlessly, through which light and air pass freely. The house stands in forested mountain surroundings, with a small stream at the foot of the property. One enters from the second story, and here, as an architectural "prelude," a reflecting pool and wide roof terrace set off one wing of the stone screen. Once inside the door, cantilevered steps lead downstairs to a central courtyard, flanked by more expanses of checkerboard stone that face the lotus pond from which the house takes its name. White and unadorned inside, the complex embraces three elements: spare interior, lush green outer grounds, and the baroque barrier of a porous stone shield.

Der Architekt Kengo Kuma verwendet Holz, Bambus, Glas, Stein, Plastik und Metall oft auf äußerst ungewöhnliche Weise. Beim Lotus House, das 2005 für den Geschäftsmann Yoichiro Ushioda erbaut wurde, dem auch die benachbarte Chizanso-Villa gehört, arrangierte Kuma schmale Travertinblöcke zu einem Schachbrettmuster, indem er die Rechtecke an einem dünnen, fast unsichtbaren Edelstahlgerüst aufhängte. Das Ergebnis ist eine fast schwerelos wirkende Steinblende. Das Haus liegt in einer bewaldeten Berglandschaft, zu Füßen des Grundstücks verläuft ein kleiner Fluss. Der Eingang befindet sich im ersten Stock, wo ein Wasserbassin sowie eine großzügige Dachterrasse einen Teil der Steinblende aufbrechen. Im Haus führen wie schwebende Stufen nach unten zu einem zentralen Innenhof mit weiteren schachbrettartigen Steinblenden und einem Lotusteich, der dem Haus seinen Namen gab. Der im Inneren weiß und schlicht gehaltene Gebäudekomplex vereint drei Elemente: minimales Interieur, üppiges Grün im Außenbereich und den verspielten Sichtschutz eines durchlässigen Schilds aus Travertin.

Entre les mains de l'architecte Kengo Kuma, le bois, le bambou, le verre, la pierre, le plastique et le métal se découvrent des usages inattendus. Dans la maison du Lotus, construite en 2005 pour l'homme d'affaires Yoichiro Ushioda (propriétaire de la villa Chizanso voisine), Kuma a conçu un treillage en étroites dalles de travertin accrochées à un mince cadre en acier presque invisible, créant un effet de paravent en pierre qui semble flotter dans le vide, laissant filtrer la lumière et l'air. La maison se dresse sur une montagne boisée, un ruisseau gargouillant à ses pieds. On entre par le premier étage où, tel un «prélude» architectural, un bassin et une vaste terrasse mettent en valeur une face du paravent de pierre. Une fois la porte franchie, des marches flottantes descendent vers la cour centrale, flanquée de surfaces en damier qui font face au bassin de lotus auquel la maison doit son nom. Avec ses intérieurs blancs et nus, le complexe associe trois éléments : une décoration sobre, une végétation luxuriante et la barrière baroque d'un paravent en pierre poreuse.

P. 255 On the second floor are an inside and an outside bath (*rotenburo*), bordered by a travertine screen, looking out at the hillside. • Im ersten Stock gibt es ein Innen- und Außenbecken (*rotenburo*). Sie werden von einer Travertinblende abgeschirmt und bieten einen schönen Blick auf die Hügel. • Le premier étage comporte un bain intérieur et extérieur (*rotenburo*). L'écran en travertin s'ouvre sur une vue des collines.

← Afternoon light casts its rays over the table in the study and music room. • Das Nachmittagslicht strömt über den Tisch des Arbeits- und Musikzimmers. • La table du bureau/salon de musique, baignée par la lumière de l'après-midi.

→ A delicate spiral staircase links the ground floor with the upstairs. • Eine grazile Wendeltreppe verbindet das Erd- mit dem Obergeschoss. • Un délicat escalier en colimaçon relie le rez-de-chaussée à l'étage supérieur.

↘ Thin cantilevered steps lead down to the marble-floored open-plan living room. The table and chairs are from Bali. Beyond the glass doors are the kitchen and dining area. • Dünne, frei tragende Stufen führen hinab zum nach vorne hin offenen Wohnraum mit Marmorboden. Der Tisch und die Stühle stammen aus Bali. Hinter den Glastüren liegen Küche und Essbereich. • De minces marches flottantes descendent dans le séjour au sol en marbre, ouvert vers l'avant. La table et les chaises viennent de Bali. Derrière les portes vitrées, la cuisine/salle à manger.

PP. 258–259 "Hanging" stairs lead down to the huge patio and the lotus pond. • Kragstufen führen hinab zum riesigen Patio mit Lotusteich. • Des marches en porte-à-faux descendent jusqu'au vaste patio qui abrite un bassin où flottent des fleurs de lotus.

KNOKKE
BELGIUM

Industrial Allure

In 2009, vintage-furniture dealer Bea Mombaers took over the thatched country house of architect Lionel Jadot, who, in the preceding years, had already gutted and extended the building. Mombaers used this modernized shell as a platform for her own interior design. With six bedrooms at her disposal, she hit upon the idea of offering bed and breakfast accommodations. Now, as well as living and working here herself, she rents out spacious rooms that welcome guests with an air of industrial charm. Together with the loft-like ambience created by concrete floors and large windows, the new furnishings offer an effortless blend of the rough and the urbane.

2009 übernahm die Vintage-Möbelhändlerin Bea Mombaers das reetgedeckte Landhaus vom Architekten Lionel Jadot. Er hatte es in den Jahren zuvor entkernt und ausgebaut. Die vorgefundene modernisierte Hülle wurde zur Grundlage für Mombaers Innenausstattung. Da das Haus sechs Schlafzimmer hat, kam sie auf die Idee, Bed & Breakfast anzubieten. Im industriellen Charme, den die großen Räume heute entfalten, fühlen sich ihre Gäste wohl, während die Hausherrin hier wohnt und arbeitet. Durch Betonböden und großflächige Fenster entsteht eine Loftatmosphäre, die dank der neuen Einrichtung ganz entspannt die Balance hält zwischen Urtümlichem und Weltläufigkeit.

Bea Mombaers, qui vend des meubles vintage, a repris en 2009 la maison de campagne au toit de chaume de l'architecte Lionel Jadot qui l'avait fait entièrement refaire et agrandir au cours des années précédentes. La coquille modernisée qu'elle a trouvée a servi de base à la décoration de Mombaers. La maison ayant six chambres, elle a eu l'idée d'offrir un Bed & Breakfast. La maîtresse de maison vit et travaille ici, et ses hôtes apprécient le charme industriel des vastes pièces. Les sols de béton et les vastes baies vitrées génèrent une ambiance de loft qui, avec le nouveau mobilier, crée un équilibre nonchalant entre l'élémentaire et le sophistiqué.

P. 261 Mombaers brought back the tree-trunk table in the dining area as a souvenir from the Philippines. • Der Baumstammtisch im Essbereich ist ein Mitbringsel von den Philippinen. • La propriétaire a rapporté des Philippines la table taillée dans un tronc, qui se dresse dans le coin repas.

↑ Washbasins and shower cubicle feature Bisazza glass mosaic tiling. • Waschbecken und Duschkabine sind mit Bisazza-Glasmosaik verkleidet. • Les lavabos et la douche sont revêtus de mosaïques de verre Bisazza.

→ Architect Lionel Jadot, the former owner designed the minimalist light fixtures on the landing walls. • Die minimalistischen Wandleuchten im oberen Flur entwarf Architekt Lionel Jadot, der Vorbesitzer. • Les appliques minimalistes dans le couloir du haut ont été conçues par l'architecte Lionel Jadot.

PP. 264–265 The Ligne Roset leather seating group and flokati rug create a contemporary chalet-style coziness. • Eine Ledersitzgruppe von Ligne Roset auf dem Flokatiteppich schafft zeitgemäße Gemütlichkeit à la Chalet. • Le canapé, les fauteuils et les poufs de Ligne Roset sur le tapis flokati génèrent un confort douillet, comme dans un chalet.

← The cast-iron spiral staircase leads up to a gallery bedroom, which is fitted with iron bars for safety reasons. • Zum Schlafplateau, das mit Eisengittern gesichert ist, führt eine gusseiserne Spindeltreppe. • Pour accéder au coin sommeil, sécurisé par des barreaux de fer, on emprunte l'escalier en colimaçon en fer forgé.

↑ The bed is separated from a Dominique Desimpel stone bath by a concrete console. • Eine Betonkonsole trennt das Bett von der steinernen Wanne, einem Werk von Dominique Desimpel. • Une console de béton sépare le lit de la baignoire en pierre, une création de Dominique Desimpel.

↓ Plastered roof beams lend the landing an almost chapel-like air. • Die Dachbalken im Obergeschoss wurden verblendet, sodass der Flur fast sakral wirkt. • À l'étage, les poutres du toit ont été crépies, ce qui donne au couloir un aspect presque sacral.

↓ An equine sculpture by Frédérique Morrel and a vintage mirror decorate the kitchen walls. • In der Küche hängen eine Pferdeskulptur von Frédérique Morrel und ein Vintage-Spiegel. • Un cheval sculpté de Frédérique Morrel et un miroir vintage décorent les murs de la cuisine.

KYMMENDÖ ISLAND
SWEDEN

A Mies Reprise

For their annual vacations in the skerries just beyond the capital, a Stockholm-based family of six wanted a house so transparent that they'd feel like they are outside. Architects Johnny Andersson and Karin Löfgren of Jordens Architects built a holiday home that appears to be little more than a glass membrane—and thus pays homage to Mies van der Rohe's Farnsworth House. The single-story structure seems almost to float above the ground, and all the rooms (except for the toilets) face out towards the landscape. What's more, the duo were as unswerving in their choice of materials as they were in their proportions: the floors are all limestone, the interior fixtures all have Douglas fir veneer.

Ein Haus, so transparent, dass man sich fühlt, als wäre man schon draußen. So wünschte es sich die sechsköpfige Stockholmer Familie für ihre alljährlichen Ferien in den Schären vor der Hauptstadt. Die Architekten Johnny Andersson und Karin Löfgren von Jordens Architects schufen daraufhin einen Ort, der kaum mehr zu sein scheint als eine Glasmembran – und erweisen damit dem Farnsworth-Haus Mies van der Rohes die Reverenz. Der eingeschossige Bau wirkt, als würde er auf einem Felsen schweben, alle Räume (bis auf die Toiletten) orientieren sich zur Landschaft hin. Ebenso konsequent wie die Proportionen ist auch die Materialwahl: Kalkstein für die Böden, Douglasien-Furnier für alle Einbauten.

Une maison si transparente qu'on a l'impression d'être dehors. Et c'est bien ce que désirait la famille stockholmoise de six personnes pour passer ses vacances annuelles dans les îlots situés devant la capitale. Les architectes Johnny Andersson et Karin Löfgren de Jordens Architects ont donc créé un endroit qui semble être à peine plus qu'une membrane de verre, rendant ainsi hommage à la maison Farnsworth de Mies van der Rohe. Le bâtiment d'un étage semble planer sur un rocher, toutes les pièces (toilettes inclues) sont orientées vers l'extérieur. Le choix des matériaux est aussi rigoureux que l'architecture : pierre calcaire pour les sols, placage de pin Douglas pour les équipements.

P. 269 At the head of the corridor on the southwestern side is a desk with Hans Wegner chairs. • Ein Arbeitsplatz mit zwei Hans-Wegner-Stühlen bildet den Auftakt zum Gang auf der Südwestseite. • Le couloir du côté sud-ouest commence par une aire de travail avec deux chaises de Hans Wegner.

← Norrvange limestone was used for the bathrooms and for all the floors in the house. • Norrvange-Kalkstein wurde für Bäder wie auch die Fußböden im ganzen Haus verwendet. • La pierre calcaire de Norrvange a été utilisée dans les salles de bains et sur tous les sols de la maison.

↗ The sun deck looks out onto the pine trees and the lagoon to the north. • Vom Sonnendeck aus geht der Blick nach Norden mit Kiefernwald und Lagune. •

De la terrasse, le regard se dirige vers le Nord, la forêt de pins et la lagune.

↓ The living room and kitchen are one open space; the three small tables were designed by Hans Bølling. • Wohnzimmer und Küche bilden einen gemeinsamen Raum, die drei Rolltischchen entwarf Hans Bølling. • Le séjour et la cuisine forment un espace commun, Hans Bølling a conçu les trois petites tables roulantes.

PP. 272–273 The children's Douglas fir-clad bunk beds are just 12 feet from the meadow. • Von den mit Douglasien-Furnier verkleideten Stockbetten der Kinder sind es nur dreieinhalb Meter bis zur Wiese. • Trois mètres et demi séparent les lits superposés des enfants, plaqués de pin Douglas, de la prairie.

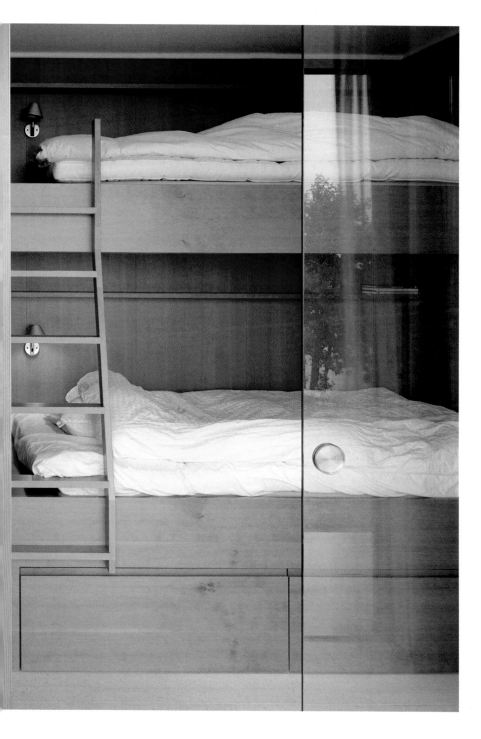

↑ In the living area, twin Natuzzi leather sofas flank a Rug Company carpet. • Im Wohnbereich liegt zwischen den Leder-sofas von Natuzzi ein Teppich von Rug Company. • Dans le séjour, un tapis de Rug Company entre des canapés en cuir de Natuzzi.

→ Like the floors, the countertop in the custom-built kitchen is Swedish limestone. • Auch die Arbeitsplatte in der maßgeschreinerten Küche ist aus schwedischem Kalkstein. • Le plan de travail de la cuisine fabriquée sur mesure est lui aussi en pierre calcaire suédoise.

LA BARRA
URUGUAY

Like a Fresh Breeze

For architect Martín Gómez, this house in the chic village of La Barra is "simply unique." Firstly, there is its location—right on the beach. Secondly, its history. It started out life more than a century ago as a customs house. "We don't have many buildings as old as this still standing," Gómez remarks. When he first saw it, the 6,500-square-foot structure was "a kind of windowless cube." The openings onto the sea had been blocked up and the inside was filled with a multitude of walls. Gomez created large, open spaces, and opted for a comfortable, relaxed look. "I didn't want something ostentatious," he says. In all, there are eight bedrooms, most of which have their own, separate entrance. "It's like a small hotel," he states. The deck in the middle of the garden, meanwhile, is rather like a raft. "It looks like it was dragged ashore and left in the middle of the lawn."

Für den Architekten Martín Gómez ist dieses Haus im schicken Badeort La Barra „schlicht einzigartig". Erstens wegen seiner Lage – direkt am Strand - und zweitens wegen seiner Geschichte. Ursprünglich hatte es nämlich als Zollhaus gedient. „Wir haben nicht viele Gebäude, die so alt sind wie dieses und immer noch stehen", meint er. Als er das Haus mit seiner Grundfläche von 600 Quadratmetern zum ersten Mal sah, erschien es ihm „wie eine Art fensterloser Würfel". Die Öffnungen zum Meer waren blockiert, und das Innere verschachtelt. Gómez schuf große offene Räume und entschied sich für einen komfortablen, entspannten Stil. „Ich wollte nichts Pompöses", sagt er. Insgesamt gibt es acht Schlafzimmer, meist mit eigenem Eingang. „Es ist wie ein kleines Hotel", stellt er fest. Die hölzerne Plattform mitten im Garten wirkt dagegen wie ein Floß. „Als wäre es an Land gezogen und auf dem Rasen vergessen worden."

Pour l'architecte Martín Gómez, cette maison dans le village huppé de La Barra est doublement unique : par son emplacement sur la plage et par son histoire. Il y a un siècle, c'était un poste de douane. « Il reste peu de bâtiments aussi vieux », explique-t-il. La structure de 600 mètres carrés était « un cube aveugle ». Les ouvertures vers la mer étaient bouchées et l'intérieur rempli d'une multitude de murs. Gómez a créé de grands espaces ouverts et opté pour un décor confortable et reposant. « Je ne voulais rien d'ostentatoire. » La plupart des huit chambres ont une entrée indépendante. « C'est comme un petit hôtel. » Au milieu du jardin se dresse une terrasse en bois, « comme un radeau qu'on aurait tiré sur le rivage et abandonné sur la pelouse ».

P. 277 The light-colored floors allow the simple, solid-wood seating to stand out. • Die einfache Sitzgruppe aus Massivholz kommt auf dem hellen Steinboden sehr gut zur Geltung. • La table et les chaises en bois massif sont bien mises en valeur par le sol de pierre claire.

↑ An outdoor terrace is provided with shade by a roof of eucalyptus branches. • Die Außenterrasse erhält durch ein Dach aus Eukalyptusästen Schatten. • Un toit en branches d'eucalyptus ombrage la terrasse extérieure.

↓ Seascapes bought locally hang above a farm table in the dining room. • Vor Ort gekaufte Seestücke hängen im Esszimmer über einem rustikalen Tisch. • Dans la salle à manger, des marines achetées dans la région sont accrochées au-dessus d'une table de ferme.

→ Gómez designed the daybed and inserted light blue panes of glass into the living-room windows. • Gómez entwarf die Chaiselongue und versah die Fenster des Wohnzimmers mit einem Band aus blauem Glas. • Gómez a dessiné le lit de repos et inséré des pans de verre bleus au-dessus des fenêtres du séjour.

↑ The kitchen is a symphony in white, with worktops made from Uruguayan marble. • Die Küche ist eine Sinfonie in Weiß mit Arbeitsflächen aus uruguayischem Marmor. • Dans la cuisine, une symphonie de blancs. Les plans de travail sont en marbre uruguayen.

↗ Linen curtains and Portuguese cotton bedcovers adorn one of the guest rooms. • Leinenvorhänge und Bettüberwurf aus portugiesischer Baumwolle in einem der Gästezimmer. • Dans l'une dechambres d'amis, des rideaux en lin et des dessus-de-lit portugais en coton.

→ The master bathroom has stucco walls and a Turkish carpet. • Im Hauptbadezimmer mit Stuccowände liegt ein türkischer Kelim. • Dans la salle de bains principale, des murs en stuc et un tapis turc.

LAMU
KENYA

Where Africa Meets Asia

More often than not, the purchase of a house is the result of a stroke of luck that occurs quite by chance. Towards the end of the 1970s, the artist Hermann Stucki had just sold a series of drawings and collages in Nairobi. His pockets were full of Kenyan shillings, a currency that cannot be taken out of the country. As luck would have it, he found himself in Lamu Town, a tumbledown port near the Somali border, built centuries ago in the mangrove swamp by Moorish slave traders. In the maze of streets lived a tiny cosmopolitan crowd originating from Persia, Yemen, Oman, Malaysia, India, Portugal, and the African mainland. In a quiet corner Stucki and his companion, Katharina Schmezer, found a house in the Arab colonial style, empty and for sale. The couple plunged into a renovation adventure that was to last for the next 15 years. In Europe, they both work, among others, for Fabric Frontline, a company specializing in the finest silks, which collaborates with the most famous fashion and interior designers. Naturally enough, the walls of their "white house" are set off by vibrant-colored fabrics, which billow in the ocean breeze. Now that their home is finished, the couple have launched themselves into the renovation of other ruins.

Der Kauf eines Hauses hängt oftmals mit einem unerwarteten Glückstreffer zusammen. Der Maler Hermann Stucki konnte Ende der 1970er Jahre in Nairobi unverhofft eine Reihe von Zeichnungen und Collagen verkaufen. Als er also gerade im Besitz dieses kleinen Vermögens in kenianischen Schilling war, das er nicht ausführen durfte, entdeckte er Lamu, eine heruntergekommene Hafenstadt, die unweit der somalischen Grenze vor Jahrhunderten von Sklavenhändlern in die Mangrovensümpfe gebaut worden war. Im Labyrinth der Gassen lebte eine kleine Gemeinschaft von Kosmopoliten, die aus Persien, dem Jemen, Oman, Malaysia, Indien, Portugal und vom afrikanischen Festland stammten. An einer idyllischen Straßenecke wartete ein Haus im arabischen Kolonialstil auf neue Besitzer. Voller Energie stürzten sich Hermann Stucki und Katharina Schmezer in die Renovierung, ein Abenteuer, das 15 Jahre in Anspruch nehmen sollte. Das Ehepaar arbeitet unter anderem für Fabric Frontline, eine Schweizer Firma, die luxuriöse Seidenstoffe herstellt und die berühmten Modehäuser beliefert. So ist es nicht verwunderlich, dass leuchtend bunte Seidenstoffe die Wände dieses „weißen Hauses" hervorheben. Seitdem sie ihr Haus fertiggestellt haben, kümmert sich das Ehepaar um die Rettung weiterer verfallener Bauten.

Souvent, l'achat d'une maison procède d'un hasard heureux. Peintre, Hermann Stucki rencontre un joli succès avec une série de collages et dessins vendus à Nairobi. À la tête d'une petite fortune en shillings kenyans, monnaie qu'il ne peut sortir du pays, il découvre, vers la fin des années 1970, Lamu Town, un port déglingué érigé il y a des siècles dans la mangrove par des négriers maures. Dans l'entrelacs de ruelles vit une petite communauté cosmopolite originaire de la Perse, du Yémen, d'Oman, de Malaisie, d'Inde, du Portugal et du continent africain. Dans un coin pittoresque, une maison de style colonial arabe attend ses nouveaux propriétaires. Hermann Stucki et Katharina Schmezer se lancent pleins d'enthousiasme dans l'aventure d'une rénovation. Une aventure qui durera 15 ans ! En Europe, le couple travaille entre autres pour la maison Fabric Frontline, fabricant suisse de tissus de soie luxueux, qui collabore avec les grands couturiers et décorateurs d'intérieur. Tout naturellement, les murs de la «maison blanche» sont relevés par les vibrantes couleurs d'étoffes gonflées par les vents marins. Leur maison achevée, le couple se lance dans l'aménagement d'autres ruines.

← Small sculptures stand in front of an open window with a matching curtain. • Vor dem geöffneten Fenster, mit farblich harmonierendem Stoffvorhang, stehen kleine Skulpturen. • De petites sculptures devant la fenêtre ouverte dont la couleur s'harmonise à celle du rideau.

↓ In the kitchen, with its cement floor, the romance of a traditional house is coupled with a contemporary character. The roof is surfaced with plaited coconut palmleaves, the crockery local. • Die Küche kombiniert die Romantik des alten Hauses mit modernen Elementen, zum Beispiel das traditionelle Geschirr und das Dach aus Kokospalmwedeln mit dem Zementboden. • Dans la cuisine, mariage réussi entre le romantisme d'une maison traditionnelle et la puissante touche contemporaine de son espace intérieur avec son sol en ciment. Toit en feuille de cocotier tressée et vaisselle traditionnelle.

→ Hermann Stucki designed the living-room furniture himself and had it made by Husseini, the most talented carpenter in Lamu whom he and Katharina have known since they were children. • Die Möbel im Salon hat Hermann Stucki entworfen und von Husseini, dem begabtesten Schreiner in Lamu und einem Freund des Paares, anfertigen lassen. • Dans le salon, Hermann Stucki a lui-même dessiné des meubles fabriqués par Husseini, le menuisier le pus doué à Lamu, que le couple connaît depuis son enfance.

P. 283 This 19th-century four-poster bed, found on the island, is upholstered in duchess silk, while the bedcover is made from a sari. Under the bed is a gorgeous *mkeka*, a rare Tanzanian rug made of palm fronds. • Das Himmelbett aus dem 19. Jahrhundert stammt von der Insel selbst. Die Decke ist aus Saristoff, der Betthimmel in Duchesseseide gepatched. Unter dem Bett liegt ein wunderschöner *mkeka*, ein aus Palmfasern handgefertigter Teppich aus Tansania. • Le baldaquin du lit, certifié 19e, découvert sur l'île, est habillé de soie duchesse, le couvre-lit est réalisé avec un sari. Sous le lit, un magnifique *mkeka*, tapis rare de Tanzanie tissé main à partir de fibres de palmier.

← Small fish swim in the *birika* to keep the water clean and to eliminate the mosquito larvae. • In der *birika* schwimmen kleine Fische, die das Wasser sauber halten und die Mückenlarven fressen. • Dans les *birika* des petits poissons gardent l'eau propre et éliminent les larves de moustiques.

↓ A bed of woven palm fronds. The bedcovers in the house are made of precious silks in an ethnic style, as are the curtains, hanging on 18th-century wooden curtain rails and dividing up the rooms. The floors are covered with traditional mosque mats. • Eine Liegestatt aus geflochtenen Palmfasern. Die Tagesdecken und raumunterteilenden Vorhänge, die an massiven Holzstangen aus dem 18. Jahrhundert hängen, sind aus Seidenstoffen im Ethnostil gefertigt. Moscheematten schmücken die Böden. • Couchette en tressage de fibres de palmes. Les dessus-de-lit de la maison sont réalisés dans des soieries type ethno ainsi que les rideaux, pendus sur des tringles 18e en bois massif, qui divisent les grandes pièces. Sols habillés d'une natte traditionnelle de mosquée.

LONDON
UK

Lofty Tradition

When Simon Upton began looking for an industrial loft in West London in the mid-1990s, he soon discovered that the market for such places was non-existent. But then his real-estate agent, rummaging around in his bottom drawer, found the details of an old warehouse. The photographer, who has lived there ever since, had everything painted white—after shooting so many great interiors around the world, he decided his own home should, first and foremost, be simple. "I didn't want it to be completely mid-century or all Georgian—although I love both styles," he explains. He has built up the furnishings gradually over the years, picking up the old antlers and animal skins, for instance, on his travels: "They have an intrinsic beauty which we often miss, due to our collective abhorrence of death."

Als Simon Upton Mitte der 1990er Jahre in West-London nach einem Industrieloft suchte, gab es für solche Immobilien noch keinen Markt. Doch in der untersten Schreibtischschublade fand sein Makler Unterlagen für eine ehemalige Lagerhalle, die der Interiorfotograf seitdem bewohnt. Upton ließ beim Umbau alles weiß streichen, denn aus Respekt vor den großartigen Interieurs, die er im Laufe seiner internationalen Karriere abgelichtet hatte, wollte er für sein eigenes Zuhause vor allem eins: Einfachheit. „Es sollte weder ganz Fifties / Sixties noch Georgian Style sein – obwohl ich beide Perioden schätze." Erst mit den Jahren füllten sich die Räume. Die alten Geweihe und Tierfelle kaufte er auf seinen Reisen: „Sie haben eine ureigene Schönheit, die wir in unserer kollektiven Angst vor dem Tod oft übersehen."

À l'époque où Simon Upton cherchait un loft industriel dans l'ouest de Londres au milieu des années 1990, il n'y avait pas encore de marché pour de tels immeubles. Et puis son agent a sorti du fond d'un tiroir des documents concernant un ancien hangar. Le photographe d'intérieur habite ici depuis et a tout fait peindre en blanc. En effet, par respect pour tous les intérieurs magnifiques qu'il a photographiés au cours de sa carrière internationale, il voulait avant tout une chose : De la simplicité. « Ni tout à fait années 1950, ni georgien – bien que j'aime ces deux styles. » Les pièces se sont remplies progressivement au cours des années. Il a acheté les bois et les peaux au cours de ses voyages : « Ils ont une beauté intrinsèque qui nous échappe souvent à cause de notre peur collective de la mort. »

P. 289 Above the living area is a gallery bedroom. The furniture consists of heirloom pieces and finds from Simon Upton's travels. • Über dem Wohnraum liegt auf einer Empore das Schlafzimmer. Die Möblierung setzt sich aus Erbstücken und Reisefunden zusammen. • La chambre à coucher sur une galerie, audessus du séjour. Les meubles ont été hérités ou trouvés au cours de voyages.

↑ "Symmetry was an important design principle," the photographer says; the objects on and next to the old fabric-cutting table were arranged accordingly. • „Symmetrie war eine wichtige Gestaltungsmaxime", sagt Upton. Entsprechend arrangierte er die Objekte auf und neben dem ehemaligen Stoffschneidetisch. • «La symétrie était importante dans la décoration», dit Upton. C'est dans cet esprit qu'il a disposé les objets sur l'ancienne table de tailleur et à côté.

→ The canopied four-poster bed has carved posts from colonial India that were discovered at a London antiques shop. • Das Himmelbett mit Zeltdach hat gedrechselte Pfosten aus dem kolonialzeitlichen Indien, die Upton bei einem Londoner Antiquitätenhändler entdeckte. • Le lit à baldaquin au toit pyramidal a des montants tournés de style colonial indien, chinés chez un antiquaire londonien.

← The kitchen units and steel-clad countertop were designed by Upton himself. In the foreground is an antique table with an Arne Jacobsen chair. • Die Küchenzeile mit stahlverkleideter Arbeitsplatte entwarf Upton selbst. Davor gesellt sich ein Stuhl von Arne Jacobsen zum antiken Tisch. • Upton a conçu lui-même la cuisine au plan de travail revêtu d'acier. Devant, une chaise d'Arne Jacobsen côtoie une table ancienne.

↓ Made from a single piece of hardwood, the coffee table was once a ceremonial bed for an Ivorian tribal chief. • Aus einem Stück Hartholz geschnitzt: das nun als Coffeetable dienende zeremonielle Bett eines Häuptlings von der Côte d'Ivoire. • Sculptée dans une seule pièce de bois dur, la table basse était autrefois le lit de cérémonie d'un chef de tribu ivoirien.

→ Discovered at Spitalfields Market, the face on the staircase wall is made of resin. The windows date back to when the former warehouse was built. • Das Kopffragment aus Kunstharz im Treppenhaus ist ein Fund vom Spitalfields Market. Die Verglasung stammt aus der Erbauungszeit der einstigen Lagerhalle. • Le fragment de tête en résine synthétique dans la cage d'escalier a été trouvé au Spitalfields Market. Le vitrage date de l'époque de construction du hangar.

"I wanted a bright, white canvas. And I didn't want to follow a certain style, or have anything jarring or offensive." SIMON UPTON

„Ich wollte Räume, die wie eine helle Leinwand wirken. Keinen fixen Stil, vielmehr die Abwesenheit von allem Lauten oder Aggressiven."
« Je voulais une toile blanche et lumineuse. Pas suivre strictement un style particulier, plutôt une absence de tout ce qui peut agresser. »

← A horn from an African kudu ante-lope and a Robbie Duff Scott drawing hang on the bathroom walls. The X-shaped side table came by way of Nicky Haslam. • Im Bad hängt außer dem Horn einer afrikanischen Kudu-Antilope eine Zeichnung von Robbie Duff Scott an der Wand. Der X-Beistelltisch stammt von Nicky Haslam. • Sur le mur de la salle de bains, une corne de koudou afri-cain et un dessin de Robbie Duff Scott. La petite table en X vient de chez Nicky Haslam.

↓ In front of the custom-made cabinets are objects Upton has collected over the years. The two chairs featuring chromed steel arms date from the 1970s. • Vor den Einbauschränken, die Upton nach Maß schreinern ließ, finden sich Sammel-objekte aus vielen Jahren. Die beiden Stühle mit verchromten Stahlbändern stammen aus den 1970ern. • Devant les placards intégrés qu'Upton a fait fabri-quer sur mesure, des objets collection-nés au fil du temps. Les deux chaises pourvues de bandes en acier chromé datent des années 1970.

LONDON
UK

Traversing Periods

"I wanted to create a space that feels contemporary, but also embraces the fact that this is an old house." Thus the London designer's aim with this, her first domestic interior, was quite clear. To achieve it, Faye Toogood revealed period features and removed unfortunate additions made in the late 1990s. "There was a lot of slightly green-tinged architectural glass going on," she cringes. The starting point for her color palette came from three photographic artworks her clients owned, as well as their love of Marni. Toogood used hues she associates with the Italian fashion brand: "slightly off colors," like fleshy rose or ochre or a moody green. The furnishings are a savvy mix of different periods and styles—"the modern, the Victorian, the rustic. I wanted the interiors to feel lived in, to feel layered." She also wanted them to be luxurious, as witnessed by the master bathroom clad in handmade enameled lava tiles. With that, she apparently drove the workmen crazy. "I gave them a specific map showing where each individual tile was to go," she recounts.

„Es sollten Räume werden, die sich zeitgenössisch anfühlen und doch das Alter des Hauses anklingen lassen", das hatte sich Faye Toogood für ihr erstes Privatprojekt vorgenommen. Also arbeitete die Londoner Designerin Details der Erbauungszeit heraus und entfernte unvorteilhafte Ergänzungen aus den 1990ern. „Wir hatten es mit einer Menge grünlichem Bauglas zu tun", stöhnt sie. Ausgangspunkt für ihre Farbwahl waren drei Foto-Arbeiten aus dem Besitz der Auftraggeber sowie deren Begeisterung für Marni. Immer wieder trifft man auf Nuancen, wie man sie von der italienischen Modemarke kennt – „leicht schräge Töne" wie Fleischrosa, Ocker oder ein verhangenes Grün. Die Möblierung mixt clever Epochen und Stile: „Das Moderne, das Viktorianische, das Rustikale. Alles sollte echt gelebt wirken, vielschichtig." Ein gewisser Luxus durfte auch nicht fehlen. So ist das Bad mit handgearbeiteten Lavasteinfliesen verkleidet, mit denen Toogood wackere Handwerker an den Rand der Verzweiflung trieb: „In meinem Plan war die Position jeder einzelnen Fliese vorgeschrieben."

« J'ai cherché à créer un espace contemporain tout en respectant l'esprit de cette vieille maison », déclare Faye Toogood à propos de son premier projet de décoration pour des particuliers. Dans ce but, elle a fait ressortir des détails d'origine et ôté des ajouts fâcheux datant de la fin des années 1990. « Il y avait beaucoup de verre architectural verdâtre », dit-elle avec une grimace. Pour sa palette de couleurs, elle s'est inspirée de trois photographies appartenant aux propriétaires ainsi que de leur passion pour Marni. Elle a repris des teintes légèrement passées propres à la marque italienne dans la chambre principale, tel que le rose chair et l'ocre. Dans le salon, elle a choisi un vert mélancolique. Le mobilier est un savant mélange d'époques et de styles : « Du moderne, du victorien, du rustique. Je voulais que ça ait l'air vécu. » Elle tenait également à ce que l'ensemble soit luxueux, comme en témoigne la salle de bains tapissée de carrelage en lave émaillée fait main. Les ouvriers ont cru devenir fous. « Je leur ai donné un plan précis indiquant l'emplacement de chaque carreau », explique-t-elle.

P. 297 A bat skeleton and ebonized console table in the living room. Metal floor lamp from Philip Thomas. • Im Wohnzimmer steht ein Fledermaus-skelett auf einer ebonisierten Konsole. Metallleuchte vom Londoner Anti-quitätenhändler Philip Thomas. • Dans le séjour, un squelette de chauve-souris est posé sur une console teintée couleur ébène. Le luminaire a été acheté chez l'antiquaire londonien Philip Thomas.

↑ Toogood installed the dining table in the kitchen. A 1950s Sputnik bulb chandelier and a trio of Hiroshi Sugimoto seascapes add to the ethereal atmo-sphere of the space. • Ein Sputnik-Lüster aus den 1950ern und Seascapes von Hiroshi Sugimoto geben der Essecke etwas Ätherisches. • La table de salle à manger est dans la cuisine. Un lustre « Spoutnik » des années 1950 et les pho-tographies de mer de Hiroshi Sugimoto ajoutent à l'atmosphère « éthérée ».

→ On the opposite end of the kitchen, a Michael Anastassiades Tube Chande-lier over an Eames table and Prouvé chairs. • Am anderen Ende der Küche: Michael Anastassiades' Tube Chandelier über einem Eames-Tisch mit Prouvé-Stühlen. • À l'autre bout de la cuisine : un lustre Tube Chandelier de Michael Anastassiades suspendu au-dessus d'une table Eames avec des chaises Prouvé.

PP. 300/301 For the walls of the living room, Toogood chose an Emery & Cie green. Both the Elements coffee table and the rug are her own designs. • Für die Wohnzimmer wählte Toogood ein raffiniertes Grün von Emery & Cie. Coffeetable Elements und Teppich entwarf sie selbst. • Pour les murs du séjour, Toogood a choisi un vert raffiné d'Emery & Cie. Elle a dessiné la table basse Elements ainsi que le tapis.

↑ Toogood used handmade, slightly irregular tiles in the bathroom. Main treading areas were highlighted with color. • Im Bad verwendete Toogood handgefertigte, leicht unregelmäßige Fliesen. Wo sie wie farbige Spuren wirken, liegen die Funktionsbereiche. • Soulignant les zones de grand passage avec de la couleur, Toogood a utilisé du carrelage fait main dans la salle de bains.

→ In the family room, two chairs from Caravane stand on a custom blue area carpet. TWB (Tailored Wood Bench) seat by Raw Edges for Cappellini. • Im Familienzimmer stehen zwei Sessel von Caravane auf dem blauen Maßteppich. Holzsitz TWB (Tailored Wood Bench) von Raw Edges für Cappellini. • Dans le séjour, deux fauteuils de chez Caravane sur un tapis bleu sur mesure. Le banc TWB (Tailored Wood Bench) a été créé par Raw Edges pour Cappellini.

← The chandelier in the bedroom is made of five Selene pendants from ClassiCon. Closets are covered in silk by De Gournay. • Im Schlafzimmer vereinen sich fünf Selene-Kugelleuchten von ClassiCon zum Lüster. Der Schrank wurde mit Seiden von De Gournay bezogen. • Le lustre de la chambre a été réalisé avec cinq plafonniers Selene de chez ClassiCon. Les placards sont tapissés de soies de chez De Gournay.

LOULÉ
PORTUGAL

Southern Comfort

When artist Christina von Rosen moved to Portugal in 1975, she held an exhibition of her work and bought a small place with the proceeds. "Houses weren't expensive back then," she recalls. Initially, her current dwelling was equally modest— a tiny, stone fisherman's house of around 320 square feet. Situated in the Ria Formosa Nature Reserve, it looks out over marshland and dunes towards the sea. Nearby is the former Roman site of Balsa. Von Rosen extended the ground floor and created guest quarters and two terraces above it. As for the decor, she says that it's an ongoing process. One evening, she painted a fish motif onto a cupboard. "My hand slipped and suddenly, one of the fish had a cigarette in its mouth!" Artistic accidents aside, her only worry is flooding: "At high tide, there aren't many inches to spare between the sea and the doorstep!"

Als die Künstlerin Christina von Rosen 1975 nach Portugal ging, veranstaltete sie dort eine Ausstellung ihrer Werke und kaufte mit dem Erlös ein kleines Haus. „Damals waren die Häuser hier sehr preiswert", erinnert sie sich. Anfänglich war ihr gegenwärtiges Heim ebenfalls bescheiden – ein winziges steinernes Fischerhaus mit einer Fläche von etwa 30 Quadratmetern. Im Naturreservat Ria Formosa gelegen, blickt es über Marschland und Dünen zum Meer. In der Nähe war die einstige römische Siedlung Balsa. Von Rosen erweiterte das Erdgeschoss und baute Gästezimmer und zwei Terrassen darüber. Die dekorative Ausgestaltung ist ihr zufolge ein sich ständig in Entwicklung befindlicher Prozess. Eines Abends malte sie ein Fischmotiv auf einen Schrank. „Meine Hand rutschte aus, und plötzlich hatte einer der Fische eine Zigarette im Maul!" Abgesehen von künstlerischen Missgeschicken ist ihre einzige Sorge ein möglicher Wasseranstieg. „Bei Flut liegen nur einige Zentimeter zwischen dem Meer und der Türschwelle."

Quand l'artiste Christina von Rosen est arrivée au Portugal en 1975, elle a exposé ses œuvres et s'est acheté une maison avec les profits. « À l'époque, ça ne coûtait pas cher », se souvient-elle. Ce n'était qu'une petite cabane de pêcheur en pierre de 30 mètres carrés située dans la réserve naturelle de Ria Formosa. Un marais et des dunes la séparent de la mer. Les ruines romaines de Balsa se trouvent à deux pas. Von Rosen a agrandi le rez-de-chaussée et créé des chambres d'amis surmontées de deux terrasses. Quant au décor, c'est une œuvre en évolution perpétuelle. Un soir, alors qu'elle peignait un poisson sur un buffet, « ma main a glissé et il s'est retrouvé avec une cigarette au bec ! ». Accidents artistiques mis à part, son seul souci est le réchauffement de la planète. « À marée haute, il ne reste plus que quelques centimètres entre la mer et le seuil de ma porte. »

P. 305　Cane was used for the enclosure and cotton for the seating area. •
Auf der Veranda wurden Schilfrohr für die Einfassung und blau-weiß gestreifte Baumwolle für die Sitzecke verwendet. •
Des cloisons en jonc pour ce coin repos tapissé d'un coton à rayures blanches et bleues.

↑　Von Rosen brought the kitchen tiles back from Morocco. The traditional stool under the window is still made by hand in the Algarve region. • Die Küchenfliesen brachte Christina von Rosen aus Marokko mit. Der traditionelle Hocker unter dem Fenster wird an der Algarveküste immer noch in Handarbeit gefertigt. • Von Rosen a rapporté le carrelage de la cuisine du Maroc. Dans la région de l'Algarve, des artisans continuent de fabriquer les tabourets traditionnels comme celui qui est sous la fenêtre.

→　An old cabinet bought at a flea market, a traditional Portuguese folding chair, and a stool found under a tree are grouped together in a corner of the sitting room. • In einer Ecke des Wohnzimmers stehen eine alte Vitrine vom Flohmarkt, ein portugiesischer Klappstuhl und ein unter einem Baum gefundener Hocker. • Dans un coin du salon, une vieille armoire chinée sur un marché aux puces, un fauteuil pliant traditionnel portugais et un tabouret découvert sous un arbre.

← A view from the outside terrace into the sitting room. The fish motifs on the cupboard were painted by von Rosen. • Blick von der Außenterrasse ins Wohnzimmer. Die Fischmotive wurden von der Hausherrin gemalt. • Le salon vu depuis la terrasse. Les poissons sur le buffet ont été peints par Christina von Rosen.

↑ The cotton mosquito net in the guest bedroom was acquired in Amsterdam, while the cotton sheets come from Greece. • Das Moskitonetz aus Baumwolle im Gästezimmer war ein Kauf in Amsterdam. Die Baumwollbettwäsche kommt aus Griechenland. • La moustiquaire en coton de la chambre d'amis vient d'Amsterdam, les draps en coton de Grèce.

MADRID
SPAIN

International Inspiration

Many different places have played a part in Eugenia Melian's life, a fact reflected in the interiors of the music producer and agent's home in Madrid, where—after sojourns in L.A. and Paris—she has lived since 2005. Situated in a historic townhouse, the apartment, which had previously been occupied by five students, was totally rundown and covered in graffiti. "Despite the state of it, I could see that the flat would be able to accommodate much of the furniture I have collected over the years." She then had it renovated by a friend according to her own specifications. The style? A rusticity inspired by the Andalusia of her childhood.

Das Leben der Musikproduzentin und Agentin Eugenia Melian hat sich an vielen Orten abgespielt. Das spiegelt auch die Ausstattung ihres Apartments, das sie - nach Stationen in L.A. und Paris - seit 2005 in Madrid bewohnt. Die damals völlig verwahrlosten Räume des historistischen Stadthauses übernahm sie, mit Graffitis beschmiert, von fünf Studenten. „Trotz des Zustandes sah ich, dass ich hier einen großen Teil meiner über die Jahre zusammengetragenen Möbelschätze unterbringen konnte." Also ließ sie alles nach ihren eigenen Vorgaben von einem Freund renovieren. Die Maxime dabei? Rustikalität wie im Andalusien ihrer Kindheit.

Eugenia Melian, productrice et agent musical, a vécu dans de nombreux endroits. L'ameublement et la décoration de son appartement montrent bien qu'elle habite depuis 2005 à Madrid, après des séjours à Los Angeles et Paris. Elle a choisi les espaces délaissés, couverts de graffitis, de la maison de ville historique, qu'occupaient auparavant cinq étudiants. « Malgré l'état des lieux, j'ai vu qu'une grande partie de mes trésors accumulés depuis des années s'intégreraient ici. » Elle a donc fait tout rénover par un ami qui a suivi ses instructions. Sur le plan stylistique, le rustique est de mise comme dans l'Andalousie de son enfance.

P. 311 A 19th-century Spanish farm-house table, combined with Eames vintage chairs, is everybody's favorite place in the kitchen. • Ein spanischer Bauerntisch des 19. Jahrhunderts bildet das Herz der Küche, kombiniert mit Vintage-Stühlen von Eames. • Associée à des chaises vintage d'Eames, la table paysanne espagnole du 19ᵉ siècle est le cœur de la cuisine.

← In the corner of a bedroom is a portrait of Melian taken in 1983 by Max Vadukul. • In einer Schlafzimmerecke

hängt ein Porträt der Hausherrin, das Max Vadukul 1983 aufnahm. • Dans un coin de la chambre à coucher, un portrait photographique de la maîtresse de maison, réalisé par Max Vadukul en 1983.

↙ The black velvet sofa by Melian Randolph fits perfectly into the striped alcove. • Das schwarze Samtsofa von Melian Randolph fügt sich perfekt in die gestreifte Wandnische ein. • Le canapé en velours noir de Melian Randolph est parfaitement intégré dans la niche murale rayée.

↓ Interiors studio Melian Randolph is owned by the music producer's sisters; they designed her bed, which was made by an upholsterer in Seville. • Die Schwestern der Hausherrin, Inhaberinnen des Einrichtungsstudios Melian Randolph, entwarfen das Bett, ein Polsterer aus Sevilla stellte es her. • Les sœurs de la maîtresse de maison, propriétaires du studio de décoration Melian Randolph, ont dessiné le lit, réalisé ensuite par un tapissier de Séville.

← The desk and insect collection are from the estate of architect Maurice Rink. • Aus dem Nachlass des Architekten Maurice Rink stammen der Schreibtisch und die Insektensammlung. • Le bureau et la collection d'insectes ont autrefois appartenu à l'architecte Maurice Rink.

↙ The bronze swallows, which have been ever-present throughout Eugenia Melian's many moves, are by Fabrice Langlade. • Fabrice Langlade entwarf die Bronzeschwalben, die Eugenia Melian bisher in jede Wohnung begleiteten. • Fabrice Langlade a conçu les hirondelles de bronze qui ont jusqu'ici accompagné Eugenia Melian dans chaque appartement.

↓ With its books, CDs, and pictures of friends, the library is also an archive of Eugenia Melian's life. • Die Bibliothek mit Büchern, CDs und Bildern von Freunden ist zugleich ein Archiv von Eugenia Melians Leben. • La bibliothèque remplie de livres, de compacts et de photos d'amis rappelle aussi les étapes de la vie d'Eugenia Melian.

→ In the guest room, a blue-black wall provides the backdrop for a 1950s Swedish desk. • Im Gästezimmer setzt eine blauschwarze Wand den schwedischen Schreibtisch aus den 1950ern in Szene. • Dans la chambre d'amis, un mur bleu-noir met en valeur la table suédoise des années 1950.

MANANTIALES
URUGUAY

In Love with Loggias

Architect Diego Félix San Martín has known the owner of this house for over 20 years. He has created several residences for her in Argentina and collaborated with her on numerous projects. "She's a very good landscape architect," he asserts. For this summer house near Punta del Este, she evoked two sources of inspiration—the Italian Renaissance and the traditional houses of Marrakech. The influence of the former can be clearly seen in the abundant use of classical arches. The latter, meanwhile, gave rise to spaces that are halfway between the indoors and outdoors. The most notable example is the 40-foot-long gallery, which is topped with a glass and cane roof, but remains open on all sides. The house also offers some wonderful axial views. As San Martín says, "the best thing is that you can see all the way through the house from one side to the other."

Die Eigentümerin dieses Hauses kennt der Architekt Diego Félix San Martín seit über 20 Jahren. Er hat in Argentinien mehrere Wohnsitze für sie gebaut und mit ihr an verschiedenen Projekten zusammengearbeitet. „Sie ist eine sehr gute Landschaftsarchitektin", erklärt er. Für dieses Sommerhaus bei Punta del Este nutzte sie zwei Quellen der Inspiration – die italienische Renaissance und die traditionellen Häuser von Marrakesch. Der italienische Einfluss zeigt sich klar in den zahlreichen klassischen Bögen, während der Gedanke an Marrakesch zu Räumen führte, die auf halbem Weg zwischen drinnen und draußen angesiedelt sind. Das bemerkenswerteste Beispiel ist die zwölf Meter lange Galerie, die mit Schilfrohr und Glas gedeckt ist, aber seitlich offen bleibt. Sie bietet einige wundervolle Sichtachsen. Wie San Martín sagt: „Das Schönste daran ist, dass man von einer Seite zur anderen durch das ganze Haus schauen kann."

L'architecte Diego Félix San Martín connaît depuis plus de vingt ans la paysagiste propriétaire de cette maison, ayant déjà construit pour elle plusieurs résidences en Argentine et collaboré avec elle sur de nombreux projets. Pour cette retraite d'été près de Punta del Este, elle a évoqué deux sources d'inspiration : la Renaissance italienne, dont l'influence est manifeste dans les nombreuses arches classiques, et les demeures traditionnelles de Marrakech, avec leurs espaces où se confondent l'intérieur et l'extérieur. L'exemple le plus frappant en est la spacieuse galerie de 12 m de long, avec un toit en jonc et verre, ouverte sur les côtés. Elle offre de merveilleuses perspectives. Comme dit San Martín : « On peut voir à travers d'un bout à l'autre de la maison. »

P. 317 A huge window next to the rustic dining table offers views of the sea. • Ein riesiges Fenster beim rustikalen Esstisch gewährt Ausblick auf das Meer. • L'immense ouverture derrière la table rustique donne sur la mer.

← The bedside table in one of the guest suites was made by a local carpenter to the owner's design. • Den Nachttisch in einer der Gästesuiten hat ein einheimischer Tischler nach einem Entwurf der Eigentümerin angefertigt. • La table de chevet dans l'une des suites des invités a été dessinée par la maîtresse de maison et réalisée par un artisan local.

↑ A breakfast room is located next to the kitchen. The countertop is made from granite. • Ein Frühstückszimmer neben der Küche, deren Arbeitsplatte aus Granit besteht. • La cuisine communique avec une petite pièce où l'on prend le petit-déjeuner. Le plan de travail est en granit.

↑ Classical lines and symmetry can also be found in the living room, where two white cotton sofas flank a pair of teak sun-bed bases, which act as coffee tables. The ottoman is upholstered in a hand-woven fabric made by Indians in northern Argentina. The concrete floors are decorated with geometric motifs in brick. • Klassische Linienführung und Symmetrie sind auch im Wohnzimmer zu finden: Dort flankieren zwei weiße Leinensofas die beiden Teakholzgestelle ehemaliger Sonnenliegen, die als Sofa-

tische fungieren. Die Ottomane ist mit einem von nordargentinischen Indianern handgewebten Stoff bezogen. In die Betonböden wurden geometrische Motive aus Ziegelsteinen eingelegt. • On retrouve les lignes classiques et la symétrie dans le séjour où deux canapés houssés de coton blanc flanquent une paire de lits de plage convertis en tables basses. Le pouf est tapissé d'une étoffe tissée par des Indiens du nord de l'Argentine. Les sols en béton sont décorés de motifs géométriques en briques.

→ The house's gallery bridges the gap between the interior and the exterior. • Die lang gestreckte Loggia-Galerie des Hauses verbindet innen und außen. • La galerie marie l'extérieur et l'intérieur.

MARRAKECH
MOROCCO

Riad Renaissance

The Arabic inscription on the wall of the main salon takes the form of a poetic statement: "This is a place for receiving friends. This is a place to listen to the singing of birds. This is a place of quiet and repose." The peace and harmony of this magnificent palace, situated in the heart of the Medina and decorated with *zelligs, ghebs* and *zouaqs*, was certainly what persuaded Frans Ankoné to come to its rescue. To sum up Ankoné's long career in a few lines is scarcely possible. Born in the Netherlands, he is a talented fashion stylist who has worked with some of the world's greatest photographers. He defined the look of such publications as *Avenue, Vogue,* and *The New York Times Magazine*, before becoming creative director for Neiman Marcus and Romeo Gigli. He had adored Marrakech since the end of the 1960s, but it was an old friend of his, the Italian stylist Alessandra Lippini, who finally helped him find and convert a riad there. Skillfully assisted by Fabrizio Bizzarri, Alessandra was able to put flesh on a number of Frans Arkoné's more daring ideas, and succeeded in translating his passion for bright colors and surprising shapes. The result is an ambience that would grace the palace of any pasha.

Die arabische Inschrift auf einer Wand im Wohnzimmer verkündet es so klar wie poetisch: „Dies ist ein Ort der Gastfreundschaft. Dies ist ein Ort, an dem man die Vögel singen hört. Und dies ist ein Ort der Ruhe und des Friedens." In der Tat rettete Frans Ankoné das herrliche Palais mitten in der Medina, um den Frieden und die Harmonie zu bewahren, die in diesem wunderschönen, mit *ghebs, zelliges* und *zouaqs* geschmückten Gebäude herrschen. Ankonés langjährige Karriere in ein paar Sätzen zusammenzufassen, ist eigentlich unmöglich. Der in den Niederlanden geborene Modestylist, der mit den größten Fotografen zusammenarbeitete, hat den „Look" von Zeitschriften wie *Avenue, Vogue* und *New York Times Magazine* geprägt, bevor er Creative Director bei Neiman Marcus und Romeo Gigli wurde. Seit Ende der 1960er Jahre liebt er Marrakesch. Eine langjährige Freundin, die italienische Stylistin Alessandra Lippini, half ihm schließlich, dort einen Riad zu finden und umzubauen. Zusammen mit Fabrizio Bizzarri verlieh sie den kühnen Ideen Ankonés Gestalt und setzte seine Leidenschaft für leuchtende Farben, überraschende Formen und eine dem Palast eines Paschas würdige Atmosphäre um.

L'inscription en caractères arabes qui orne l'un des murs du salon principal est formelle : « Voici un endroit pour recevoir ses amis. Voici un endroit d'où on entend chanter les oiseaux. Et voici un endroit paisible propice au repos.» Frans Ankoné a-t-il sauvé ce splendide palais situé au cœur de la médina pour pouvoir jouir pleinement de la paix et de l'harmonie qui règnent dans ce lieu magnifique décoré de *ghebs*, de *zelliges* et de *zouaqs* ? Résumer la longue carrière de Frans en quelques lignes est impossible. Né aux Pays-Bas, ce styliste de mode talentueux qui a travaillé avec les plus grands photographes a défini le «look» de magazines tels que *Avenue, Vogue* et le *New York Times Magazine*, entre autres, avant de devenir Creative Director chez Neiman Marcus et Romeo Gigli. Il adorait Marrakech depuis la fin des années 1960, mais c'est une amie de longue date, la styliste italienne Alessandra Lippini, qui l'a aidé à y trouver un riyad. Secondée par Fabrizio Bizzarri, elle a su donner forme aux idées les plus audacieuses de Frans et réussi à traduire sa passion pour les couleurs éclatantes, les formes surprenantes et pour une ambiance digne du palais d'un pacha.

P. 323 Fabrizio Bizzarri designed this fireplace in one of the guest bedrooms. It is crowned by an onion dome with a Turkish crescent made of gilded metal. • Diesen Kamin in einem der Gästezimmer entwarf Fabrizio Bizzarini. Der zwiebelförmiger Aufsatz ist mit einer vergoldeten Sichel verziert. • Fabrizio Bizzarini a dessiné cette cheminée dans une des chambres d'amis. Elle est couronnée d'un bulbe décoré d'un croissant doré.

← The bedroom corridor boasts a mosaic floor, and the lanterns were made by Moroccan craftsmen. • Ein Mosaik bedeckt den Boden im Korridor zum Schlafzimmer, die Lampen schmiedeten marokkanische Handwerker. • Le sol du corridor de la chambre à coucher est revêtu de mosaïques, les lampes ont été forgées par des artisans marocains.

↑ The room traditionally reserved for men, where they went to smoke or meditate, was beautifully restored by Alessandra Lippini and Fabrizio Bizzarri. • Das „Herrenzimmer", in das man sich einst zurückzog, um zu rauchen oder nachzudenken, wurde von Alessandra Lippini und Fabrizio Bizzarri meisterhaft restauriert. • « La chambre des hommes » où ceux-ci se réunissaient jadis pour fumer ou méditer a été magistralement restaurée par Alessandra Lippini et Fabrizio Bizzarri.

← A 1950s chair under the arches of the patio is decorated with Arabic inscriptions. • Der Stuhl aus den 1950er Jahren, der unter den Bögen im Patio steht, wurde mit Inschriften in arabischen Lettern bestickt. • Sous les arches du patio, une chaise des années 1950 est décorée d'inscriptions en caractères arabes.

→ In the kitchen are 1950s coffee-house chairs that Ankoné discovered in Morocco. • In der Küche stehen Kaffeehausstühle aus den 1950ern, die Ankoné in Marokko fand. • Dans la cuisine, des chaises de café des années 1950 qu'Ankoné a trouvées au Maroc.

"I love all the handcrafted details in this old house, which we have restored with great care." FRANS ANKONÉ

„Ich liebe all die handgearbeiteten Details des alten Hauses, die wir achtsam restauriert haben."
« Dans la vieille maison, j'aime tous les détails faits à la main que nous avons restaurés avec soin. »

MÉRIDA
MEXICO

Walking on History

The streets of Yucatán's capital are a treasure trove of colonial architecture. Eyes never grow weary of contemplating late 19th-century wonders such as the Paseo de Montejo, lined with ornate stucco-decorated palaces and cut through with numerous alleyways filled with brightly colored houses. The renowned Mexican architect Salvador Reyes Rios and his wife, designer Josefina Larraín Lagos, live here with their two children in a low-rise residence adorned with classical pilasters. Salvador and Josefina have restructured their turn-of-the-century home, giving it a resolutely contemporary feel, but their modern makeover integrates several historical features, such as cement flagstones and a beautiful colonnade leading onto the patio. The couple's purist tastes have also influenced the interiors. They have maintained a rustic spirit in the kitchen, a sober but comfortable style in the bathroom, and decorated their home with stylishly minimalist furniture throughout. Their remarkable metamorphosis is completed with eye-catching details such as a striking section of blue wall, a strelitzia arranged in a vase, and an elegant bathtub placed in the middle of the garden.

Wer in der Hauptstadt von Yucatán spazieren geht, kann die Schätze der Kolonialarchitektur des späten 19. Jahrhunderts bewundern. Man wird es einfach nicht satt, die Blicke über den Paseo de Montejo schweifen zu lassen. Viele mit Stuck verzierte Paläste stehen dort, und unzählige Gassen, in denen sich Häuser in leuchtenden Farben reihen, kreuzen ihn. Salvador Reyes Rios, ein bekannter Architekt, und seine Frau Josefina Larraín Lagos, Designerin, bewohnen mit ihren beiden Kindern ein recht niedriges Haus, das mit klassischen Pfeilern geschmückt ist. Unter Erhaltung einiger Details dieser Epoche, wie der Zementfliesen und des Säulengangs zum Patio, haben die Besitzer die Räumlichkeiten jenseits der Toreinfahrt völlig neu gegliedert und dieses Haus aus der Jahrhundertwende resolut in die Gegenwart geholt. Die Interieurs wirken nun klar und großzügig: Das Paar hat die rustikale Küche behalten, ein komfortabel-funktionales Badezimmer eingerichtet und Möbel von mustergültiger Schlichtheit ausgesucht. Ein blauer Mauerabschnitt, eine Strelitzie in einer Vase, die Badewanne im Garten – alles hier komplettiert diese bemerkenswerte Metamorphose.

Se promener dans la capitale du Yucatán, c'est pouvoir admirer des trésors de l'architecture coloniale de la fin du 19e siècle. On ne se lasse pas de contempler le Paseo de Montejo bordé de palais décorés de «pâtisseries» en stuc et traversé de ruelles où s'alignent des maisons aux couleurs vives. Salvador Reyes Rios, un architecte connu, et son épouse Josefina Larraín Lagos, designer, habitent avec leurs deux enfants une maison assez basse ornée de pilastres classiques. Au-delà de l'entrée cochère, les maîtres des lieux ont restructuré les espaces tout en gardant quelques détails d'époque comme les dalles de ciment et la colonnade qui donne accès au patio. Ils ont conféré à cette demeure fin de siècle une ambiance résolument contemporaine. L'intérieur montre le même souci de simplicité. Le couple a gardé la cuisine rustique, créé une salle de bains dépouillée et confortable et choisi des meubles d'une sobriété exemplaire. Un pan de mur bleu, un strelitzia dans un vase et une baignoire au milieu du jardin complètent cette métamorphose remarquable.

P. 329 The bathroom opens onto the bedroom, where old French roof tiles are arrayed on shelves. • Vom Bad aus kann man ins Schlafzimmer blicken, wo auf einem Regal alte französische Dachziegel stehen. • De la salle de bains on peut regarder dans la chambre où une étagère accueille de vieilles tuiles françaises.

← A canopy is draped above the paved courtyard, providing shade from the sun. • Ein Sonnensegel schützt im gepflasterten Hof vor der Mittagshitze. • Un vélum protège la cour pavée du grand soleil.

→ The owners have kept original design features in the kitchen, such as the traditional Mexican tilework and the impressive chimney hood. • In der Küche sind die traditionelle mexikanische Kachelung und der großzügig bemessene Dunstabzug erhalten geblieben. • La cuisine a conservé son carrelage traditionnel mexicain et sa hotte aux dimensions généreuses.

"With its 20-foot-high ceilings, the hacienda is truly beautiful. We just had to rescue it from ruin."

JOSEFINA LARRAÍN LAGOS

„Die Hazienda ist wunderschön mit ihren sechs Meter hohen Räumen. Wir mussten sie einfach vor dem Verfall bewahren."
« L'hacienda est merveilleuse avec ses pièces de six mètres de haut. Nous devions tout simplement les préserver de la dégradation. »

← Dating from around 1906, the tiles in the portico are part of the original architecture. The oil and acrylic painting is by Josefina Larraín Lagos. • Die Fliesen der Veranda sind originaler Bestandteil des Hauses und stammen aus der Zeit um 1906. Das Olacrylbild malte Josefina Larraín Lagos. • Les carreaux sous le portique sont d'origine et datent d'environ 1906. Le tableau à l'huile et l'acrylique a été peint par Josefina Larraín Lagos.

↑ The furniture Salvador Reyes Rios designed for the living room reflects this architect's love of pure, clean lines. • Im Wohnzimmer kündet das vom Architekten selbst entworfene Mobiliar von seiner Vorliebe für klare Formen. • Dans le séjour, le mobilier dessiné par l'architecte reflète sa prédilection pour les lignes pures.

MEXICO CITY
MEXICO

Viva Vintage

Mexico is famous for its colorfully painted houses. For the living spaces of Casa M. Herrera, interior designer Emmanuel Picault translated that positive energy into an elegant color scheme of red, gold, and black. The villa, planned by Jaime Guzman and completed in 2007, is situated close to a canyon, above the city. The furniture was sourced entirely from Picault's gallery Chic by Accident and comprises 20th-century pieces by both local and international designers. And with client and designer having embarked on scouting tours together even before the house was finished, there's a highly personal feel to the interiors.

Mexiko ist berühmt für seine farbig bemalten Hauswände. Deren positive Energie überführte Interiordesigner Emmanuel Picault mit einem Farbschema aus Rot, Gold und Schwarz auf elegante Weise in die Räume der Casa M. Herrera. Die 2007 nach Plänen von Jaime Guzman fertiggestellte Villa liegt an einem Canyon über der Stadt. Die gesamte Möblierung stammt von Chic by Accident, der Galerie von Picault, und besteht aus Stücken einheimischer wie internationaler Designer aus dem 20. Jahrhundert. Schon bevor das Haus stand, gingen Besitzer und Gestalter gemeinsam auf Möbelsuche, und es hat sich gelohnt: Das Ambiente wirkt tatsächlich wie langsam gewachsen und individuell.

Le Mexique est célèbre pour ses façades peintes de couleurs vives. Utilisant une palette de rouge, d'or et de noir, l'architecte d'intérieur Emmanuel Picault a élégamment fait passer leur énergie positive dans les pièces de la Casa M. Herrera. Achevée en 2007, la villa construite d'après des plans de Jaime Guzman est située près d'un canyon au-dessus de la ville. Le mobilier composé de pièces de designers mexicains et internationaux du 20ᵉ siècle vient de chez Chic by Accident, la galerie de Picault. La maison n'existait pas encore que le propriétaire et le décorateur partaient ensemble à la recherche de meubles, créant ainsi une ambiance absolument personnelle.

P. 335 In the living room, a gold-leaf screen by Arturo Pani stands next to a Don Shoemaker table. • Im Wohnzimmer leuchtet der Blattgoldparavent von Arturo Pani neben einem Tisch von Don Shoemaker. • Dans le séjour, le paravent à la feuille d'or d'Arturo Pani brille à côté de la table de Don Shoemaker.

↑ The shelf unit in the bedroom was designed in 1955 by the Mexican firm Ras-Martin. • Das Regal im Schlafzimmer ist ein Entwurf der mexikanischen Firma Ras-Martin aus dem Jahr 1955. • L'étagère de la chambre à coucher est une création de la maison mexicaine Ras-Martin et date de 1955.

→ On the classical rug is a mahogany partition by Erwin Hauer. • Auf dem neoklassizistischen Teppich steht ein Mahagoniraumteiler von Erwin Hauer. • Sur le tapis néoclassique, une cloison de séparation en acajou d'Erwin Hauer.

← The slatted ceiling allows natural light to fall on the bathroom's washbasin and granite floor. • Im Bad fällt durch Deckenlamellen das Sonnenlicht auf Waschblock und Granitfußboden. • Dans la salle de bains, les lames du plafond laissent passer la lumière du jour sur le lavabo encastré et le sol en granit.

↓ On the wall behind the ensemble of Mexican vintage chairs is a photograph by Seydou Keïta. • Hinter dem Ensemble aus mexikanischen Vintage-Stühlen hängt an der Wand eine Fotografie von Seydou Keïta. • Au premier plan, un groupe de chaises vintage mexicaines ; sur le mur, une photographie de Seydou Keïta.

MIAMI
USA

Captain's Cabin

Coming from Miami and headed for the beach and the pleasures of the water, you cross a curving bridge that links the mainland to a sunny island. Around here, the green, lush islands bearing the fragrant names of blossoms seem to peek inquisitively out of the azure seas like little green noses. On one of these islands, bearing the name Hibiscus, a European has created a tasteful beach house as a vacation home for himself and his family. Passionate about seafaring since his boyhood, he conceived the house along the lines of a yacht, with a row of cabins, and even portholes. The pool is also long and sleek, and excellent for diving. "I feel like the captain aboard my 'steamer,'" he jokes. In the rooms, a host of maritime objects, valuable model ships, nautical literature, and ancient sea charts tempt visitors to linger over them. Pure inspiration to set sail and take course for faraway places with exotic names.

Wer von Miami in Richtung Strand und Wasserfreuden düst, dessen Weg führt über eine kurvig geschwungene Brücke, die das Festland vom sonnigen Eiland trennt. Neugierig lugen hier üppig bewachsene Inseln mit duftigen Blütennamen wie grüne Flecken aus dem azurblauen Meer. Auf einer dieser Inseln mit dem Namen „Hibiskus" gestaltete ein Europäer geschmackvoll ein Strandhaus als Feriendomizil für sich und seine Familie. Von Kind auf mit Passion der Schifffahrt verbunden, glich er die Linienführung des Hauses einem schlanken Boot mit aneinandergereihten Kajüten an und ließ sogar ein Bullauge einbauen. Selbst der Pool ist lang gezogen und eignet sich zum Tauchen. „Ich fühle mich hier wie der Kapitän auf seinem Dampfer", scherzt er fröhlich. Die Räume bestückte er mit vielen maritimen Objekten, wertvollen Schiffsmodellen, nautischer Literatur und antiken Seekarten, die zum Studieren einladen. Da wächst die Lust, einfach die Segel zu setzen und Kurs zu nehmen auf ferne Orte mit geheimnisvollen Namen.

Celui qui part de Miami pour la plage, rêvant déjà des joies de la baignade, se retrouve irrévocablement sur un pont sinueux qui relie la terre ferme aux îles ensoleillées. Ici, les îlots à la végétation luxuriante qui portent des noms de fleurs parsèment comme des points verdoyants la mer d'azur. Sur l'une de ces îles, nommée Hibiscus, un Européen a aménagé avec goût une maison de plage où il passe ses vacances en compagnie de sa famille. Passionné depuis l'enfance par la navigation, il a donné à sa maison les lignes d'une embarcation élancée, dotée de cabines alignées, et même d'un hublot. La piscine est toute en longueur et se prête à la plongée. « Je me sens comme le capitaine sur son ‹vapeur› », plaisante-t-il joyeusement. Il a décoré les pièces de nombreux objets déclinant le thème marin, de maquettes de bateau de grande valeur, de livres et d'anciennes cartes maritimes qui invitent à y fureter. Il ne reste plus qu'à hisser les voiles et à mettre le cap sur des contrées lointaines et mystérieuses.

P. 341 Unlike the Rietveld classic they were inspired by, the dining-room chairs are more S-shape than zigzag. • Die Stühle im Esszimmer formen keine Zickzacklinie wie beim berühmten Rietveld-Vorbild, sondern eher ein S. • Les chaises de la salle à manger ne forment pas une ligne en zigzag comme celles du célèbre modèle de Rietveld mais plutôt un S.

↑ The combination of wood and light linen lends the living room an air of coziness. • Die Kombination von hellem Leinen und blondem Holz macht das Wohnzimmer gemütlich. • Le mariage de lin clair et de bois rend le séjour confortable et douillet.

→ An oil painting of the *Tilikum* by Susanne Fournais hangs over the Brazilian wood desk. • Ein Ölgemälde des Schiffes *Tilikum* von Susanne Fournais hängt über dem Arbeitstisch aus brasilianischen Hölzern. • Une huile représentant le *Tilikum* signée Susanne Fournais est suspendue derrière la table en bois brésilien.

← To keep things cool, there is a skylight and a ceiling fan with canvas blades. The paintings in the room are all by artist Julie Polidoro. In the hatch to the dining room is a model of the battleship *Potemkin*, widely known from Sergei Eisenstein's silent movie made in the 1920s. • Damit die Hitze sich nicht staut, wurden ein Oberlicht und ein Ventilator mit Leinen-flügeln eingebaut. Die Gemälde im Raum stammen alle von der Malerin Julie Polidoro. Im Durchbruch zum Esszimmer

steht ein Modell des Panzerkreuzers *Potemkin*, bekannt auch durch Sergej Eisensteins Stummfilm der 1920er Jahre. • Une lucarne et un ventilateur aux ailes de lin ont été intégrés pour éviter que la chaleur ne stagne. Les toiles accrochées dans la pièce sont signées Julie Polidoro. Dans l'ouverture sur la salle à manger, une maquette du cuirassé *Potemkine*, immortalisé dans les années 1920 par le film muet de Sergueï Eisenstein.

↑ The desk in the small maritime-themed study is an old card table. • Der alte Kartentisch wird in dem kleinen, ma-ritim dekorierten Arbeitszimmer zum Schreibtisch. • Dans le cabinet de travail au décor maritime, la vieille table à cartes se transforme en bureau.

MIAMI
USA

Meet Me at the Poolhouse

It was love at first sight for author Tom Healy when he and entrepreneur Fred Hochberg set eyes on this house, designed by architect Russell Pancoast on one of the Sunset Islands. Built in 1938 as a pleasure pavilion for the main residence on the adjoining lot, it had a ballroom, bar, and changing rooms, which Tom and Fred proceeded to adapt to their own purposes. The inside, created by interior designer Alison Spear, is painted in light shades enlivened by individual bright splashes and colorful abstract paintings. The garden, laid out by landscape architect Robert Parsley, adheres to the clear lines of the architecture. In the modestly sized guest rooms, in the tradition of the American motel, friends feel simultaneously "at home" and "on the road."

Es war Liebe auf den ersten Blick bei Autor Tom Healy, als er gemeinsam mit dem Unternehmer Fred Hochberg auf einer der Sunset Islands das vom Architekten Russell Pancoast entworfene Haus erspähte. 1938 als Vergnügungspavillon des auf dem benachbarten Grundstück stehenden Haupthauses gebaut, war es mit Tanzsaal, Bar und Umkleidekabinen ausgestattet, die nun von Tom und Fred umfunktioniert wurden. Das insgesamt hell gehaltene Interieur, von Innenarchitektin Alison Spear geschaffen, beleben Akzente in kräftigen Farben und abstrakte Gemälde. Der Garten, ein Werk des Landschaftsarchitekten Robert Parsley, folgt den klaren Linien der Architektur. In den kleinen Gästezimmern, die in der Tradition amerikanischer Motels ausgestattet wurden, fühlen sich Freunde „at home" und „on the road" zugleich.

Tom Healy, auteur, et Fred Hochberg, entrepreneur, ont eu le coup de foudre devant cette maison conçue par l'architecte Russell Pancoast sur l'une des Sunset Islands. Ce pavillon de plaisance construit en 1938 à côté de la maison principale située sur le terrain adjacent, était doté d'une salle de bal, d'un bar et de cabines de bain que Tom et Fred ont tout simplement détournés de leur vocation première. Les espaces aux teintes claires, conçus par l'architecte d'intérieur Alison Spear, sont égayés par quelques notes multicolores isolées et des tableaux abstraits colorés. Le jardin aménagé par le paysagiste Robert Parsley respecte les lignes sobres de l'architecture. Dans les petites chambres, les amis se sentent à la fois « at home » et « on the road » dans la tradition des motels américains.

P. 347 Above the orange velvet chaise longue hangs a painting by Tom Sachs. • Über der Chaiselongue mit orangefarbenem Samtbezug hängt eine Arbeit von Tom Sachs. • Au-dessus de la chaise longue habillée de velours orangé, un tableau de Tom Sachs.

↖ The high wooden ceiling of the living room evokes the romantic atmosphere of a chalet. In the background is the bar. • Das Wohnzimmer mit Blick auf die Bar. Die hohe Decke aus Holz erzeugt eine romantische Chalet-Atmosphäre. • Le séjour avec vue sur le bar. Le haut plafond en bois évoque un chalet romantique.

← On Tom and Fred's bed is a cashmere Hermès counterpane, which just happens to feature the same initial as the two owners' surnames. • Auf Toms und Freds Schlafzimmerbett liegt eine Kaschmirdecke von Hermès, die wie zufällig dieselbe Initiale wie die Nachnamen der Hausbesitzer trägt. • Sur le lit de Tom et Fred, un plaid Hermès en cachemire où s'inscrit, belle coïncidence, l'initiale des maîtres de maison.

↑ "Clean and glassy" best describes the dining room. The table was designed by Monica Armani and the chairs are by Antonio Citterio. • „Clean und gläsern", so lautete das Motto für das Esszimmer. Der Tisch ist ein Entwurf von Monica Armani und wurde mit Stühlen von Antonio Citterio kombiniert. • La salle à manger de lumière et de verre. La table signée Monica Armani est mariée à des chaises d'Antonio Citterio.

← One of the guest rooms which were furnished in the style of a motel. • Eines der Gästezimmer, die im Stil eines Motels eingerichtet wurden. • Une des chambres d'amis meublées et décorées dans le style des motels.

→ A white bathroom, which features Giampaolo Benedini's tub, Spoon by Agape. • Ein weißes Bad mit der Designwanne Spoon von Agape. • Une salle de bains blanche avec la baignoire Spoon de Giampaolo Benedini pour Agape.

↓ The guest bathroom was decorated with dark-red mosaic tiles. • Dunkelrote Mosaikfliesen wurden für das Gästebad verwendet. • Des mosaïques couleur pourpre pour la salle de bains des invités.

↙ With their natural color, the staircase's wooden treads stand out against the otherwise white surfaces. • Die hölzernen Trittstufen der Treppe setzen sich durch ihren natürlichen Ton von den weißen Flächen ab. • La couleur naturelle des marches en bois de l'escalier contraste avec les murs blancs.

MIAMI
USA

Wild Style

The neighbors have been speculating for years about what exactly lies concealed here behind the thick stone walls. But even a nosy peek through the ornate wrought-iron railings reveals little more than creepers and Royal Palm trunks. In fact, the lush vegetation on this modest plot hides one of South Beach's most distinctive Art Deco villas. The owner, Brian Antoni, author of *Paradise Overdose*, lives here in a flamboyantly colorful artistic realm of his own creation. He himself describes the house as "haunted," and surrounds himself with Caribbean pirate motifs, weird and wonderful furniture, and wild, fabulous creatures made of papier-mâché. The house was used as a location by photographer Helmut Newton and has been a rendezvous for numerous American artists. Primarily, though, this place serves as a source of inspiration for its creative owner, who is a dedicated and passionate activist for the conservation of historic buildings in Miami's South Beach district.

Viele Nachbarn rätseln schon seit Jahren, was sich nun genau hinter den dicken Steinmauern verbirgt. Doch neugierige Blicke durch das schmiedeeiserne Gitter gewähren lediglich Aussicht auf wuchernde Schlingpflanzen und Königspalmenstämme. Tatsächlich befindet sich auf dem dicht bewachsenen Stückchen Land eine der originellsten Art-déco-Villen von South Beach. Der Besitzer, Brian Antoni, Autor des Buches *Paradise Overdose*, lebt hier in seiner von ihm geschaffenen, poppig überladenen, bunten Kunstwelt. Sein Haus beschreibt er selbst als verwunschen. Er umgibt sich mit karibischem Piratenflair, mehr als ausgefallenem Mobiliar und wilden Fabelwesen aus Pappmaché. Das Haus diente schon als Kulisse für den Fotografen Helmut Newton sowie als Treffpunkt vieler amerikanischer Künstler. Vor allem aber ist dieser Ort eine stetige Inspirationsquelle für den kreativen Hausbesitzer, der mit viel Engagement und Leidenschaft den Denkmalschutz für die historischen Häuser von South Beach unterstützt.

Il y a des années que les voisins se demandent ce que dissimulent les épais murs de pierre, mais les regards curieux à travers le portail en fer forgé ne révèlent que des plantes grimpantes et des troncs de palmiers. En fait, le terrain où croît une végétation dense abrite une des villas Art Déco les plus originales de South Beach. C'est ici que vit Brian Antoni, auteur du livre *Paradise Overdose*, dans un monde artificiel multicolore, au décor surchargé et tapageur, qu'il a créé de sa main. Il dit lui-même que sa maison est enchantée et s'entoure d'un monde de pirates des Caraïbes, de meubles inusités, uniques et de créatures fabuleuses en papier mâché. La maison a déjà servi de décor à Helmut Newton, et de nombreux artistes américains s'y sont rencontrés. Mais l'endroit est avant tout une source d'inspiration pour son propriétaire qui s'engage avec ferveur pour sauvegarder les demeures historiques à South Beach.

P. 353 The "ugly" portraits, of which Brian is an obsessive collector, cover every inch of the dining-room wall. • Eine Ansammlung von „hässlichen" Porträts, die Brian wie besessen sammelt, bedecken die Esszimmerwand. • Les « vilaines têtes » que Brian collectionne avec passion recouvrent entièrement le mur de la salle à manger.

↑ "Alligator Wrestling" —after Hurricane Andrew, Brian found the sign in a pile of rubble. Now it adorns one of his bedrooms. • „Alligator Wrestling" — dieses Schild fand Brian nach einem Wirbelsturm in einem Trümmerhaufen, jetzt dekoriert es eines seiner Schlafzimmer. • « Alligator Wrestling » – Brian a trouvé l'écriteau qui décore une des chambres sur un tas de décombres après le passage d'une tornade.

→ Dried palm leaves, a wire globe, a Yul-Brynner-like head on the cabinet door: Brian Antoni collects objects of all kinds. • Getrocknete Palmblätter, ein Globus aus Draht, ein Yul-Brynner-Kopf am Schrank: Brian Antoni sammelt alles. • Un pied de bananier desséché, un globe terrestre en fil de fer, une tête style « Yul Bynner » sur la porte du petit meuble : Brian Antoni collectionne tout.

← The bedroom decor mixes sunflowers and seahorses. • Im Schlafzimmer kombiniert der Hausherr Sonnenblumen mit Seepferdchen. • Dans la chambre, les tournesols et les hippocampes font bon ménage.

↑ In the country-style kitchen, painted blue units contrast with yellow tiling. • Die Küche ist im Landhausstil gehalten. Ihre blau gestrichenen Schränke kontrastieren mit den gelben Fliesen. • La cuisine est de style campagnard. Ses armoires peintes en bleu contrastent avec les carreaux jaunes.

↓ Even the bed linen has sunflower motifs, while a bucolic landscape lends a calming touch. • Selbst die Bettwäsche passt zum Thema des Raums, und eine bukolische Landschaft begleitet den Schlaf. • Même la literie correspond au thème de la collection, et les paysages bucoliques accompagnent le dormeur.

MIAMI
USA

A Collector's Retreat

It took some time for Carlos Cisneros, a businessman and collector of Persian and Venezuelan extraction, to find the right house, a house where his collection of art and furniture would fully come into its own. The building dating from the 1950s was painstakingly restored to its present condition by John Keenen of the New York architects' bureau of Keenen/Riley. Waterside seating, generously planned and deliberately simple, fits in—both in shape and color—with the landscape setting and blends into the background. Landscape designer Edwina von Gal adopted this architectural leit-motif for her biomorphic garden design and established palm groupings, bamboo screens, and stone seas. With its at-mosphere of tranquillity and equilibrium, the splendid residence now acts like a tonic to the creative energies of the press-shy, sensitive owner.

Es dauerte einige Zeit, bis Carlos Cisneros, Unternehmer und Sammler persisch-venezolanischer Herkunft, das pas-sende Haus fand – ein Haus, in dem seine Kunst- und Möbelsammlung optimal zur Geltung kommen könnte. Der Bau stammt aus den 1950er Jahren und wurde mit viel Sorgfalt von John Keenen vom New Yorker Architekturbüro Keenen/Riley in seinen jetzigen Zustand gebracht. Großzügige und bewusst einfach gestaltete Sitzgruppen am Wasser integrieren sich in Form und Farbgebung in die Landschaft, ja verschmelzen mit dem Hintergrund. Die Landschaftsdesignerin Edwina von Gal führte das architektonische Leitmotiv in ihrem biomorphen Gartendesign wei-ter und schuf Palmeninseln, Bambuswände, Steinmeere. Die puristische Umgebung überträgt innere Ruhe und Ausgeglichenheit – und damit genau die Art von Inspiration, die sich der pressescheue, sensible Besitzer gewünscht hatte.

Trouver la maison qui mette le mieux en valeur sa collection d'œuvres d'art et de meubles a demandé quelque temps à Carlos Cisneros, un entrepreneur et collectionneur d'origine perso-vénézuélienne. Le bâtiment qu'il a choisi date des années 1950 et doit son état actuel aux soins méticuleux de John Keenen, du bureau d'architectes new-yorkais Keenen/ Riley. Les formes et les couleurs des groupes de sièges conçus avec générosité et une simplicité délibérée au bord de l'eau s'intègrent parfaitement au paysage et se fondent dans l'arrière-plan. La paysagiste Edwina von Gal a prolongé le fil conducteur architectural dans son jardin biomorphique et créé des îlots de palmiers, des parois de bambou et des mers de pierre. L'environnement puriste génère une paix intérieure et une égalité d'humeur qui ont une influence posi-tive sur la créativité du maître des lieux, un homme sensible qui fuit plutôt les journalistes.

P. 359 A painting by Ross Bleckner fills the wall next to the dining table. • Neben dem Esstisch hängt ein wandfüllendes Bild von Ross Bleckner. • À côté de la table à repas, un tableau de Ross Bleckner recouvre tout le mur.

↑ The stool by Eero Saarinen stands within the curve of the swinging Plexiglas door. Dense bamboo affords the bather privacy. To the rear is the main bedroom. • Der Hocker von Eero Saarinen steht in der Rundung der Schwingtür aus Plexiglas. Dichter Bambus gibt dem hier Badenden Sichtschutz. Im Hintergrund ist das Schlafzimmer zu sehen. • Le tabouret d'Eero Saarinen se dresse dans l'entrée arquée de la porte pivotante en plexiglas. Un rideau de bambous dissimule les baigneurs. À l'arrière plan, la chambre à coucher.

→ The interior of the owner's private library is governed by a masculine aesthetic. *Blue Net* by Ross Bleckner harmonizes with the 1960s sofa by Poul Kjærholm. • Die Einrichtung der privaten Bibliothek des Hausherrn wird von einer maskulinen Ästhetik bestimmt. Die Arbeit *Blue Net* von Ross Bleckner harmoniert mit dem Sofa von Poul Kjærholm aus den 1960er Jahren. • Une esthétique masculine définit la bibliothèque privée du maître de maison. Le tableau *Blue Net* de Ross Bleckner dialogue harmonieusement avec le canapé sixties de Poul Kjærholm.

← The bathroom wall and Plexiglas door are gently curved. • Die Badezimmerwand samt Plexiglastür ist sanft geschwungen. • Le mur de la salle de bains et sa porte en Plexiglas sont légèrement arrondis.

↑ Bed and bedside tables were designed by Keenen / Riley, the architect's firm. In the reading nook in the background sits a pouf by Massimo Morezzi for Edra. • Bett und Nachttische sind Entwürfe des Architekturbüros Keenen / Riley. In der Lesenische hinten steht ein Ottoman von Massimo Morezzi für Edra. • Le lit et les tables de nuit ont été conçus par le cabinet d'architecture Keenen / Riley. Dans le coin lecture, à l'arrière-plan, un pouf de Massimo Morezzi pour Edra.

→ The corridor links the living room and bedroom; to the left is the pool. • Der Flur verbindet Wohn- und Schlafzimmer, links geht es zum Pool. • Le couloir relie le séjour à la chambre à coucher. À gauche, on va vers la piscine.

MIAMI
USA

A Colorful Collection

In 1958, Miami's legendary architect Morris Lapidus, best known for his Eden Roc and Fontainebleau hotels, built one of only two private residences he ever constructed, on the Biscayne Bay waterfront. The current owners, Kim and Al Eiber, feel that this Lapidus-built house with its flat roof and geometrical façade is uniquely suited to their singular collection of design treasures. With a playful and colorful air, the 1950s and 1960s furniture and *objets d'art*, mostly Italian, seem to be giving a contemporary response to the architect's belief in allowing a free rein to excess. In their lifestyle, Kim and Al have fully embraced Lapidus's motto that "too much is never enough." This is also true of their particularly interesting collection of lamps, of which they have a total of 95 unusual models.

Miamis Architekturikone Morris Lapidus, bekannt durch die legendären Hotelbauten Eden Roc und Fontainebleau, baute 1958 eines seiner zwei Privathäuser an der Ozeanfront der Biscayne Bay. Die beiden heutigen Besitzer Kim und Al Eiber finden, dass sich ihre einzigartigen Designschätze nirgendwo so harmonisch einfügen wie in die Architektur ihres Hauses, das Lapidus mit Flachdach und geometrischer, kubenreicher Außenfassade gestaltete. Verspielt und farbenfroh erwidern die meist italienischen Möbel und Objekte aus den 1950er und 1960er Jahren bis heute das Credo des Architekten, dem Überfluss freien Lauf zu lassen. Kim und Al leben hier frei nach Lapidus' Motto: „Too much is never enough". Dies betrifft auch ihre besonders interessante Lampenkollektion – sie besitzen insgesamt 95 außergewöhnliche Leuchtenmodelle.

L'architecte de l'après-guerre Morris Lapidus, devenu une véritable idole à Miami, et dont on connaît les légendaires hôtels Eden Roc et Fontainebleau, a également construit en 1958 l'une des deux maisons particulières qui font face à l'océan à Biscayne Bay. Les deux propriétaires actuels, Kim et Al Eiber, sont convaincus que les trésors du design, uniques en leur genre, qu'ils ont rassemblés au fil des années ne s'intègrent nulle part de manière aussi harmonieuse que dans cette maison que Lapidus a pourvue d'une toiture plate et d'une façade géométrique, agrémentée de nombreuses formes cubiques. Ludiques et hauts en couleurs, les meubles et les objets des années 1950 et 1960, la plupart italiens, correspondent jusqu'à ce jour à la devise de l'architecte convaincu qu'il faut laisser le champ libre à l'abondance. Kim et Al vivent selon l'adage de Lapidus « Too much is never enough », en témoigne par exemple leur intéressante collection de lampes qui comprend 95 modèles sortant de l'ordinaire.

P. 365 The shelving units, the enormous foot, the table, and the lamp are all by Gaetano Pesce. The metal pillars were formerly part of a purification plant and are used as a room partition. • Regalsystem, überdimensionaler Fuß, Tisch und Lampe sind von Gaetano Pesce. Die Metallsäulen waren Bestandteil einer Kläranlage und werden als Raumteiler benutzt. • Le système de rangement, le pied monumental, la table et le luminaire sont de la main de Gaetano Pesce. Les colonnes en métal faisaient partie d'une station d'épuration, et les Eiber les utilisent pour diviser les pièces.

↑ In front of the curved wall of the breakfast room are Broadway chairs and a table by Gaetano Pesce. • Im Frühstücksraum mit geschwungenen Wänden stehen Broadway-Stühle und ein Tisch von Gaetano Pesce. • Dans la pièce du petit-déjeuner aux murs courbes, des chaises Broadway et une table de Gaetano Pesce.

→ The yellow and red circular lamp is designed by Gaetano Pesce. • Die gelb-rote runde Lampe ist ein Entwurf von Gaetano Pesce. • La lampe ronde jaune et rouge est signée Gaetano Pesce.

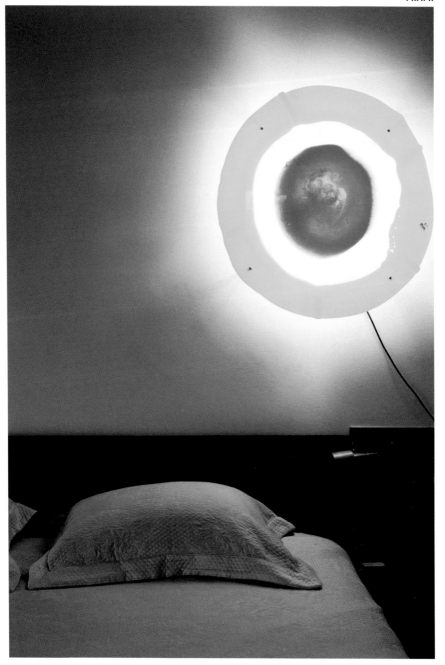

←← The house's entrance is shielded by a wide overhang and a round-hole screen. • Der Hauseingang ist durch einen breiten Dachüberstand und ein Lochgitter geschützt. • L'entrée de la maison est protégée par la grande avancée du toit et un panneau à claire-voie.

← Ralph, the house mascot, is sitting in Eero Aarnio's Bubble chair. • Ralph, das Maskottchen des Hauses, sitzt in dem Sessel Bubble von Eero Aarnio. • Ralph, la mascotte, se repose dans le fauteuil Bubble d'Eero Aarnio.

← The pool in the glass-walled extension looks out onto Biscayne Bay. • Aus dem verglasten Anbau mit Pool schaut man über die Biscayne Bay. • De la véranda qui abrite une piscine on peut voir Biscayne Bay.

↓ As if expressly created for Florida, Gaetano Pesce's heavily laden Miami Sound shelving sprawls colorfully along the wall. The armchairs are by Florence Knoll, while Al Eiber's favorite lamps were designed by Yonel Lébovici and are called The Welders. • Wie für Florida geschaffen, steht das übervolle Regal Miami Sound von Gaetano Pesce an der Wand. Die Sessel sind von Florence

Knoll. Al Eibers Lieblingslampen wurden von Yonel Lébovici entworfen und The Welders betitelt. • L'étagère Miami Sound de Gaetano Pesce, pleine à craquer et jetant des éclats de couleur dans la pièce, semble faite pour la Floride. Les fauteuils sont de Florence Knoll, les lampadaires préférés d'Al Eiber sont signés Yonel Lébovici et s'appellent The Welders.

← A vintage chair from the Lounge
Seating collection by Florence Knoll,
co-founder of the furniture firm that
bears her name. • Ein Vintage-Sessel
aus dem Lounge-Seating-Programm
von Florence Knoll, der Mitbegründerin
des gleichnamigen Möbelherstellers. •
Un fauteuil vintage du programme
Lounge-Seating de Florence Knoll, la
cofondatrice du fabricant de meubles.

↑ The leopard-skin Safari sofa by
Archizoom dates from 1967. The Patroclo lamp is by Gae Aulenti. • Hinten
das Safari-Sofa (1967) von Archizoom,
links eine Patroclo-Lampe von Gae
Aulenti. • Le canapé habillé de peau
de panthère Safari d'Archizoom (1967)
et, à gauche, une lampe Patroclo de
Gae Aulenti.

→ The Gazelle dining suite is by American Dan Johnson. The wickerwork
doors are original. • Die Esstischgar-
nitur nennt sich Gazelle und stammt
von dem Amerikaner Dan Johnson.
Die Türen aus Rohrgeflecht sind Origi-
nalbestand des Hauses. • L'Américain
Dan Johnson a dessiné la table et les
chaises Gazelle. Les portes en rotin
sont d'origine.

MIAMI
USA

Party Palace

This house was once the home of wacky American TV star Jackie Gleason who settled in Miami in 1967. For eight years, Craig Eberhardt had coveted this architectural marvel of the 1960s, and when the chance came he snapped it up—against the advice of all his friends. The exterior resembles an ocean liner, with its two symmetrical bay wings—but the interior, when Craig acquired it, was a complete disaster. He embarked on a massive program of renovation, which transformed the 16 tiny, shoe-box rooms and four pokey bathrooms into a veritable feast for the eyes. A majestic flight of white terrazzo stairs now leads up to a breathtaking, sumptuous entrance in the decadent colors typical of Miami Art Deco: old rose, pastel green, stucco white, and silver. The parties in the basement can be pretty wild in an Austin Powers kind of way, and it was in fact Mike Myers who inspired Craig Eberhardt in the design of what has to be the craziest private bar in all of Florida.

Dieses Haus war das Heim des schrägen TV-Stars Jackie Gleason, der mit seiner Show Millionen von Amerikanern zum Lachen brachte und sich 1967 in Miami niederließ. Craig Eberhardt hatte das architektonische Wunderwerk aus den 1960ern acht Jahre lang im Visier, dann schlug er entgegen der Warnungen aller Freunde zu. Das Innere des Baus, der von außen mit seinen zwei symmetrischen, bauchigen Seitenflügeln an einen Seedampfer erinnert, präsentierte sich das Innere zunächst als völliges Desaster. Doch durch umfangreiche Restaurierungsarbeiten wurde aus 16 winzigen, schuhkartonartigen Zimmern und vier kleinen Bädern ein wahrer Augenschmaus. Ein grandioser Treppenaufgang aus weißem Terrazzo führt zu dem atemberaubend großzügigen Entree, das in den typischen Farben des Art déco von Miami gehalten ist: Puderrosa, Blassgrün, Weiß und Silber. Im Partykeller geht es dagegen poppig bunt à la „Austin Powers" zu - tatsächlich inspirierte Mike Myers Craig Eberhardt bei der Einrichtung dieser wohl verrücktesten Privatbar Floridas.

Cette maison a appartenu à Jackie Gleason, star excentrique de la télé, dont le show a fait rire des millions d'Américains et qui s'établit en 1967 à Miami. Pendant huit ans, Craig Eberhardt a attendu son heure et acheté - sans se soucier des avertissements de ses amis - ce merveilleux bâtiment des années 1960 qui évoque un paquebot avec ses deux ailes ventrues symétriques. L'intérieur de la demeure était quant à lui dans un état désastreux. Mais de vastes travaux de restauration ont transformé seize pièces minuscules, de véritables cartons à chaussures, et quatre petites salles de bains, en un lieu exquis. Un escalier grandiose en terrazzo blanc mène à l'entrée spectaculaire qui arbore les couleurs rose poudre, vert pâle, blanc et argent, typiques de l'Art Déco à Miami. En revanche, au sous-sol, là où on fait la fête, le ton est plus criard, bigarré à la « Austin Powers ». Et de fait, Craig Eberhardt a bien pensé à Mike Myers en aménageant le bar privé le plus déjanté de Floride.

← Reclining inside the transparent Perspex case is a soft-toy leopard. The circular picture over the sofa features a host of colorful parrots. • In der durchsichtigen Plexiglastruhe liegt ein weicher Plüschleopard, über dem Sofa hängt ein kreisrundes Bild, das von bunten Papageien bevölkert wird. • Une panthère en peluche toute douce se prélasse dans le coffre en plexiglas transparent. Au-dessus du canapé, un tableau circulaire peuplé de perroquets aux couleurs vives.

↓ The ballroom has been restored to its original glory. Seven crystal chandeliers dating from 1959 hang in the center above the dining table, which is encircled by a delicate wrought-aluminum balustrade. • Der Tanzsaal erstrahlt wieder in seinem alten Glanz. Sieben Kristalllüster aus dem Jahre 1959 hängen in der Mitte über dem Esstisch, der von einer kunstvoll geschmiedeten Balustrade aus Aluminium umgeben wird. • La salle de bal a retrouvé sa splendeur d'antan. Sept lustres de cristal de 1959 sont suspendus au-dessus de la table entourée d'une balustrade en aluminium aux volutes sophistiquées.

P. 373 The shape of the pool echoes the room's curved walls. In the background is the party room. • Die Form des Pools folgt den Wänden des Raumes, im Hintergrund das Partyzimmer. • La forme de la piscine est adaptée aux murs courbes de la pièce. À l'arrière-plan, le *party room*.

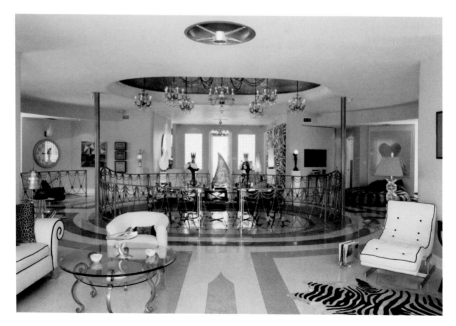

↖ The home cinema, with an arrangement of coordinated yellow gladioli and deep soft orange flokati rugs. The ceiling lamp, once a coffee table, was simply redefined and painted red and yellow. • Das Heimkino mit farblich passenden Gladiolen und orangerotem Flokati. An der Decke hängt ein zur Lampe umfunktionierter, rot-gelb bemalter Coffeetable. • Le home cinema avec, couleur oblige, un bouquet de glaïeuls jaunes et un tapis genre flokati vermillon. En guise de plafonnier, une table basse peinte en jaune et rouge.

← The Austin Powers films inspired the design of the kitchen, which has a mirrored end wall. • Die Austin-Powers-Filme beeinflussten das Design der Küche mit ihrer verspiegelten Rückwand. • Les films Austin Powers ont influencé le design de la cuisine qui a un mur-miroir.

↑ Behind Mies van der Rohe's MR 20 cantilevered chairs is a curved window that looks out onto the garden. • Die Freischwinger MR 20 von Mies van der Rohe stehen vor der geschwungenen Fensterfront mit Gartenblick. • Des chaises luges MR 20 de Mies van der Rohe devant la baie vitrée courbe avec vue sur le jardin.

→ A round mirror complements the soft curves of Eero Saarinen's Tulip table and chairs. • Die weich geschwungene Tulip-Esstischgruppe von Eero Saarinen wird mit einem runden Spiegel kombiniert. • La table à repas et les chaises Tulip aux lignes douces d'Eero Saarinen sont associées à un miroir rond.

MILAN
ITALY

Shock of the New

The locals called it Ca' Brutta ("ugly house"), and yet it is one of the city's architectural masterpieces: this 1922 apartment building by Giovanni Muzio was, despite its classical design language, simply too modern for the conservative Milanese. Interior designer and furniture manufacturer William Sawaya, however, fell in love with the building's spatial character and dignified appearance. He purchased Muzio's own former apartment and, over a period of one and a half years, restored it to its former elegant glory. "Time had fossilized the interiors, covering everything in sandy shades," Sawaya recalls. He also gave the place a new identity courtesy of furniture by his own company Sawaya & Moroni, which produces spectacular creations by some of today's best-known designers.

Der Volksmund nannte es Ca' Brutta („hässliches Haus"), dabei zählt es zu den architektonischen Meisterwerken der Stadt: 1922 von Giovanni Muzio erbaut, war das Wohnhaus trotz seiner klassischen Formensprache den konservativen Mailändern einfach zu modern. Wegen seiner raumbildenden würdevollen Anmutung verliebte sich der Interiordesigner und Möbelproduzent William Sawaya in den Solitär. Er kaufte das einstige Apartment von Muzio in dem Block und legte dessen alte Eleganz in eineinhalb Jahre dauernden Restaurierungsarbeiten frei. „Die Zeit hatte den Innenraum fossilisiert, alles schien in sandige Farbtöne getaucht", erinnert er sich. Gleichzeitig gab er dem Ort eine neue Identität durch die Möbelobjekte seiner Designmanufaktur Sawaya & Moroni, die spektakuläre Entwürfe der bekanntesten Gestalter unserer Zeit realisiert.

Appelée communément Ca'Brutta (« maison laide »), elle est en fait l'un des chefs-d'œuvre architecturaux de la ville. Construite en 1922 par Giovanni Muzio, la maison était trop moderne pour les Milanais conservateurs en dépit de son vocabulaire formel classique. L'architecte d'intérieur et fabricant de meubles William Sawaya est tombé amoureux du bâtiment à cause de la majesté de ses formes. Il a acheté l'ancien appartement de Muzio dans l'immeuble et lui a rendu son élégance d'antan au cours de travaux de restauration qui ont duré un an et demi. « Le temps avait fossilisé l'intérieur en baignant tout dans des teintes sableuses », se souvient-il. En même temps, il a donné à l'endroit une nouvelle identité en y plaçant les meubles de sa manufacture de design Sawaya & Moroni qui réalise les créations les plus spectaculaires des concepteurs de notre époque.

P. 379 On the living room wall is a painting by Luciano Bartolini, whereas the two cocktail tables are by Sawaya himself. • Die beiden Cocktailtische im Wohnzimmer entwarf der Besitzer selbst, das Gemälde stammt von Luciano Bartolini. • Le propriétaire a dessiné les deux tables à cocktail du séjour, le tableau est signé Luciano Bartolini.

↑ The Maxima chair in front of the bedroom desk is another of Sawayas's own designs. • Vor dem Schreibtisch im Schlafzimmer steht der Stuhl Maxima, ebenfalls ein Entwurf Sawayas. • Dans la chambre à coucher, devant le bureau, une chaise Maxima, dessinée elle aussi par Sawaya.

↗ Wooden wall paneling, which conceals a cupboard and drawers, dates back to 1922 and forms part of architect Giovanni Muzio's interior fixtures. • Die Holzvertäfelung an der Wand, hinter der sich teilweise Schubladen und Schrank verbergen, stammt aus dem Erbauungsjahr 1922 und wurde von Giovanni Muzio entworfen. • La boiserie, qui dissimule en partie des tiroirs et une armoire, date de 1922, année de construction de la maison, et a été conçue par Giovanni Muzio.

→ The hall, which still has Muzio's original mosaic flooring, features a bird cage in the shape of an architectural model that recreates a church in St. Petersburg. • Auf dem originalen Flurmosaik von Muzio steht eine Voliere, deren Miniaturarchitektur einer Kirche in St. Petersburg nachempfunden ist. • Dans le couloir qui a conservé son sol d'origine en mosaïque de Muzio, une cage à oiseaux recrée en miniature l'architecture d'une église de Saint-Pétersbourg.

← The early 19th-century fireplace was installed when the building was constructed in 1922. • Der Kamin aus dem frühen 19. Jahrhundert wurde schon beim Bau des Hauses eingefügt. • La cheminée du début du 19ᵉ siècle a été intégrée pendant la construction de la maison en 1922.

↑ Sawaya designed both the bar stools and the units in the kitchen. • Die Barstühle wie auch die Küchenmöbel entwarf der neue Besitzer selbst. • Le nouveau propriétaire a lui-même dessiné les tabourets de bar ainsi que les meubles de cuisine.

↓ The curving sofa is part of a collection by architect Zaha Hadid for Sawaya & Moroni. • Das kurvige Sofa stammt aus einer Edition der Architektin Zaha Hadid für Sawaya & Moroni. • Le canapé curviligne fait partie d'une édition de l'architecte Zaha Hadid pour Sawaya & Moroni.

← A light sculpture by Zaha Hadid and Patrik Schumacher hangs above a 1950s glass table. • Über einem Glastisch aus den 1950ern hängt eine Lichtskulptur von Zaha Hadid und Patrik Schumacher. • Au-dessus d'une table en verre des années 1950, une sculpture lumineuse de Zaha Hadid et Patrik Schumacher.

↙ The marble wall cladding and the mosaic floor are part of the original building design. • Die Marmorwandverkleidung wie auch das Bodenmosaik sind Teil der ursprünglichen Bausubstanz. • Le revêtement mural de marbre et les mosaïques du sol font partie de la structure d'origine.

↓ Next to a painting by Richard Texier is an obelisk sculpture that Sawaya created himself. • Vor dem Gemälde von Richard Texier steht eine Obeliskenskulptur von der Hand des Besitzers. • À côté du tableau de Richard Texier, une sculpture obélisque de la main du propriétaire.

→ The installation *Marrakech Butchery* by Ferdi Giardini adds vibrant color to the dining-room wall. • Eine Wand des Esszimmers belebt die Installation *Marrakech Butchery* von Ferdi Giardini. • L'installation *Marrakech Butchery* de Ferdi Giardini égaie un mur de la salle à manger.

MILAN
ITALY

A Drawing in Space

In the city's Navigli district, amidst other creatives, the designer Elia Mangia, in collaboration with architect Roberto Murgia, has turned the office building of a former precision-tools factory into a home and studio. Its ground floor now contains his work space and kitchen, while, above, he installed a new upper level for the bedroom, bathroom, and guest room. Black grooves and bars provide the only contrast to the white backdrop, rather like lines drawn on a blank piece of paper. As Mangia explains, he has "to deal with new drafts every day, so I wanted spaces that were visually unsullied."

Da, wo früher Präzisionswerkzeug hergestellt wurde, im Navigli-Viertel, erwarb der Designer Elia Mangia die Bürohalle eines alten Fabrikkomplexes. In der Nachbarschaft anderer Kreativer baute er sie zum Wohn- und Werkstatthaus um. Während er das Erdgeschoss in ein Arbeitsstudio mit Küche verwandelte, ließ er durch seinen Architekten Roberto Murgia auf einer zweiten Ebene Schlafzimmer, Bad und Gästeraum einziehen. Dabei setzen nur schwarze Schattenfugen und Geländer Akzente, ähnlich der Zeichenlinien auf weißem Papier. „Da ich mich täglich mit neuen Entwürfen beschäftige", erklärt Mangia, „wollte ich als Ausgleich dazu Räume, die visuell unverschmutzt sind."

Dans le quartier des Navigli, là où on fabriquait autrefois des instruments de précision, le designer Elia Mangia a acheté les bureaux d'un ancien complexe industriel. Dans le voisinage d'autres créateurs il l'a converti en maison d'habitation et atelier. Avec la collaboration de Roberto Murgia, il a transformé le rez-de-chaussée en studio de travail avec cuisine, et intégré la chambre à coucher, la salle de bains et la chambre d'amis au niveau supérieur. Seuls des joints et des rampes noirs posent des accents, comme des signes sur du papier blanc. « M'occupant tous les jours de nouveaux projets, je voulais chez moi des espaces visuellement vierges », explique Mangia.

P. 387 The former office building is now a white living space in which black lines provide a minimalist contrast. • Eine alte Halle wurde zum weißen Wohnraum, in dem nur schwarze Linien einen Kontrast setzen. • Seules les lignes noires offrent un contraste dans l'espace blanc.

↑ A model boat bears witness to Mangia's passion for sailing; above it hangs *What we want, Phi Phi Ley* by Francesco Jodice. • Die Segelleidenschaft des Besitzers zeigt sich im Modellboot, darüber hängt *What we want, Phi Phi Ley* von Francesco Jodice. • La maquette de voilier reflète la passion du propriétaire, audessus *What we want, Phi Phi Ley* de Francesco Jodice.

↗ The drill and other tools in the ground floor studio are used for making prototypes. • Zur Herstellung von Prototypen gibt es im Erdgeschossatelier eine Bohrmaschine. • Dans l'atelier du rez-de-chaussée une perceuse et d'autres outils servent à fabriquer des prototypes.

→ Jasper Morrison designed the green and beige sofas, the photo titled *What we want, Osaka* is by Francesco Jodice. • Die grünen und beigefarbenen Sofas sind Entwürfe von Jasper Morrison, das Foto *What we want, Osaka* ist von Francesco Jodice. • Les canapés verts et beiges sont signés Jasper Morrison, la photo *What we want, Osaka* est de Francesco Jodice.

PP. 390–391 On the upper level are more intimate spaces; the middle section houses the bathroom. • Intime Wohnräume befinden sich auf einer erhöhten Ebene, in der mittleren Raumbox wurde das Bad untergebracht. • Les espaces réservés à l'intimité se trouvent sur un niveau supérieur. La salle de bains est intégrée dans l'espace fermé central.

← The lounge corner on the gallery offers views across the space. • Aus der Lounge-Ecke der oberen Ebene lässt sich der Raum gut überblicken. • Du coin repos du niveau supérieur, on peut voir tout l'espace.

→ A folding door gives access to a walk-in wardrobe that has its own wash-basin and bath. • Durch eine Falttür betritt man den begehbaren Schrank mit Waschbecken und Badewanne. • Une porte pliante s'ouvre sur l'armoire accessible qui abrite un lavabo et une baignoire.

"I applied a designer's perspective to all the architectural elements, treating them as individual objects." ELIA MANGIA

„Alle architektonischen Elemente entwarf ich ebenfalls mit dem Blick des Designers: als eigenständige Objekte."
« J'ai également conçu tous les éléments architectoniques avec le regard du designer : comme des objets autonomes. »

MONTE
ARGENTINA

Farm of Charm

With a career in fashion design, an aristocratic name, two wonderful children and successful businessman Federico Álvarez Castillo fora husband, Paula Cahen D'Anvers embodies the sophisticated feminist ideal. Following in the tradition of her grandmother and mother, she has built a country house some 60 miles from the center of Buenos Aires on land adjacent to her family's property. The dwelling consists of various rooms, a vast garden filled with rose-covered pergolas, an orchard, and a magnificent swimming pool. The whole property was designed by Paula and in particular by her husband Federico. The building comprises different, independent, yet connected spaces for the greater comfort of occupants and guests. The decor has been carefully thought through, down to the smallest detail, and re-creates the tranquillity of the past but without abandoning modern amenities. "We looked for a style that would bring new life to the traditional approach, with antique touches that create the feeling that this house has been standing here for many years," the owners explain.

Mit einer Karriere als Modedesignerin, einem aristokratischen Namen und zwei prächtigen Kindern verkörpert Paula Cahen D'Anvers, die mit dem erfolgreichen Unternehmer Federico Álvarez Castillo verheiratet ist, das romantische Ideal souveräner Weiblichkeit. Mutter und Großmutter folgend hat sie sich etwa 100 Kilometer von Buenos Aires entfernt ein Haus auf dem Land neben dem Anwesen ihrer Familie bauen lassen. Der Wohnsitz umfasst verschiedene Nebengebäude, einen riesigen Garten mit rosenbewachsenen Pergolen sowie einen Obst- und Gemüsegarten. Der Komplex wurde von Paula und vor allem von ihrem Mann Federico entworfen. Er besteht aus verschiedenen unabhängigen, aber miteinander verbundenen Baukörpern, sodass sich Bewohner und Gäste nie gegenseitig stören können. Die Dekoration ist bis ins kleinste Detail durchdacht und lässt die Gemütlichkeit vergangener Tage aufkommen, ohne auf zeitgemäßen Komfort zu verzichten. „Wir suchten einen Stil, der das Traditionelle verjüngt, aber mit historischen Anklängen den Eindruck entstehen lässt, dass dieses Haus schon viele Jahre hier steht", erklären die Hausherren.

Avec une carrière de styliste de mode, un nom aristocratique, deux superbes enfants et un mariage avec le brillant homme d'affaires Federico Álvarez Castillo, Paula Cahen D'Anvers incarne l'idéal d'un féminisme sophistiqué. Suivant l'exemple de sa grand-mère et de sa mère, elle s'est fait construire une maison de campagne sur un terrain jouxtant le domaine familial, à cent kilomètre de la capitale. Elle compte plusieurs dépendances, un immense jardin parsemé de pergolas envahies de rosiers, un potager et une magnifique piscine. Paula et son mari ont voulu une maison qui soit pratique à vivre pour eux et leurs invités : elle est composée de plusieurs volumes indépendants mais reliés entre eux. La décoration, soignée dans ses moindres détails, vise à recréer la quiétude du passé sans renoncer en rien au confort moderne. « Nous cherchons un style qui rajeunisse la vision du traditionnel, avec des touches anciennes qui donnent l'impression que cette maison existe depuis toujours », expliquent les propriétaires.

P. 395 In the kitchen the same aesthetic rules as in the rest of the house: vintage table, lamps, and flooring. • In der Küche herrscht dieselbe Ästhetik wie im übrigen Haus: Tisch und Leuchter sind antik, die Fliesen genau wie einst verlegt. • Dans la cuisine, la même esthétique que dans le reste de la maison : tables, lampes et sols anciens.

← The pink of the hall wall is picked up by the curtains of the four-poster bed; in the background the en-suite bathroom. • Das Rosa der Flurwand wird durch die Vorhänge des Himmelbettes wieder aufgenommen; ganz hinten das anschließende Bad. • On retrouve le rose des murs du couloir dans le voilage du lit à baldaquin, derrière se trouve une salle de bains.

→ The fire surround in the living-room is made from timber sourced from old beams; while the wall above is covered in pictures and family photos. "We wanted it to be very welcoming, as we love using this space," explains Cahen D'Anvers. • Im Wohnzimmer wurde der Kamin mit dem Holz alter Balken umkleidet, während die Wand mit Bildern und Fotos der Familie bedeckt ist. „Wir wollten es gemütlich haben, da wir diesen Raum sehr gern nutzen", berichtet Cahen D'Anvers. • Dans le salon, une cheminée dont le cadre a été réalisé avec du bois de récupération. Aux murs, des tableaux et photos de famille. « Nous l'avons voulu le plus chaleureux possible car c'est là que nous passons le plus de temps », confie Cahen D'Anvers.

↑ Paula Cahen D'Anvers already had
the furniture when the house was built. •
Die Möbel besaß Paula Cahen D'Anvers
schon, bevor das Haus überhaupt fertig
war. • Paula Cahen D'Anvers possédait
les meubles avant que la construction de
la maison ne soit terminée.

→ The living area—pictured here is the
dining corner—has an airy feel thanks to
the exposed inner roof construction. •
Der Wohnraum reicht bis unter die offen
liegende Dachkonstruktion, hier der Essbereich. • Le séjour se prolonge jusque
sous la construction ouverte du toit, ici le
coin repas.

← The master bedroom with adjoining bathroom. The checkerboard floor tiles are reclaimed. • Das Hauptschlafzimmer hat sein eigenes Badezimmer. Die schachbrettartig verlegten Fliesen stammen aus Abrisshäusern. • La chambre principale communique avec sa salle de bains. Le sol en damier a été réalisé avec des carreaux de récupération.

↓ A fitted cabinet for books covers the wall opposite the living-room fireplace. • Im Wohnzimmer wurde gegenüber dem Kamin ein breiter Bücherschrank eingebaut. • Dans le séjour, une large armoire encastrée face à la cheminée.

MOSCOW
RUSSIA

Living à la Kandinsky

Before the journalist and author Alexander Timofeevsky moved into his flat on the top floor of a 1913 apartment buildings, it had been a typical Soviet communalka, a state-owned communal apartment. Having grown up in the same central area of Moscow close to the Garden Ring orbital road, he couldn't resist the charm of its old rooms, which have since been transformed by the set designer and artist Nikola Samonov, a friend of Timofeevsky. His interiors carefully incorporate the writer's heirloom items and art collection and, with their juxtaposition of red painted doors and coffered ceilings featuring dark green wood beams, create a sophisticated ambience: "We wanted to reinterpret the Art Deco interior—as a mixture of palace and factory."

Als der Journalist und Schriftsteller Alexander Timofeevsky diese Wohnung in der obersten Etage eines Mietshauses von 1913 übernahm, war sie eine typisch sowjetische Kommunalka, eine staatliche Wohngemeinschaft. Da er in derselben zentralen Gegend am Moskauer Gartenring aufgewachsen war, fühlte er sich vom Charme der alten Zimmer angezogen. Der Bühnenbildner und Künstler Nikola Samonov, ein Freund Timofeevskys, machte aus den Räumen Interieurs, in die sich die Erbstücke und die Kunstsammlung des Besitzers wirkungsvoll einfügen. Durch die Kassettierung der Decken mit dunkelgrün gestrichenen Holzbalken, die mit den rot lackierten Türen kontrastieren, gelang ihm eine raffinierte Gesamtwirkung: „Wir wollten das russische Art déco neu interpretieren – als eine Mischung aus Palast und Fabrik."

Lorsqu'Alexander Timofeevsky, journaliste et écrivain, a emménagé dans cet appartement situé au dernier étage d'un immeuble locatif de 1913, il s'agissait d'une kommunalka typique, un appartement communautaire. Comme il avait grandi dans le même coin, au centre, dans « l'anneau des jardins » de Moscou, le charme des vieilles pièces l'a séduit. L'artiste et décorateur de théâtre Nikola Samonov, un ami de Timofeevsky, a transformé les espaces en un intérieur qui met en valeur les objets dont a hérité le propriétaire et sa collection d'œuvres d'art. Avec les grilles de bois peintes en vert foncé du plafond qui contrastent avec les portes laquées de rouge, il a réussi à créer un effet vraiment distingué : « Nous voulions réinterpréter l'Art Déco – comme un mélange de palais et d'usine. »

P. 403 Historic coffered ceilings inspired the half-timbered look of Samonov's interior surfaces. • Als Vorbild für die fachwerkartige Gliederung der Räume dienten Samonov historische Kassettendecken. • Samonov s'est inspiré des plafonds à caissons historiques pour diviser les pièces avec des charpentes apparentes.

← As in the aristocratic Russian homes of old, poplar-wood veneer was applied to some of the living room's timber frames. • Wie in den russischen Adels-

häusern von einst wurden einige Holzrahmen im Wohnzimmer mit Pappelholz furniert. • Les cadres de bois du séjour ont été plaqués en peuplier comme dans les maisons aristocratiques russes de jadis.

↑ The table in the studio is a Muscovite re-edition of a Charles Rennie Mackintosh design. • Der Tisch im Atelier ist die Moskauer Reedition eines Entwurfes von Charles Rennie Mackintosh. • La table de l'atelier est une réédition moscovite d'une création de Charles Rennie Mackintosh.

↗ In the study, a bust of Apollo watches over Russian literary classics. • Im Arbeitszimmer wacht eine Apollobüste über Klassiker der russischen Literatur. • Dans le cabinet de travail, un buste d'Apollon veille sur les classiques de la littérature russe.

PP. 406–407 Bits of old Art Deco bedroom furniture were reused to make the guest room's sofa. • Für das Gästesofa wurden Elemente aus alten Art-déco-Schlafzimmermöbeln recycelt. • Pour le canapé des amis, on a recyclé des éléments de vieux meubles de chambres à coucher Art Déco.

↑ From the guest bedroom, the living room can be seen through the glass partition wall. • Durch eine gläserne Trennwand kann man vom Gästezimmer in den Wohnraum blicken. • De la chambre d'amis, une cloison de séparation en verre permet de voir le séjour.

→ Above the divan are paintings by Nikola Samonov, on the left is the picture *Satyr in the Farmer's House*. • Über dem Diwan hängen Gemälde von Nikola Samonov, links *Satyr im Haus des Bauern*. • Au-dessus du divan, des tableaux de Nikola Samonov, à gauche *Satyre dans la maison du paysan*.

NAGANO
JAPAN

Light as a Feather

Old-style Japanese houses stand on wooden supports raised a few feet above the ground. Architect Kengo Kuma's Forest Floor House reinvents this tradition of translucence, fragility, and openness. With its main supporting column hidden deep under the house, the cubical superstructure appears to rest on slim tubes placed around the sides, so frail as to hardly seem capable of bearing weight. The steps and railings are so insubstantial as to almost disappear. Above this floats not so much a series of rooms as an open floor, a glassed-in viewing platform overlooking the woods outside. Accentuating the sense of lightness, the house is entirely white, both outside and inside, with pale wooden floors. "I want to recover the Japanese tradition, not of 'monuments,' but of 'weaker' buildings," says Kuma. In this house, what is man-made is thin, fragile, white, flat, and transparent—a delicate raft afloat in a sea of verdant nature.

Historische japanische Häuser werden auf Holzpfählen errichtet und ihre Wohnräume liegen so deutlich über dem Erdboden. Das Forest Floor House des Architekten Kengo Kuma hat diese Tradition neu interpretiert. Dabei handelt es sich um eine Bauform, die ganz stark durch Lichtdurchlässigkeit, Zerbrechlichkeit und Offenheit geprägt ist. Während der stützende Hauptpfeiler tief unter dem Haus verborgen ist, scheint der viereckige Aufbau einzig und allein auf rundum angeordneten, schlanken Röhren zu ruhen. Ein großer, offener Raum bietet einen herrlichen Blick in die Wälder. Um diese Leichtigkeit zu betonen, ist das Haus sowohl außen als auch innen ganz in Weiß gehalten und verfügt über helle Holzböden. „Ich möchte die japanische Tradition neu entdecken – aber nicht die der ‚Denkmäler', sondern die von ‚schwächeren' Gebäuden", so Kuma. In diesem Haus ist alles, was von Menschenhand geschaffen wurde, dünn, fragil, weiß, flach und durchsichtig – als wäre es ein Floß, das in einem Meer von Grün treibt.

Les anciennes maisons japonaises sont légèrement surélevées sur des supports en bois, vestiges de leurs origines, quand elles étaient perchées sur de hauts pilotis dans la forêt. Forest Floor, bâtie par l'architecte Kengo Kuma, réinvente cette tradition. Tout est transparence, fragilité et ouverture. Son principal pilier de soutien étant caché sous la maison, la superstructure cubique paraît posée sur les minces tubes qui la bordent, si délicats qu'elle semble légère comme une plume. Les marches et les rampes minimalistes disparaissent presque. Au-dessus flotte un espace ouvert, un balcon en verre dominant les bois environnants. Pour renforcer cette impression de légèreté, la maison est peinte en blanc, au-dedans comme au-dehors, avec des parquets en bois clair. « Je veux renouer avec la tradition, pas les ‹ monuments › mais les bâtiments plus ‹ simples › ... », explique Kuma. Dans ce vaisseau délicat flottant dans un océan de verdure, tout ce qui a été façonné par l'homme est mince, fragile, blanc, plat et transparent.

← Fragile white steel steps lead up to a white slatted balcony. • Zierliche weiße Stahlstufen führen zu einem Balkon mit weißen Holzlamellen hoch. • De délicates marches en acier blanc mènent au balcon protégé d'un store à lamelles.

↓ The architecture is so transparent that the line between inside and outside seems to blur. • Die Architektur ist so transparent, dass sich die Trennung zwischen Innen- und Außenraum aufzulösen scheint. • L'architecture est si transparente qu'on ne sait pratiquement plus distinguer le dedans du dehors.

→ Thick-cushioned headrest, lamp, and forest—who needs more? • Weiche Daunenkissen, eine Lampe und der Wald – was braucht man mehr? • D'épais appuis-tête moelleux, une lampe et la forêt – que faut-il de plus ?

↘ The white-themed living room is basically a platform for viewing the forest. • Der ganz in Weiß gehaltene Wohnraum wirkt wie eine Aussichtsplattform für den Wald. • Le salon blanc est un espace transparent, une plateforme d'où contempler la forêt.

P. 411 Outside, the parquet flooring gives way to wooden boards. Next to the door is Sori Yanagi's Butterfly Stool. • An der Türschwelle werden die Holzplanken von Parkett abgelöst. Neben der Tür steht ein Butterfly-Hocker von Sori Yanagi. • Sur le seuil, le plancher cède la place à un parquet. À côté de la porte, un tabouret Butterfly de Sori Yanagi.

PP. 412–413 The angular kitchen with chairs and glass table, topped with a skylight, continues the theme of whiteness. • Die kantige Küche mit Glastisch und Stühlen, die von einem Oberlicht beleuchtet werden, führt das Thema „Weiß" fort. • La cuisine tout en angles avec des chaises et une table en verre, couronnée d'une lucarne, poursuit le thème de la blancheur.

414

NAGUABO
PUERTO RICO

The Artist as Architect

When psychiatrist César Reyes and his wife Mima bought a plot of land on Puerto Rico's east coast, they decided to commission a work from artist Jorge Pardo. Instead of asking him to create a painting, they requested that he build a house. Pardo was greatly inspired by the "devastatingly beautiful" location. "It's a very dramatic, tight site," he says. "The challenge was to get as much sky and sea as possible and yet maintain a maximum of privacy." He decided not to use any glass. Instead, he left the concrete structure open and wrapped it in ornate metal screens. "It gets wet inside," he admits, "but it also dries quickly. That's how it is in the tropics." Other striking features include the blood-red swimming pool and the gradually shifting color of the floor tiles—they start off yellow at the front of the house and end up blue at the back.

Als der Psychiater César Reyes und seine Frau Mima ein Grundstück an der Ostküste von Puerto Rico kauften, beschlossen sie, den Künstler Jorge Pardo statt mit einem Gemälde mit dem Bau eines Hauses zu beauftragen. Pardo war stark inspiriert von der „überwältigend schönen" Lage. „Es handelt sich um ein sehr dramatisch gelegenes, relativ schmales Grundstück", sagt er. „Die Herausforderung bestand darin, so viel Himmel und Meer wie möglich einzube- ziehen und dennoch ein Maximum an Privatsphäre zu bewahren." Er beschloss, keinerlei Glas zu verwenden. Stattdessen legte er die Betonstruktur offen an und umgab sie mit dekorativen Metallgittern. „Bei Regen gibt es innen einen nassen Streifen", gibt er zu, „aber das trocknet auch schnell wieder. So ist es eben in den Tropen." Weitere verblüf- fende Hingucker sind die blutrote Swimmingpool und die Farben der Fußbodenfliesen – an der Vorderseite des Hauses setzen sie mit Gelb ein, um an der Rückseite in Blau zu enden.

Après avoir acheté un terrain sur la côte est de Puerto Rico, le psychiatre César Reyes et sa femme Mima ont contacté l'artiste Jorge Pardo. Au lieu de commander un tableau, ils lui ont demandé de leur construire une maison. Pardo fut très inspiré par la beauté « ravageuse » du site. « Il est spectaculaire, escarpé. Le défi consistait à y faire entrer le plus de ciel et de mer possible tout en préservant l'intimité des occupants. » Délaissant le verre, il a opté pour une structure en béton ouverte ceinte d'écrans métalliques ouvragés. « Il pleut à l'intérieur », admet-il, « mais ça sèche vite. On est sous les tropiques. » Parmi les autres détails saisissants : une piscine rouge sang et le carrelage aux couleurs changeantes. Il passe du jaune sur le devant de la maison au bleu à l'arrière.

P. 417 A still life with Mexican folk masks and Elizabeth Peyton portraits of Liam Gallagher and Kurt Cobain. • Mexikanische Masken und Elizabeth Peytons Porträts von Liam Gallagher und Kurt Cobain. • Des masques mexicains anciens et des portraits de Liam Gallagher et de Kurt Cobain signés Elizabeth Peyton.

PP. 418–419 The kitchen units were custom-made from laminated cedar wood. The rocking chairs are by Charles and Ray Eames. • Die Küchenmöbel wurden aus laminiertem Zedernholz gefertigt. Schaukelstühle von Charles und Ray Eames. • Les éléments de cuisine sont en cèdre laminé et les rocking chairs de Charles et Ray Eames.

↑ A George Nelson Bubble lamp hangs above a four-poster bed in the master bedroom. • Eine Bubble-Lampe von George Nelson „schwebt" über dem Pfostenbett mit Netzbaldachin. • Dans la chambre des maîtres, un lit à baldaquin. Au-dessus, une lampe Bubble de George Nelson.

↗ An Eames Lounge Chair and Ottoman on a terrace outside. • Ein Lounge Chair mit Ottomane von Eames auf einer Terrasse. • Un fauteuil Lounge Chair de Eames avec son repose-pieds, sur une terrasse.

→ The large artwork, titled Hola Carola, was created by Pardo in homage to the owners' daughter. • Das große Gemälde mit dem Titel Hola Carola ist eine Hommage Pardos an die Tochter der Besitzer. • La grande toile, intitulée Hola Carola, est un hommage de Pardo à la fille des maîtres de maison.

NEW YORK CITY
USA

Vroom! Flash! Make a Splash!

Perspective is everything, as the two art-world luminaries occupying this 2,700-square-foot three-bedroom residence high above Central Park know well. The couple had been content in the traditional Upper East Side apartment they exchanged for a skybox over Columbus Circle. But, as one of them says, life at the top "changes your aesthetic expectations. Living 66 floors above the worries of the city liberates your mind." It's also a great catalyst for unorthodox design, as the irregular spaces demonstrate. To create a place suited to visual experimentation, including the freedom to make mistakes, and to show off an art collection focused on life's prime forces, Eros and Thanatos, they lined the apartment's core in plywood. "That stage of construction is pregnant with possibilities," one owner says. "Plus, you can rehang pictures, and holes don't matter."

Perspektive ist alles: Das wissen die beiden Größen der Kunstwelt, die diese über 250 Quadratmeter große Residenz mit drei Schlafzimmern hoch über dem Central Park bewohnen. Das Paar war zwar mit dem traditionellen Apartment, das zuvor an der Upper East Side bewohnte, glücklich, dennoch lockte das Leben hoch über dem Columbus Circle. „In der 66. Etage schwebt man über den Sorgen und der Hektik dieser Stadt. Das ist befreiend für den Geist, und es verändert die Vorstellungen von Ästhetik", erklärt einer der Bewohner. Die luftige Höhe und unregelmäßig gewinkelten Wände scheinen auch zu ungewöhnlichen Lösungen zu inspirieren. So wurde das Kernstück der Wohnung mit Sperrholz ausgekleidet – dies erlaubt visuelle Experimente und war ein guter Ausgangspunkt für die Hängung der Kunstsammlung der Bewohner rund um die Urkräfte „Eros" und „Thanatos". Oder wie einer der Besitzer anmerkte: „Auf diesen Wänden ist das Umhängen und Rearrangieren der Bilder nach Belieben möglich, denn Löcher sind nicht weiter auffällig."

Comme le savent les deux sommités de l'art qui occupent cet espace de 250 mètres carrés dominant Central Park, tout est dans la perspective. Ils ont échangé l'eur appartement traditionnel du Upper East Side contre ce skybox au-dessus de Columbus Circle. Comme le dit l'un deu : « Vivre 66 étages au-dessus des soucis de la ville modifie votre sens esthétique et libère votre esprit. » Cela sert également de catalyseur à une architecture originale qui se reflète dans les formes irrégulières des pièces. Pour créer un lieu adapté à l'expérimentation esthétique et exhiber une collection basée sur les forces primaires de la vie, « éros » et « thanatos », ils ont tapissé le cœur de l'appartement de contreplaqué. « C'est un matériau de construction riche de possibilités. En outre, vous pouvez accrocher et décrocher des œuvres à loisir sans vous préoccuper des trous. »

← Like many of the apartment's other rooms, the art library and study is an irregular shape. • Das Arbeitszimmer mit Studiertisch hat – wie die meisten Räume hier – unregelmäßig gewinkelte Wände. • Comme de nombreuses pièces de l'appartement, la bibliothèque/bureau a une forme irrégulière.

↑ A work by Adam McEwen leans against the Shelves near a Jonathan Meese ceramic assemblage. • Am Regal lehnt eine Arbeit von Adam McEwen, rechts eine Keramikassemblage von Jonathan Meese. • Une œuvre d'Adam McEwen est posée contre les étagères. Assemblage en céramique de Jonathan Meese.

P. 423 *The Clairvoyant*, a John Currin painting in an early 17th-century Florentine frame, hangs over an 18th-century chest topped by a Tony Duquette pagoda lamp. • Eine Pagodenlampe von Tony Duquette steht auf einer Kommode aus dem 18. Jahrhundert. Darüber hängt in einem florentinischen Rahmen aus dem frühen 17. Jahrhundert das Bild *The Clairvoyant* von John Currin. • *The Clairvoyant*, de John Currin, dans un cadre florentin du début du 17ᵉ siècle, est accroché au-dessus d'une commode du 18ᵉ siècle sur laquelle est posée une lampe pagode de Tony Duquette.

PP.426—427 A 19th-century Chinese daybed with a Huanuco fur cover dominates the media room. The chair is by Chicago architect Ron Krueck. • Ein chinesisches Daybed aus dem 19. Jahrhundert mit einem Überwurf aus Guanako-Fell ist ein Blickfang im Media Room. Der Stuhl ist ein Entwurf des Chicagoer Architekten Ron Krueck. • Un lit chinois du 19ᵉ siècle, avec un dessus-de-lit en fourrure Huanuco, domine la médiathèque. Le fauteuil est de l'architecte Ron Krueck, originaire de Chicago.

↑ British art duo Tim Noble and Sue Webster's light-bulb dollar sign hangs in the entry with a Barry McGee wall installation. The striped carpet is used throughout. • Dollarzeichen aus Glühbirnen vom britischen Künstlerduo Tim Noble und Sue Webster im Foyer mit Wandinstallation von Barry McGee. Der gestreifte Teppich zieht sich durchs ganze Apartment. • Dans l'entrée, le dollar en ampoules lumineuses du duo artistique britannique Tim Noble et Sue Webster ; l'installation murale est de Barry McGee . La même moquette rayée est utilisée partout.

→ Like its colorful cousin, the black and white mural *Tom Cruising* in the master bedroom is by Assume Vivid Astro Focus. • Wie die bunten Wände im Hauptraum ist auch die schwarz-weiße Wandarbeit *Tom Cruising* von Assume Vivid Astro Focus. • Comme les murs en couleur de la pièce principale, *Tom Cruising*, la peinture murale noire et blanche, est également d'Assume Vivid Astro Focus.

NEW YORK CITY
USA

Mirror, Mirror Overall ...

Remodeled four decades ago by the late architect Paul Rudolph, this 5,000-square-foot apartment is a time capsule of avant-garde 1970s design. The owner has preserved the major rooms of the flat exactly as Rudolph created them. That means curving floor platforms, complex ceiling treatments, innovative lighting, and idiosyncratically installed art and collectibles (a display wall in the dining room is punctured with lighted circular niches holding pieces of blue-and-white china). In the living room, Rudolph applied narrow strips of mirror to the base of a built-in sofa so that it seems to levitate. More mirror strips radiate from a Jean Arp work on the office ceiling, while tiny round dentist's mirrors form decorative graphics on the kitchen cupboards. "The man's brilliance was so clear," says the delighted owner.

Vor vier Dekaden gestaltete der Architekt Paul Rudolph dieses fast 500 Quadratmeter große Apartment im Avantgarde-Look der 1970er. Die heutige Besitzerin hat fast alle Räume im Originalzustand belassen, samt ihren Bodenplattformen, mondänen Deckengestaltungen und ungewöhnlich installierten Kunst- und Sammelobjekten. So wird im Esszimmer eine Wand von individuell beleuchteten Rundnischen durchbrochen, in denen blau-weißes Porzellan ausgestellt ist. Und weil Rudolph den unteren Teil des Einbausofas im Wohnzimmer mit schmalen Spiegelstreifen versehen hat, sieht es aus, als würde es schweben. Im Arbeitszimmer glitzern rund um einWerk von Hans Arp an der Decke ebenfalls schmale Spiegelstreifen. Und auf den Küchenschränken blitzen kleine, runde Zahnarztspiegel. „Die Brillanz des Mannes ist einfach nicht zu übersehen", kommentiert die begeisterte Eigentümerin.

Rénové il y a quarante ans par l'architecte Paul Rudolph, aujourd'hui disparu, cet appartement de 500 mètres carrés est comme une fenêtre temporelle sur le design d'avant-garde des années 1970. La propriétaire actuelle a conservé presque toutes les pièces dans leur état d'origine, avec leurs plates-formes, leur plafonds ornementés sophistiqués et des objets d'art et de collection disposés de manière insolite. Ainsi un mur de la salle à manger est percé de niches rondes éclairées abritant des porcelaines blanches et bleues. Dans le séjour, d'étroites bandes de miroirs sur le socle du sofa encastré semblent le faire léviter. Dans le bureau, d'autres bandes de miroir irradient d'une œuvre de Jean Arp collée au plafond, tandis que de minuscules miroirs de dentiste forment un motif décoratif sur les placards de la cuisine. La maîtresse des lieux est toujours aussi enthousiaste : « Rudolph avait un sens des matières inouï. Il était brillant. »

P. 431 The study's ceiling boasts a Jean Arp relief within a sunburst of mirrors by Rudolph. • An der Decke des Arbeitszimmers prangt ein Werk von Hans Arp mitten in der Spiegelstrahlensonne von Rudolph. • Sur le plafond du bureau, Rudolph a créé un rayonnement de miroirs autour d'une œuvre de Jean Arp.

← The bed in the master bedroom is placed in a niche. • Das Bett im Schlafzimmer wird durch eine Nischenwand abgeschirmt. • Dans la chambre principale, le lit est encastré dans une niche.

↑ Rudolph applied mirror-strips like tiles to walls. The living room includes Dutch paintings in gilded frames and, in the corner, an important construction by Larry Rivers. • Rudolph applizierte Spiegelstreifen fliesenartig auf die Wände. Im Wohnzimmer hängen altniederländische Gemälde in vergoldeten Rahmen. In der Ecke steht eine Installation von Larry Rivers. • Rudolph a tapissé le bas des murs de miroirs. Dans le salon, des tableaux hollandais dans des cadres dorés côtoient une construction polychrome de Larry Rivers.

P. 434 A hallway serves as art gallery for lithographs. • Der Flur dient als Galerie, hier hängt eine ganze Reihe von Lithografien. • Un couloir accueille une collection de lithographies.

P. 435 The ceramics collection is also displayed on bedroom shelves. • Die blau-weiße Keramiksammlung hat auch auf den Regalen im Schlafzimmer Platz gefunden. • La collection de porcelaines se poursuit sur les étagères de la chambre.

↑ Russian *matryoshkas* line the kitchen counter under cabinet doors emblazoned with decorative graphics made of round dentist's mirrors. • In der Küche reihen sich russische *Matroschkas* unter den Schränken, die Muster aus runden Zahnarztspiegeln tragen. • Sur le comptoir de la cuisine, des *matriochkas* russes sous des portes de placards décorées de petits miroirs de dentiste.

→ Beneath a ceiling-mount starburst chandelier, the dining table is modular. • An der Decke über dem dreiteiligen Esstisch ist ein sonnenförmiger Leuchter installiert. • Dans la salle à manger, sous un plafonnier rayonnant, une table modulaire.

NEW YORK CITY
USA

A Loft for Life

This 4,860-square-foot loft, belonging to a writer and her video editor husband, sits on top of a working factory in the Garment District. The neighborhood retains its blue-collar character. "We still have three butchers and two fishmongers within three blocks," notes the husband. The loft had been an artist's studio and raw living space "built by students in the 1970s." The couple asked Resolution: 4 Architecture to upgrade the interiors without stripping them of their industrial feel. Concrete floors and steel-framed windows were refurbished, while kitchen, baths, and storage were gathered into a central box that left half the apartment open. A growing family is accommodated in three bedrooms, separated by big sliding doors.

Das 450 Quadratmeter große Loft über einem Fabrikbetrieb im Garment District gehört einer Schriftstellerin und ihrem Mann, einem Video-Cutter. In dieser Nachbarschaft herrscht noch Arbeiterviertelatmosphäre: „Wir haben in Fußnähe drei Metzger und zwei Fischhändler", bemerkt der Ehemann. Das Loft wurde in den 1970ern von Studenten gebaut und diente ursprünglich als Künstleratelier, sodass der Wohnbereich nicht wirklich wohnlich war. Das neue Besitzerpaar beauftragte das Büro Resolution: 4 Architecture, das Loft aufzuwerten, ohne sein industrielles Flair zu zerstören. Also wurden Betonböden und stahlgerahmte Fenster renoviert, und Küche, Badezimmer und Stauraum in einer zentralen Box zusammengefasst. Dadurch blieb viel offener Raum - etwa die Hälfte der gesamten Wohnfläche - erhalten. Ideal für rasante Dreiradfahrten der Kids! Und hinter großen Schiebetüren sind die drei Schlafzimmer der Familie untergebracht.

Ce loft de 450 mètres carrés qui appartient à un écrivain et son mari vidéaste, est perché au sommet d'une usine du quartier de la confection. Ce dernier conserve son caractère populaire : « Nous avons encore trois bouchers et deux poissonniers dans le coin », s'émerveille le mari. L'espace était autrefois un atelier d'artiste « récupéré et habité » par des étudiants dans les années 1970. Le couple a demandé au cabinet d'architecture Resolution: 4 Architecture de le réaménager tout en préservant son côté industriel. Les sols en béton et les fenêtres en acier ont été remis en état ; la cuisine, les salles de bains et les espaces de rangement ont été rassemblés dans un bloc central. Les trois chambres sont séparées par des portes coulissantes. Quand toutes ces cloisons sont ouvertes, les enfants peuvent faire la course en tricycle tout autour de l'appartement.

P. 439 Droog Design's amusing chest of drawers is an assemblage of boxes held together by a canvas strap. • Die Kommode von Droog Design besteht aus einer Assemblage unterschiedlicher Schubladen, die von einem Leinengurt zusammengehalten werden. • Cette amusante commode de Droog Design est un assemblage de boîtes retenues par une sangle en toile.

← The original concrete floor was refurbished. • Der originale Betonboden wurde ausgebessert und poliert. • Le sol original en béton a été remis en état.

↗ In the kitchen area, an Eero Saarinen chair and oiled walnut table sit under a 1960s Italian pendant light. • Stühle und Tisch mit geölter Nussbaumplatte, alles Eero Saarinen, und eine italienische Leuchte aus den 1960ern im Küchenbereich. • Dans le coin cuisine, une chaise d'Eero Saarinen et une table en noyer huilé sous un plafonnier italien des années 1960.

↓ The husband sewed together thrift-shop cashmere sweaters to make a witty patchwork coverlet for the master bedroom. • Aus alten Kaschmirpullovern, die er in Secondhandläden kaufte, nähte der Hausherr einen originellen Patchwork-überwurf fürs Elternbett. • Pour la chambre principale, le mari a cousu de vieux pulls en cachemire trouvés dans des fripes pour créer un dessus-de-lit original.

PP. 442–443 The service block and the white lacquered kitchen island create a large sculptural form at the middle of the loft. • Wie eine Skulptur mitten im Loft: die weiß lackierte Kücheninsel vor dem zentralen Block mit Stauraum und Bädern. • Le bloc central et l'îlot de cuisine laqué blanc créent une grande forme sculpturale au milieu du loft.

NEW YORK CITY
USA

Freedom of Expression

Manhattan real-estate broker Jan Hashey sees many great apartments. But when she was marketing six lofts in a 1909 former stables and got depressed at each sale, Hashey realized she had to have one of the condominiums herself. So she bought 3,000 square feet of raw space in the West Village building, and hired architect Deborah Berke to turn it into the home Hashey now shares with her husband, Yasuo Minagawa. "Deborah listened to our needs and wrapped a serene and delicate plan around them," says Hashey of the three-bedroom, two-bath layout. Muscular elements like the building's industrial windows remained, though Berke covered the concrete floors with pine planking. More than a decade later, Hashey says, "I've never seen any apartment I'd trade it for."

Jan Hashey ist eine sehr erfolgreiche Immobilienmaklerin in Manhattan und sieht in ihrem Job so manches tolle Apartment. Als sie die sechs Lofts in den ehemaligen Stallungen von 1909 auf den Markt brachte, war sie nach jedem Verkauf nicht etwa glücklich, sondern traurig. Schnell wurde klar: Sie musste eines dieser Lofts im West Village für sich und ihren Ehemann Yasuo Minagawa kaufen. Für den Ausbau der 280 Quadratmeter großen Rohbaufläche engagierte sie die Architektin Deborah Berke, eine Meisterin der elegant-strengen Moderne. Hashey über die Gestaltung der Räumlichkeiten mit drei Schlaf- und zwei Badezimmern: „Deborah hörte sich unsere Bedürfnisse an und entwickelte daraus einen souveränen, sensiblen Plan." An kraftvollen Elementen wie den Industriefenstern änderte Berke wenig. Der Betonboden allerdings wurde mit dunkel gebeizten Kieferndielen belegt. Auch nach mehr als zehn Jahren sagt Hashey: „Mir ist seitdem kein Apartment untergekommen, das ich dafür eintauschen würde."

La courtière immobilière Jan Hashey a l'habitude des affaires en or mais, en voyant partir comme des petits pains une série de six lofts logés dans d'anciennes écuries de 1909 dans le West Village, elle a compris qu'il lui en fallait un avant qu'il ne soit trop tard. Elle a acheté 280 mètres carrés d'espace vide, puis a demandé à l'architecte Deborah Berke d'en faire l'appartement de trois chambres et deux salles de bains qu'elle partage à présent avec son mari, Yasuo Minagawa. « Deborah a écouté nos besoins et les a traduits en un plan serein et délicat », déclare-t-elle. Berke a conservé les éléments robustes de la structure tels que les fenêtres industrielles mais a recouvert les sols en béton d'un plancher en pin. Plus de dix ans plus tard, Hashey affirme : « Je n'ai jamais vu un appartement contre lequel je serais prête à échanger celui-ci. »

P. 445 The floors of the loft feature dark-stained pine boards. • Dunkel gebeizte Kieferndielen bedecken den Boden des Lofts. • Un plancher de pin brun foncé recouvre le sol du loft.

← In Jan Hashey's home office, the shelves and desk unit are designs by Dieter Rams for Vitsœ. • Die Regale und der Schreibtisch in Jan Hasheys Arbeitszimmer wurden von Dieter Rams für Vitsœ entworfen. • Dans le bureau de Jan Hashey, les étagères et le bureau ont été dessinés par Dieter Rams pour Vitsœ.

← The loft's curtainless, industrial-style windows are close replicas of the century-old building's original fenestration. • Die vorhanglosen Industriefenster sind möglichst exakte Repliken der Originalfenster des hundert Jahre alten Gebäudes. • Les fenêtres industrielles, sans rideaux, sont de proches répliques du fenêtrage original du bâtiment, vieux d'un siècle.

↑ In the dining area, laser-cut chairs by Ineke Hans surround a table custommade by George Smith. The photograph is by Jessica Craig-Martin, Hashey's daughter. • Per Laser geschnittene Stühle der Designerin Ineke Hans stehen um einen Maßtisch von George Smith. Das Foto stammt von Hasheys Tochter Jessica Craig-Martin. • Dans le coin salle à manger, des chaises découpées au laser par Ineke Hans entourent une table réalisée par George Smith. La photographie est de Jessica Craig-Martin, la fille de Hashey.

← An Elizabeth Peyton monoprint in the bathroom. • Der Monoprint im Bad ist von Elizabeth Peyton. • Dans la salle de bains, un monotype d'Elizabeth Peyton.

↓ Yasuo Minagawa is a master framemaker, and all the wash paintings in the study are his own work. • Yasuo Minagawa ist nicht nur ein virtuoser Rahmenbauer, auch alle Aquarelle in seinem Arbeitszimmer stammen von ihm. • Maître encadreur, Yasuo Minagawa est l'auteur de toutes les aquarelles dans l'atelier.

→ In the interiors and on the stairs, the concrete joists of this former stable block were left exposed. • Die Betonträger des einstigen Stallgebäudes liegen im Treppenhaus und in den Innenräumen offen. • Les supports en béton de l'ancienne écurie sont visibles dans la cage d'escalier et les espaces intérieurs.

NEW YORK CITY
USA

Precious Space

Architect Lee Mindel's spectacular loft occupies what was the dark top floor of a Flatiron District hatmaker. "It was very tough to build, both structurally and mechanically," says Mindel, whose firm, Shelton, Mindel & Associates, collaborated with Reed A. Morrison Architect on the difficult job. The space had few windows, so the architects broke ten large ones through the masonry walls to bring in light and panoramic views. Now, being in the apartment, "you understand that Manhattan is an island because you can see the Hudson and the East rivers," Mindel says. The new entry rotunda is wrapped by Mindel's double-helix stainless-steel and concrete staircase, which leads to a glass-enclosed solarium lounge. The airy structure echoes the shape of the adjacent rooftop water tower, though Mindel admits it also recalls for him the crown on the Statue of Liberty.

Das spektakuläre Loft des Architekten Lee Mindel liegt im obersten Stockwerk einer ehemaligen Hutmanufaktur im Flatiron District. Für den Umbau arbeitete Mindels Firma Shelton, Mindel & Associates mit dem Architekten Reed A. Morrison zusammen. „Ein schwieriges Unterfangen, strukturell wie auch mechanisch", sagt Mindel im Rückblick. Die Räume waren düster, hatten kaum Fenster. Um Licht und Ausblick zu schaffen, brachen die Architekten zehn große Fenster aus den Mauern. Mindel: „Nun blickt man auf den Hudson und den East River, und man kann erkennen, dass Manhattan eine Insel ist." In der neuen Eingangsrotunde führt eine Doppelhelix-Treppe aus Stahl und Beton, von Mindel entworfen, aufs Dach in die verglaste Solarium-Lounge. Die luftige Konstruktion ähnelt der Form des Wassertanks nebenan, obschon Mindel sagt, sie erinnere ihn auch an den Strahlenkranz der Freiheitsstatue.

Le loft spectaculaire de Lee Mindel est perché au sommet d'une ancienne usine à chapeaux dans le quartier du Flatiron. « Les travaux ont été un vrai casse-tête, tant structurel que mécanique », avoue-t-il. Pour mener à bien la tâche ardue, son cabinet d'architecture, Shelton, Mindel & Associates, s'est associé à celui de Reed A. Morrison. Pour pallier le manque de fenêtres, dix grandes ouvertures ont été percées dans les murs en maçonnerie afin de faire entrer la lumière et de jouir de vues panoramiques. Désormais, on ne peut plus douter que Manhattan soit une île car, nous dit Mindel, « d'un côté on voit le Hudson et de l'autre, East River ». Dans la nouvelle rotonde de l'entrée, le grand escalier en colimaçon en acier et béton de Mindel mène à un salon solarium ceint de verre. La structure claire et spacieuse rappelle la citerne voisine sur le toit ou, selon le maître des lieux, la couronne de la Statue de la Liberté.

P. 451 In the rotunda entrance is a re-edition of an Antoni Gaudí bench. • In der Eingangsrotunde steht die Neuauflage einer Bank von Antoni Gaudí. • Dans le pavillon d'accès rond, une nouvelle édition d'un banc d'Antoni Gaudí.

↓ A pair of vintage Hans Wegner Ox chairs sits near one of the ten new windows created in the loft. A French Cubist plaster maquette rises on the corner table. • Zwei Ox-Sessel von Hans Wegner flankieren eines der zehn neu eingebauten Loftfenster. Auf dem Beistelltisch in der Ecke steht eine kubistische Gipsskulptur aus Frankreich. • Deux fauteuils Ox de Hans Wegner à côté d'une des nouvelles dix fenêtres du loft. Sur la table, dans le coin, une maquette en plâtre cubiste française.

→ A curving staircase leads up to the glass-walled solarium lounge. • Eine geschwungene Treppe führt hinauf in die verglaste Solarium-Lounge. • Un escalier courbe mène au salon-solarium vitré.

↘ Small bulbs have been fitted into the bobèches of the Lobmeyr candle chandelier above the dining table. • Über dem Esstisch ein Kerzenleuchter von Lobmeyr. Anstelle von Kerzen sind in den Manschetten nun kleine Glühbirnen. • De petites ampoules ont été vissées dans les bobèches du chandelier de Lobmeyr au-dessus de la table de salle à manger.

PP. 454–455 A seating group, including a Frits Henningsen armchair, is lighted by a Flos wall lamp, a Fontana Arte table lamp, and floor lamp by Serge Mouille. • Eine Wandlampe von Flos, eine Tischlampe von Fontana Arte und eine Stehlampe von Serge Mouille beleuchten die Sitzgruppe mit einem Sessel von Frits Henningsen. • Ce coin salon, qui inclut un fauteuil de Frits Henningsen, est éclairé avec une applique de Flos, une lampe de Fontana Arte et un lampadaire de Serge Mouille.

↑ The sun deck on the roof offers clear
views of the New York skyline. • Vom
Sonnendeck auf dem Dach hat man
freien Blick auf die Skyline der Stadt. •
Du toit-terrasse, on a une vue panoramique de la ville.

→ An early Tom Dixon table with a
chromed wire base stands in the entrance rotunda. • Ein Frühwerk von Tom
Dixon: der Tisch mit verchromtem Draht-
gestell in der Eingangsrotunde. • Dans
la rotonde de l'entrée, une table de Tom
Dixon avec un pied en fil de fer chromé,
une œuvre de ses débuts.

NEW YORK CITY
USA

A Kid's Dream for Grown-ups

For the renovation of computer consultant Josh Morton's bachelor pad, architects LOT-EK bought a 72,000-gallon oil-truck tank—appropriately, since Morton's 1,000-square-foot West Village apartment is located in a former truck parking garage. LOT-EK, which is inspired by heavy industry, transformed the tank into twin sleeping pods, each just big enough to accommodate a king-size mattress. A crane swung the pods into the apartment, where they were installed as a mezzanine bridging the high-ceilinged space. Another slice of the tank was installed vertically to house a pair of double-decker bathrooms. A narrow catwalk links the upper bathroom to the mezzanine. All that makes the apartment look like the crewquarters of a ship, and is now an efficient family home. As Morton's wife, Susan Weinthaler, says, "Living here quickly seemed rather normal."

Das Architekturbüro LOT-EK erwarb für den Umbau der ehemaligen Junggesellenbude des Computerberaters Josh Morton den 272 550-Liter-Oltank eines Tankwagens. Und das passte ganz gut, denn Mortons 95 Quadratmeter großes Apartment im West Village liegt in einem ehemaligen Lastwagen-Parkhaus. Die Architekten von LOT-EK, die sich oft von der Schwerindustrie inspirieren lassen, bauten in den Riesenzylinder zwei Schlafzellen – jede so groß, dass gerade eine Doppelmatratze reinpasst. Die Zellen wurden mit einem Kran in das Apartment gehievt, wo sie als Zwischenetage den hohen Raum überqueren. Ein anderes Stück des Tanks wurde vertikal eingebaut, darin befinden sich auf zwei Ebenen übereinander die beiden Bäder. Nur ein schmaler Laufsteg verbindet das obere Badezimmer mit der Zwischenetage. Was wie das Crew-Quartier eines Schiffs aussieht, ist nun eine Familienwohnung. Denn inzwischen hat Morton geheiratet, und seine Frau Susan Weinthaler sagt: „Hier zu leben, erschien ganz schnell normal."

Pour transformer sa garçonnière dans le West Village en un foyer fonctionnel de 95 mètres carrés, le consultant en informatique Josh Morton a fait appel au cabinet LOT-EK. Ce dernier y a fait entrer une citerne de camion de 272 550 litres, ce qui était approprié puisque l'endroit était autrefois un garage de poids lourds. LOT-EK, qui s'inspire de l'industrie lourde, en a fait deux lits capsules, chacun assez grand pour accueillir un matelas à deux places. Il a fallu une grue pour les hisser dans l'appartement, et les déposer sur une mezzanine qui enjambe le haut espace. Une autre section de la citerne a été installée verticalement pour accueillir deux salles de bains superposées, celle du dessus étant reliée à la mezzanine par une étroite passerelle. Ce qui ressemble au quartier d'un équipage est maintenant un appartement familial car Morton s'est marié entretemps et sa femme, Susan Weinberg, déclare : « On s'y fait très rapidement. »

P. 459 Only a narrow catwalk con-
nects the two sleeping pods to the
mezzanine bathroom. • Der schmale
Laufsteg ist die einzige Verbindung der
beiden Schlafzellen mit dem Bad auf der
Zwischenetage. • Une étroite passerelle relie les deux lits capsules à la salle
de bains en mezzanine.

P. 460 Bathroom interiors feature the
same canary colored baked-on car
paint (LOT-EK named it Safety Yellow)
as the pods. • Die Badezimmer sind im
selben kanarienvogelgelben Autolack
wie das Innere der Schlafzellen gestrichen. LOT-EK bezeichnet die Farbe als
„Sicherheitsgelb". • L'intérieur des
salles de bains est peint de la même
laque de carrosserie jaune canari que
les capsules ; LOT-EK l'appelle « jaune
sécurité ».

P. 461 Two bathrooms are installed, one
above the other, in an upended section
of the tank. • In einem umgestülpten
Teil des Tanks wurden übereinander
zwei Badezimmer installiert. • Les deux
salles de bains sont installées l'une sur
l'autre dans une section verticale de la
citerne.

← The pods have gull-wing doors on
both sides that open using hydraulic pis-
tons. • Die Türen auf beiden Seiten der
Zellen erinnern an Klappdeckel, sie lassen sich hydraulisch öffnen. • Les capsules sont équipées de portes papillons
qui s'ouvrent à l'aide d'un piston hydrau-
lique.

→ The oil-tank mezzanine spans the
entire width of the apartment over the
dining area's custom-made resin table. •
Der einstige Öltank spannt sich als Zwischenetage über die ganze Breite des
Apartments. Darunter steht ein maß-
gefertigter Tisch aus Kunstharz. • La
mezzanine occupe toute la largeur du
loft. Dessous se trouve la salle à manger,
avec une table en résine réalisée sur
mesure.

NIIGATA
JAPAN

Turrell's Temple

James Turrell is known worldwide as "the artist of light." His painstakingly calibrated installations take time to experience, time to take in the passage of time and changing shades of light. So in 2000, as part of the First Echigo-Tsumari Triennial art event in Niigata Prefecture near the Japanese Sea coast, Turrell designed an inn where one can spend a day and a night enveloped in his world of light and shadow. Architect Daigo Ishii planned the building in the traditional Japanese style with tatami-matted rooms, wooden-floored corridors, verandas, and yukimi-shoji, paper doors with cutout windows for viewing the deep snow for which the Niigata region is known. Into these traditional surroundings, Turrell brought soft overhead lighting in various hues. The "Outside-In" room features an aperture that slides open to the sky, surrounded by a computer-coordinated ceiling that changes color as sunset progresses. At night, the house comes into its own, as stairways, door frames, and even the edges of the bath glow with surreal light.

James Turrell ist weltweit als Lichtkünstler berühmt. Um seine Kunstwerke zu begreifen, muss man sich Zeit nehmen – Zeit, um das Verstreichen der Zeit und das sich verändernde Licht zu erleben. Als er 2000 von der Präfektur Niigata an die Küste des Japanischen Meers eingeladen wurde, entwarf Turrell ein Gästehaus, wo man einen Tag und eine Nacht in seiner Welt aus Licht und Schatten verbringen kann. Der Architekt Daigo Ishii gestaltete das Gebäude im japanischen Stil: Räume, die mit Tatami-Matten ausgelegt sind, Flure aus Holzdielen, Veranden und yukimi-shoji, Papiertüren mit ausgesparten Fenstern, durch die man die tief verschneite Landschaft betrachten kann, für die die Präfektur Niigata so berühmt ist. In diese traditionelle Umgebung integrierte Turrell eine sanfte Deckenbeleuchtung in verschiedenen Farbschattierungen. Der „Outside-In-Room" verfügt über eine zur Seite gleitende Oberlichtblende, die den Blick auf den Himmel freigibt, umgeben von einer computergesteuerten Decke, die ihre Farbe während des Sonnenuntergangs verändert.

James Turrell est connu dans le monde entier comme « l'artiste de la lumière ». Il faut du temps pour apprécier ses œuvres, celui de suivre le passage du temps et les nuances changeantes de la lumière. C'est pourquoi, invité en 2000 par la préfecture de Niigata, il a conçu une auberge près de la mer du Japon où l'on peut s'immerger une journée et une nuit dans son monde d'ombres et de lumière. L'architecte Daigo Ishii a construit le bâtiment dans le style japonais avec des pièces tapissées de tatamis, des couloirs en parquet, des vérandas, des yukimi-shoji, des portes en papier percées de fenêtres donnant sur l'épais tapis de neige qui fait la réputation de la région. Dans cet environnement traditionnel, Turrell a créé un éclairage par le haut tout en nuances changeantes. Le plafond de la pièce « Dehors-dedans », qu'un ordinateur fait changer de couleur à mesure que le soleil se couche, possède une trappe coulissante qui s'ouvre sur le ciel. La nuit, l'escalier, les cadres de portes et même le bord de la baignoire luisent d'une lumière surnaturelle, révélant la maison dans toute sa splendeur.

P. 465 Yellow light from the ceiling and light from outside shining through the *shoji* doors reflect on the wooden floors of the entryway. • Die gelbe Deckenbeleuchtung sowie das Tageslicht, das durch die papierbespannten Türen *(shoji)* fällt, mischt sich auf den Holzdielen des Eingangsbereichs. • L'éclairage jaune du plafond et la lumière extérieure filtrée par les portes *shoji* se reflètent dans le parquet de l'entrée.

← Solid planks of wood line the corridor leading to the ground-floor bathroom. The pool is lit by natural light from a window to the left. • Wände aus massiven Holzdielen säumen den Durchgang zum Bad im Erdgeschoss. Links erkennt man Tageslicht, das durch ein Fenster fällt. • Au rez-de-chaussée, des cloisons en planches épaisses bordent le couloir qui mène à la salle de bains. À gauche, la lumière naturelle tombe sur le bassin par une fenêtre vitrée.

↑ In lieu of a tiled backsplash, the kitchen has panes of glass protecting the paper in the Japanese partition walls. • Wo sich sonst Fliesen befinden, schützen in dieser Küche Glasscheiben die papierbespannten Schiebewände. •

Là où se trouvent normalement des carreaux, des vitres protègent dans la cuisine les cloisons de séparation japonaises tendues de papier.

PP. 468–469 Guest bedding in what appears to be a traditional Japanese room, but is actually under a retractable roof skylight that opens slowly for observing the sky at night. • Ein Gästeschlaflager in einem vermeintlich traditionellen japanischen Zimmer. Doch es befindet sich unter einem Oberlicht, das sich nachts langsam öffnet, um den Sternenhimmel freizugeben. • Dans la chambre d'amis au décor traditionnel, le plafond s'ouvre lentement sur une vue du ciel nocturne.

PANTAI SESEH
INDONESIA

Feminine Paradise

While residing for most of the 1980s in a secluded, traditional village in eastern Bali, the Dutch-born Conchita Kien and her mother cultivated a deep understanding of Balinese culture. By the 1990s, Conchita had become a jewelry designer and moved closer to the expatriate community living near the beaches of southern Bali. The construction of her first house was planned on a meager budget of $10,000. She pioneered new architectural techniques and reinvented others, creating inspiring designs and changing the future of her own career. Eventually, she was even hired to build private villas and spas—such as the famous Bodyworks—as well as boutiques, such as Milo's. In constructing her own new home, Villa Matisse, Conchita Kien employed terrazzo in muted colors with chips of glimmering mother of pearl for the walls and floors, along with mosaics of broken mirrors and lots of polished silver-gray cement. The ocean side of the two-story villa has no continuous walls at all—that's what we call a breezy approach to life.

Conchita Kien stammt ursprünglich aus den Niederlanden und lebte in den 1980ern acht Jahre lang mit ihrer Mutter in einem traditionellen und abgeschiedenen Dorf im Osten Balis. Dort begann sie, Schmuck zu entwerfen, und zog später an die Südküste der Insel, wo sie mit einem mageren Startkapital von 10 000 Dollar ihr erstes eigenes Haus entwarf. Mit Mut und Kreativität erfand sie damals völlig neue Techniken, die ihr Gebäude einzigartig machten und ihr zu einer Karriere als Architektin und Designerin verhalfen. Sie wurde für die Gestaltung von Privatvillen auf der Insel engagiert, entwarf das Spa Bodyworks und Boutiquen wie Milo's. Für sich selbst baute Conchita Kien die Villa Matisse: Hier verzierte sie die Terrazzowände und -böden mit glitzerndem Perlmutt, dazu kamen Spiegelmosaik und polierter Beton. Den Blick in die umliegende Natur und auf den Ozean ließ sie sich nicht nehmen: Eine Seite der zweistöckigen Villa kommt sogar ganz ohne durchgehende Außenwand aus. Das nennt man einen luftigen Lifestyle.

Ayant passé huit ans dans un village traditionnel de l'est de Bali au cours des années 1980, la jeune Hollandaise Conchita Kien et sa mère ont acquis une connaissance profonde de la culture balinaise. Devenue ensuite créatrice de bijoux, Conchita s'est rapprochée de la communauté des expatriés installés près des plages du sud de Bali. Elle a imaginé les plans de sa première maison, avec un budget de 10 000 $, lançant et réinventant des techniques et des éléments architecturaux qui ont su séduire. Sa carrière a alors pris un nouveau tournant et on lui a peu à peu confié la construction de villas particulières, de centres thermaux, comme le célèbre Bodyworks, et de boutiques comme Milo's. Pour édifier la Villa Matisse, Conchita a utilisé des techniques comme celle qui consiste à incorporer dans un revêtement de sols et de murs décoratif en terrazzo aux tons fondus des éclats de nacre ou de mosaïques de miroir avec quantité de ciment poli gris argent. Une façade de cette villa à deux étages donnant sur l'océan est dépourvue de murs.

← With its archetypal simplicity and the coolness of the polished, white concrete, the bath with shower stall conveys a sense of freshness. • Die Schlichtheit der Duschnische im Bad wirkt mit der Kühle des polierten Weißbetons erfrischend. • Dans la salle de bains, l'alcôve pour la douche, d'une simplicité archaïque, véhicule une impression de fraîcheur avec son béton blanc poli.

↓ The fusion of styles in the living room reflects Conchita's innovative approach; the hand-painted floral patterns on the wall pick up on the dominant theme of deep, sensuous red. • Das Wohnzimmer zeigt Conchitas freien, eklektischen Stil: Alles ist in sattes, sinnliches Rot getaucht und eine Wand trägt handgemalte Blüten. • Dans le salon de style éclectique, bien que fidèle à la veine créatrice de Conchita, un remarquable revêtement mural peint à la main constitue, avec ses motifs floraux, une toile de fond en harmonie avec les tons de rouge profond et sensuel qui dominent.

→ Shocking pink in two nuances brightens the guesthouse bedroom overlooking the river. • Knallige Pinktöne bringen das Gästeschlafzimmer mit Blick auf den Fluss zum Leuchten. • Le mariage osé de deux tons de rose donne sa tonalité à la chambre du pavillon réservé aux amis, qui donne sur la rivière.

P. 471 The riverside guesthouse features a table and chairs with mosaic patterns made of chipped mirrors, inspired by Indian crafts. • Im Gästehaus am Fluss findet man einen Tisch und Stühle mit einem Mosaik aus Spiegelscherben nach indischem Vorbild. • Le pavillon des invités en bordure de rivière est agrémenté d'une table et de chaises revêtus d'une mosaïque d'éclats de miroir d'inspiration indienne.

↑ In a corner of the exposed upper level, a hole in the floor allows a tree to continue to grow. • In einer Ecke des oberen Stockwerks befindet sich ein Loch, durch das der Baumstamm weiterwachsen kann. • Dans un coin de l'étage ouvert, un arbre poursuit sa croissance grâce à un trou ménagé dans le plancher chaulé.

↑ The clean lines framing the washbasins in the bathroom reflect structural patterns of design found throughout the house. • Die reduzierten Linien des Waschbeckenbereichs fügen sich ideal in die klaren Strukturen des Hauses. • Les lignes épurées du bloc-lavabos reflètent le design général clair de la maison.

↓ This pillowed sitting area without walls affords a panoramic view of the forest, river, and ocean beyond. • Der wandlose, gepolsterte Sitzbereich erlaubt einen Panoramablick über den Urwald, den Fluss und das Meer dahinter. • Assis sur des coussins dans l'espace salon ouvert sur l'extérieur, on embrasse du regard la forêt, la vallée et l'océan dans le lointain.

↑ Ocean breezes gently blow through the upstairs bedroom in luminous shades of gray, silver, and white. • Das Schlafzimmer im oberen Stockwerk wird von einer frischen Meeresbrise durchweht und bildet einen hellen Farbklang aus Grau, Silber und Weiß. • À l'étage, camaïeu lumineux de gris, argent et blanc dans la chambre rafraîchie par la brise marine.

→ In Ruby's nursery her clothes hang open like in a fairy-tale showroom. • In Rubys Kinderzimmer hängen ihre Kleider offen wie in einem märchenhaften Showroom. • La chambre de Ruby semble tout droit sortie d'un conte de fées.

PP. 476–477 The terrace of the main house overlooks the annex below. • Von der Terrasse des Haupthauses blickt man auf das niedrige Nebengebäude. • De la terrasse de la maison principale on voit les annexes situées plus bas.

PARIS
FRANCE

Small Is Splendid

Decorator Jean-Louis Deniot is a world traveler. He has projects in places like Delhi and Colombia, and five residences between France and the United States. Among them is a 485-square-foot pied-à-terre in the Saint-Germain-des-Prés district, which perfectly reflects his philosophy about small spaces—that you should bestow them with great refinement. "That way," he says, "you compensate for the lack of space." He covered the walls with fake parchment and had the doors stylishly painted to resemble rosewood. He also filled the two main rooms with a plethora of objects. "If you do something too minimalist, small apartments immediately look like shoe boxes," he opines. Most cleverly, he integrated a maximum of storage throughout. In the bedroom, he devised two walk-in closets and created drawers in the base of the bed. He also hid a small office space and a tiny kitchen behind doors in the living room.

Der Innenausstatter Jean-Louis Deniot ist ein Mann von Welt. Er hat Projekte in Delhi und Kolumbien sowie fünf Wohnsitze zwischen Frankreich und den USA. Dazu gehört auch ein Pied-à-terre mit ganzen 45 Quadratmetern im Viertel Saint-Germain-des-Prés, das seine Philosophie hinsichtlich kleiner Räume perfekt illustriert – nämlich, dass man sie mit großer Raffinesse einrichten sollte: „Auf diese Weise kann man den Platzmangel hervorragend kompensieren." Er tapezierte die Wände mit Pergament-Imitat und ließ die Türen so bemalen, dass sie an Palisander erinnern. Außerdem dekorierte er die beiden Haupträume mit einer Fülle von Objekten, denn: „Wenn man zu minimalistisch vorgeht, sehen kleine Apartments schnell aus wie Schuhschachteln." Höchst geschickt hat er überall ein Maximum an Stauraum geschaffen. Im Flur beherbergt ein Schrank die Waschmaschine, im Schlafzimmer installierte Deniot zwei begehbare Kleiderschränke und integrierte Schubladen in den Bettsockel. Hinter Türen im Wohnzimmer versteckte er sogar ein Mini-Büro und eine winzige Küche.

Jean-Louis Deniot est un décorateur globe-trotter, sillonnant la planète de New Delhi à la Colombie. Parmi ses cinq résidences réparties entre la France et les États-Unis, son pied-à-terre de 45 mètres carrés à Saint-Germain-des-Prés reflète parfaitement sa philosophie des petits espaces : un raffinement extrême permet de compenser le manque de place. Les murs sont tapissés de faux parchemin et les portes peintes en trompe-l'œil de bois de rose. Les deux pièces principales sont remplies d'objets. « Trop minimalistes, les petits appartements ressemblent à des boîtes à chaussures », observe-t-il. Partout, il a imaginé des espaces de rangement astucieux : dans la chambre, il a conçu deux dressings et des tiroirs encastrés dans le sommier du lit ; dans le salon, des portes cachent un petit bureau et une kitchenette.

P. 479 The wall behind the bed is covered with a striped silk from Dominique Kieffer. The 1940s clock was bought at a Paris flea market. • Eine gestreifte Seidentapete von Dominique Kieffer schmückt die Wand hinter dem Bett. Die Uhr aus den 1940er Jahren stammt von einem Pariser Flohmarkt. • Le mur derrière le lit est tapissé d'une soie rayée de Dominique Kieffer. L'horloge des années 1940 a été chinée au marché aux puces de Paris.

← A plaster sculpture of a dancer stands in front of the gilded mirror from Denmark. • Vor einem teilvergoldeten dänischen Spiegel steht eine Tänzerin aus Gips. • Une sculpture en plâtre devant un miroir danois doré.

↑ An early 20th-century copy of a Titian portrait hangs above a Louis XVI sofa. In the background, a 1930s plaster bas-relief can be seen on one wall of the bedroom. • Die Tizian-Kopie aus dem frühen 20. Jahrhundert hängt über einem Louis-XVI-Sofa. Im Hintergrund sieht man ein Gipsrelief aus den 1930ern an einer der Schlafzimmerwände. • Une copie d'un portrait du Titien datant du début du 20ᵉ siècle au-dessus d'un canapé Louis XVI. Dans le fond, on aperçoit un bas-relief en plâtre des années 1930 sur le mur de la chambre.

PP. 482–483 Both the chairs with velvet seats and the elegant stone fireplace were designed by Deniot. • Sowohl die Sessel mit Samtsitz als auch der elegante Kamin sind Entwürfe von Deniot. • Deniot a dessiné les fauteuils en velours et l'élégante cheminée en pierre.

← Above the velvet armchair is a shell-shaped wall lamp by Serge Roche. The recessed cupboard contains a small kitchen. • Über einem Samtsessel hängt die muschelförmige Wandlampe von Serge Roche. In dem Nischenschrank verbirgt sich eine kleine Küche. • Au-dessus d'un fauteuil de velours est suspendue l'applique en forme de coquillage de Serge Roche, une kitchenette est dissimulée dans le placard.

→ A 1940s coffee table and a 1920s plaster column stand on a rug with stripes by Madeleine Castaing. • Ein Couchtisch aus den 1940er und eine Gipssäule aus den 1920er Jahren stehen auf einem gestreiften Teppich, der nach einem Entwurf von Madeleine Castaing gefertigt wurde. • Une table basse des années 1940 et un socle en plâtre des années 1920 sur un tapis aux couleurs vives dessiné par Madeleine Castaing.

"I wanted spaces that recall a Parisian boudoir from the 1940s, a mix of classicism and Art Deco."
JEAN-LOUIS DENIOT

„Ich wollte Räume wie in einem Pariser Boudoir der 1940er Jahre, eine Mischung aus Klassizismus und Art déco."
« Je voulais que les pièces ressemblent à des boudoirs parisiens des années 1940, un mélange de néoclassique et d'Art Déco. »

PARIS
FRANCE

Creative Luxury

Art dealers and collectors Cathy and Paolo Vedovi originally planned to redecorate their Parisian pied-à-terre themselves. That is until Cathy stopped by the Parisian gallery of interior designer Chahan Minassian. "Everything there was so perfect," recalls the co-founder of the Galerie Emmanuel Perrotin in Miami. "I said to myself, I'll never manage to do something like that." Within 15 minutes, she'd bought a coffee table, two side tables, and various lamps and ceramics. She had also hired Minassian for the project. Inspiration came from a photo of the swimming pool of the Rhoul Palace in Marrakech—the chevron motif of the tiles was copied for the living room rug, while the dining room was fitted out with three tiled tables and a banquette which Minassian refers to as "a stretched chair." The whole process apparently went swimmingly, too. As Cathy Vedovi says, "It was as if someone had waved a magic wand!"

Ursprünglich wollten die Kunsthändler und Sammler Cathy und Paolo Vedovi ihr Pariser Pied-à-terre selbst neu einrichten. Aber das war, bevor Cathy die Pariser Galerie des Interiordesigners Chahan Minassian betreten hatte. „Dort war einfach alles perfekt", erinnert sich die Mitbegründerin der Galerie Emmanuel Perrotin in Miami. „Ich dachte: So was kriegst du allein niemals hin." Innerhalb einer Viertelstunde war sie stolze Besitzerin eines Couchtisches, zweier Beistelltischchen und diverser Lampen und Keramiken. Außerdem hatte sie Minassian für das Projekt angeheuert. Als Inspiration diente beiden ein Foto des Pools im Palais Rhoul in Marrakesch: Das zackige Fliesenmotiv wurde für den Wohnzimmerteppich entlehnt, während man das Esszimmer mit drei Mosaiktischen und einer Bank bestückte, die Minassian als „extrem langen Sessel" bezeichnet. Der Einrichtungsprozess lief wie von selbst. Wie sagt Cathy Vedovi noch so schön: „Es war, als habe jemand über der Wohnung den Zauberstab geschwungen!"

Marchands et collectionneurs d'art, Cathy et Paolo Vedovi comptaient initialement décorer eux-mêmes leur pied-à-terre parisien. Puis Cathy est passée à la galerie du décorateur Chahan Minassian. « Tout y était tellement parfait. Je me suis dit que je n'arriverai jamais à faire quelque chose comme ça. » Un quart d'heure plus tard, elle en ressortait avec une table basse, deux consoles, plusieurs lampes et céramiques, et avait engagé Minassian. Elle s'inspira d'une photo de la piscine du palais Rhoul à Marrakech. Le motif de son carrelage fut copié pour le tapis du salon et la salle à manger fut aménagée avec trois tables de mosaïque et une banquette que Minassian qualifie de « chaise étirée ». Depuis, les Vedovi se sentent comme des poissons dans l'eau dans leur nouveau décor. Comme dit Cathy : « C'était comme si quelqu'un avait agité une baguette magique. »

P. 487 A 1950s ceramic lamp stands on a desk created by a student of Gio Ponti. • Eine Keramiklampe aus den 1950er Jahren steht auf einem Schreibtisch, der von einem Schüler Gio Pontis entworfen wurde. • Une lampe des années 1950 en céramique posée sur un bureau créé par un élève de Gio Ponti.

↑ The furniture blends harmoniously with the room's parquet floor. • Das Parkett harmoniert perfekt mit der Möblierung des Zimmers. • Le parquet est en parfaite harmonie avec les meubles de la pièce.

→ In the dining room, three tables stand —bistro style—on a Bedouin rug from Morocco. The painting is by Bernard Frize. • Im Esszimmer reihen sich drei Tische à la Bistro auf einem Beduinenteppich aus Marokko. Das Gemälde ist von Bernard Frize aus der Galerie Emmanuel Perrotin. • Dans la salle à manger, trois tables sont posées sur un tapis bédouin marocain. Le tableau est de Bernard Frize de la Galerie Emmanuel Perrotin.

PP. 490–491 Two imposing Vladimir Kagan sofas and a Salviati glass chandelier dominate the living room. In the far corner is Takashi Murakami's *Kinoko Isu* sculpture, made from fiberglass, steel, and acrylic paint. • Zwei imposante Vladimir-Kagan-Sofas und ein Glaslüster von Salviati beherrschen das Wohnzimmer. Hinten am Fenster sieht man Takashi Murakamis *Kinoko Isu* aus Fiberglas, Stahl und Acrylfarbe. • Deux imposants canapés de Vladimir Kagan et un lustre en verre Salviati dominent le séjour. Au fond, une sculpture de Takashi Murakami, *Kinoko Isu*, en fibre de verre, acier et peinture acrylique.

← The glass and granite coffee table was created by the Brazilian designer Amaury Cardoso. The two paintings on the mantle are from Murakami's *Dokuro* series. • Der Couchtisch aus Glas und Granit ist ein Entwurf des brasilianischen Designers Amaury Cardoso. Die beiden Bilder auf dem Kaminsims stammen aus der *Dokuro*-Serie von Murakami. • La table basse en verre et granit a été créée par le designer brésilien Amaury Cardoso. Les deux tableaux sur le manteau de la cheminée appartiennent à la série *Dokuro* de Murakami.

→ The oil painting above the antique recamier is from the series *Concrete Cabin* by Peter Doig. • Das Ölbild über einer antiken Récamiere stammt aus der *Concrete-Cabin*-Serie von Peter Doig. • Le tableau peint à l'huile au-dessus d'une récamière ancienne fait partie de la série *Concrete Cabin* de Peter Doig.

↓ Next to the master bed are Karl Springer snakeskin lamps and a 1940s Lucite chair upholstered with ocelot fur. • Neben dem großen Bett stehen Lampen von Karl Springer und ein Plexiglassessel aus den 1940er Jahren mit Ozelotfellbezug. • Près du lit dans la chambre principale, lampes en peau de serpent de Karl Springer et un fauteuil en Plexiglas tapissé d'ocelot des années 1940.

PARIS
FRANCE

Gold, Silver, and Steel

Gerald Schmorl works as a consultant to several luxury-goods houses and lives in an apartment in the 9th arrondisse-ment, the decor of which he conceived as a showcase for his collection of contemporary art. The discreet color scheme is dominated by various shades of gray. The mix of classical elements and geometric motifs is inspired by the late David Hicks. In the entrance hall greets a grisaille scenic wallpaper by Zuber, while the dining-room walls are covered with a swirling, graphic design created in situ by Swiss artist Stéphane Dafflon. And the movable art? It's mainly American. Particularly striking is a gold painting with an elaborate damask motif by New York-based artist Rudolf Stingel. Placed next to a puristic John McCracken plank sculpture, it perfectly illustrates Schmorl's style. As he himself says: "My taste ranges from the minimalist to the very baroque."

Beruflich ist Gerald Schmorl Berater für mehrere Luxusfirmen. Privat wohnt er im 9. Arrondissement in einem Apartment, in dem er seine Sammlung zeitgenössischer Kunst perfekt zur Geltung bringt. Dessen zurückhaltendes Farbschema besteht überwiegend aus verschiedenen Grautönen, während die Mischung aus klassischen Elementen und geometrischen Motiven von dem legendären Interiordesigner David Hicks inspiriert wurde. Schmorls Flur schmückt eine Panoramatapete von Zuber und die Esszimmerwände ein schwungvolles, grafisches Motiv, das der Schweizer Künstler Stéphane Dafflon direkt vor Ort kreiert hat. Und die bewegliche Kunst? Sie ist überwiegend ameri-kanisch. In Erinnerung bleibt vor allem ein goldenes Gemälde mit opulentem Damastmotiv, ein Werk des in New York lebenden Künstlers Rudolf Stingel. Typisch Schmorl ist, dass er es neben eine puristische Plankenskulptur von John McCracken gehängt hat. Wie sagt er so schön: „Mein Geschmack reicht von Minimalismus bis hin zu Barockem."

Gerald Schmorl, consultant pour plusieurs maisons de luxe, habite dans un appartement du 9e arrondissement dont le décor sert d'écrin à sa collection d'art contemporain. Discrète, la palette de couleurs est dominée par des nuances de gris. Le mélange d'éléments classiques et de motifs géométriques s'inspire de feu David Hicks. Un papier peint panora-mique de Zuber vous accueille dans l'entrée. Les murs de la salle à manger sont ornés d'arabesques graphiques peintes in situ par l'artiste suisse, Stéphane Dafflon. L'art, lui, est principalement américain. Parmi les œuvres les plus frappantes, une peinture dorée à motif de brocart signée du New-yorkais Rudolf Stingel est placée près d'une sculpture planche puriste de John McCracken, illustrant parfaitement le style Schmorl. Comme il le dit lui-même : « Mon goût varie du minimaliste au très baroque. »

494

P. 495 The scenic wallpaper in the hall is by the French firm Zuber. • Die Panoramatapete im Flur stammt von der französischen Manufaktur Zuber. • Le papier peint panoramique du couloir vient de la manufacture française Zuber.

PP. 496–497 The living room acts as a showcase for Schmorl's collection of contemporary art. From left: a work by Peter Halley called *Silver Prison*, a John McCracken plank sculpture entitled *Cool One*, and a 2004 oil and enamel on canvas by Rudolf Stingel. The Louis XVI-style chair is from Potsdam. • Das Wohnzimmer dient als Showroom für

Schmorls Sammlung zeitgenössischer Kunst. Von links: *Silver Prison* von Peter Halley, eine Plankenskulptur von John McCracken mit dem Titel *Cool One* und ein Werk in Öl und Lack von Rudolf Stingel aus dem Jahr 2004. Der Sessel im Louis-XVI-Stil stammt aus Potsdam. • Le séjour sert de vitrine à la collection d'art contemporain de Schmorl. De gauche à droite, une œuvre de Peter Halley intitulée *Silver Prison*, une sculpture planche de John McCracken, *Cool One*, et une huile et émail sur toile peinte par Rudolf Stingel en 2004. Le fauteuil de style Louis XVI vient de Potsdam.

↑ The study's fireplace and large mirror. • Der Kamin mit großem Spiegel befindet sich im Arbeitszimmer. • La cheminée surmontée d'un grand miroir se trouve dans le cabinet de travail.

→ Schmorl's brushed-steel-and-bronze four-poster bed dates from the 1970s. • Schmorls Bett aus gebürstetem Stahl und Bronze stammt aus den 1970er Jahren. • Le lit en acier brossé et bronze date des années 1970.

← To the left is a John Tremblay painting titled *Silver Curtain*. The ornate chandelier is 18th-century Italian. • Links hängt ein Gemälde von John Tremblay mit dem Titel *Silver Curtain*. Der Kristalllüster aus dem 18. Jahrhundert stammt aus Italien. • À gauche, une toile de John Tremblay intitulée *Silver Curtain*. Le beau lustre italien date du 18ᵉ siècle.

← The motifs on the dining-room walls are the work of Swiss artist Stéphane Dafflon. On the Eero Saarinen table stands an 18th-century Fürstenberg porcelain urn. The stool front right is by Carlo Mollino and the black wall sculpture by Vincent Szarek. • Das schattenähnliche Motiv auf den Esszimmerwänden ist eine Arbeit des Schweizer Künstlers Stéphane Dafflon. Auf dem Tisch von Eero Saarinen steht eine Porzellanurne aus dem 18. Jahrhundert von

Fürstenberg. Der Hocker vorne rechts ist von Carlo Mollino und die schwarze Wandskulptur von Vincent Szarek. • Les motifs sur les murs de la salle à manger ont été peints par l'artiste suisse Stéphane Dafflon. Sur la table d'Eero Saarinen, une urne en porcelaine du 18ᵉ siècle de la manufacture de Fürstenberg. Le tabouret au premier plan à droite est de Carlo Mollino et la sculpture noire sur le mur de Vincent Szarek.

↓ Two André Arbus chairs flank an antique English mahogany desk in Schmorl's office. • Zwei Sessel von André Arbus stehen in Schmorls Arbeitszimmer an einem antiken englischen Mahagonitisch. • Dans la pièce de travail de Schmorl, deux fauteuils d'André Arbus flanquent un vieux bureau anglais en acajou.

PARIS
FRANCE

Home of an Interiors Hero

Christian Liaigre is one of Europe's most lauded living designers—a real star of his métier. Among his most celebrated projects to date are The Mercer Hotel in New York and apartments for Calvin Klein and Rupert Murdoch. When it comes to his own apartment in Paris, he claims not to make that much effort. If that is the case, then it certainly doesn't show! The eight-room duplex in the Marais district was formerly home to a clothing factory. Liaigre ripped everything out and created a wonderfully elegant shell for his ever-changing arrangements of furniture. "As it's my profession, I quickly get tired of things," he admits. What remains, however, are his works of art and the objects he brings back from his travels. They include such diverse treasures as a Buddha head, which he found in Thailand 30 years ago, and sculpted coconut shells from Saint Barths.

Christian Liaigre ist einer von Europas meistgepriesenen zeitgenössischen Interiordesignern. Zu seinen bekanntesten Projekten zählen das Mercer Hotel in New York sowie grandiose Wohnungen für Calvin Klein und Rupert Murdoch. Bei seinem eigenen Apartment in Paris habe er sich nicht so angestrengt, behauptet er. Davon ist allerdings nichts zu merken! In dem Acht-Zimmer-Domizil im Marais war einst eine Kleiderfabrik untergebracht. Liaigre riss alles raus und schuf eine wunderbar elegante Hülle für seine sich stets ändernde Einrichtung. „Ich bekomme die Dinge sehr schnell satt, eine Art Berufskrankheit", gibt er zu. Was bleibt, sind seine Kunstwerke und Reisesouvenirs. Dazu gehören so unterschiedliche Schätze wie der Kopf eines Buddhas, den er vor 30 Jahren in Thailand fand, sowie mit Schnitzereien verzierte Kokosnussschalen aus Saint Barths.

Christian Liaigre est un des décorateurs vivants les plus admirés de l'Europe. Ses réalisations célèbres incluent l'hôtel Mercer à New York et les appartements de Calvin Klein et de Rupert Murdoch. Pour sa propre résidence à Paris, il affirme ne pas s'être donné beaucoup de mal. À la voir, on ne le dirait pas ! Son duplex de 8 pièces dans le Marais était autrefois une usine de confection. Il a abattu tous les murs et créé un élégant écrin pour son mobilier en évolution constante. « Comme c'est mon métier, je me lasse vite », avoue-t-il. En revanche, il tient à ses œuvres d'art et aux objets qu'il rapporte de ses voyages. Parmi eux, une tête de bouddha trouvée en Thaïlande il y a 30 ans et des noix de coco sculptées venant de Saint Barths.

P. 503 Numerous Liaigre designs can be found in the sitting room. Among them are the *Galet* coffee table pouf and the *Bazane* stool. The photograph is by Peter Beard. • In Liaigres Wohnzimmer trifft man auf viele seiner Entwürfe – den Couchtisch-Pouf *Galet* und den Hocker *Bazane*. Die Fotoarbeit ist von Peter Beard. • Dans le séjour, de nombreuses créations de Liaigre, dont une table basse *Galet* et un tabouret *Bazane*. Les photos sont de Peter Beard.

← The study is decorated with African stools and wickerwork. The blinds are made from linen. • Das Arbeitszimmer schmücken afrikanische Hocker und Körbe, Rollos aus Leinen. • Le bureau est décoré avec des tabourets et de la vannerie africains. Les stores sont en lin.

→ Both the chestnut stools and iron kitchen table were created by Liaigre. • Sowohl die Hocker aus Kastanienästen als auch der eiserne Küchentisch sind Entwürfe von Liaigre. • Les tabourets en châtaignier et la table en fer sont des créations de Liaigre.

↓ Liaigre also designed the sofa and the *Latin* lounge chair—in the generous, perfect proportions that are his trademark. • Liaigre entwarf auch das Sofa und den *Latin*-Klubsessel – in den so großzügigen wie perfekten Proportionen, die seine Signatur sind. • Liaigre a aussi dessiné le canapé et le fauteuil club *Latin*, dotés des proportions généreuses et parfaites qui sont sa signature.

← In the sitting room, a Chinese table stands in front of a picture of a colocynth by Jacques Martinez. The paper frieze is by the same artist. • Im Wohnzimmer steht ein chinesischer Tisch vor dem Gemälde einer Koloquinte von Jacques Martinez. Der Papierfries stammt vom selben Künstler. • Dans le séjour, une table chinoise devant un tableau représentant une coloquinte de Jacques Martinez. La frise en papier est du même artiste.

↑ The marble bathroom plays with cuboid forms. • Das Marmorbad spielt mit kubischen Formen. • La salle de bains en marbre joue avec les formes cubiques.

↑ The 1,300-square-foot garden can be seen behind a copy of a Greek head. • Hinter der Kopie eines griechischen Kopfes erhascht man einen Blick in den 120 Quadratmeter großen Garten. • On aperçoit le jardin de 120 mètres carrés derrière une copie d'une tête grecque.

PARIS
FRANCE

Vive la Créativité!

Clémence and Didier Krzentowski are the owners of Paris's hippest design gallery, Kreo, where they represent the likes of the Bouroullec brothers, Martin Szekely, and Marc Newson. They are also avid collectors. He believes he has the largest number of lights designed by Gino Sarfatti, and has two other principal passions—Pierre Paulin furniture and mirrors created by artists. Their apartment is certainly jam-packed with an anarchic mix of objects. Among them, several artistic installations, the most striking of which is Richard Jackson's *Accidents in Abstract Painting*. Created in situ, it consists of a large model airplane on a paint-spattered sheet. "When he switched on the propellor," recalls Krzentowski enthusiastically, "paint went absolutely everywhere!"

Clémence und Didier Krzentowski sind die Besitzer von Kreo, der hippsten Designgalerie von Paris. Dort vertreten sie unter anderen die Bouroullec-Brüder, Martin Szekely und Marc Newson. Außerdem sind sie begeisterte Sammler. Nach eigener Auskunft besitzt er die größte Kollektion von Lampen des Designers Gino Sarfatti. Er hat aber auch noch zwei andere große Leidenschaften: Möbel von Pierre Paulin und von Künstlern geschaffene Spiegel. Die Wohnung des Paars ist voll bis unter die Decke mit einem anarchischen Mix von Objekten. Dazu zählen Künstlerinstallationen, von denen Richard Jacksons *Accidents in Abstract Painting* sicherlich die auffälligste ist. Sie entstand direkt vor Ort und besteht aus einem großen Modellflugzeug, das über einem farbbespritzten Laken schwebt. „Als er den Propeller anmachte", erinnert sich Didier Krzentowski mit Begeisterung, „spritzte die Farbe absolut überall hin!"

Clémence et Didier Krzentowski sont les propriétaires de la galerie de design super branché Kreo où ils représentent, entre autres, les frères Bouroullec, Martin Szekely et Marc Newson. Ce sont aussi d'avides collectionneurs notamment de meubles de Pierre Paulin, de miroirs d'artistes et de luminaires dont la plus grande collection de Gino Sarfatti. Leur appartement est bondé d'un mélange anarchique d'objets. Parmi eux, plusieurs installations artistiques dont la plus frappante est *Accidents in Abstract Painting* de Richard Jackson. Créée in situ, c'est une grande maquette d'avion sur un drap éclaboussé de peinture. « Quand il a mis l'hélice en route », se souvient Didier, « il y a eu de la peinture partout ! ».

← Vases by Ettore Sottsass, Wieki Somers, and Hella Jongerius are displayed on a Martin Szekely bookshelf. • Vasen von Ettore Sottsass, Wieki Somers und Hella Jongerius schmücken ein Regal von Martin Szekely. • Des vases d'Ettore Sottsass, de Wieki Somers et d'Hella Jongerius exposés dans une étagère de Martin Szekely.

P. 509 The master bedroom features globes by Ange Leccia and an array of colored rectangles by Allan McCollum. • Das große Schlafzimmer versammelt Globen von Ange Leccia sowie viele bunte Rechtecke von Allan McCollum. • Dans la chambre de maître, des globes d'Ange Leccia et un arrangement de rectangles de couleurs d'Allan McCollum.

← Richard Jackson's plane seems to hover in front of a seating group with a Marc Newson Orgone coffee table. • Richard Jacksons Flugzeug vor einer Sitzgruppe mit Orgone-Sofatisch von Marc Newson. • L'avion de Richard Jackson semble planer devant les fauteuils groupés autour de la table Orgone de Marc Newson.

↓ The living room is dominated by the Richard Jackson installation *Accidents in Abstract Painting*, which features a model airplane. • Im Wohnzimmer ist das Modellflugzeug von Richard Jacksons Installation *Accidents in Abstract Painting* der Blickfang. • L'installation *Accidents in Abstract Painting* de Richard Jackson, dont fait partie une maquette d'avion, domine le séjour.

↑ A red bench by the Bouroullecs and a yellow Pierre Paulin chair are grouped around the Szekely coffee table. The *U.S. Historians* artwork is by Sam Durant. • Eine rote Bank von den Bouroullec-Brüdern und ein gelber Stuhl von Pierre Paulin stehen um den Couchtisch von Szekely. Das Bild *U.S. Historians* stammt von Sam Durant. • Autour de la table basse de Szekely, un banc rouge des Bouroullec et un siège jaune de Pierre Paulin. Au mur, une œuvre de Sam Durant, *U. S. Historians*.

→ The boat-like bathtub was created by Wieki Somers. • Die Badewanne in Form eines aufgebockten Boots stammt von Wieki Somers. • La baignoire bateau est une œuvre de Wieki Somers.

PP. 514–515 On top of a Maarten van Severen sideboard, a parade of vases by artist-designers like Hella Jongerius, the Bouroullecs, and Jerszy Seymour. The glass-ball ceiling light is by Gino Sarfatti. • Vasen von Hella Jongerius, den Bouroullec-Brüdern und Jerszy Seymour wurden auf einem Sideboard von Maarten van Severen arrangiert. Die mittlere Deckenleuchte ist von Gino Sarfatti. • Des vases d'Hella Jongerius, des Bouroullec et de Jerszy Seymour sont regroupés sur une desserte de Maarten van Severen. Au centre, un lustre de Gino Sarfatti.

PARIS
FRANCE

Le Chic Historique

If modernity is a question of mixing styles, then this apartment is certainly of the present. For its former occupants, Jacques Garcia created an ornate, Neo-Gothic decor—there are 19th-century fabrics on the walls, rich colors, and kitchen cupboards made from the wood paneling of an old chapel. The master bathroom, meanwhile, is kitted out with a throne from a St. Petersburg palace and antique Roman onyx. The present owner has changed very little. He has even kept the curtains and some of his predecessors' old-style furniture. He did, however, bring with him an exceptional collection of 20th-century design pieces by Jean Royère, Gaetano Pesce, and the like. It took about two years for everything to find its place. Now that it has, each piece looks perfectly at home. As the owner says, "The mix may be daring, but it's also extremely harmonious."

Wenn Modernität bedeutet, Stile zu mischen, ist diese Wohnung mit Sicherheit zeitgemäß. Für ihre vorherigen Bewohner schuf Jacques Garcia ein opulentes, neugotisches Dekor. Es gibt Stofftapeten aus dem 19. Jahrhundert, leuchtende Farben und Küchenschränke, die aus der Holzvertäfelung einer alten Kapelle gefertigt wurden. Das Bad ist mit einem Thron aus einem St. Petersburger Palast ausgestattet sowie mit antikem römischem Onyx. Der heutige Eigentümer hat daran nur wenig verändert – er behielt sogar die Vorhänge sowie einige Stilmöbel seiner Vorgänger. Dafür brachte er eine außergewöhnliche Sammlung von Designerstücken des 20. Jahrhunderts mit, Objekte von Jean Royère, Gaetano Pesce und anderen. Es dauerte zwei Jahre, bis alles seinen Platz fand, aber jetzt stimmt das Gesamtbild. Oder wie der Besitzer sagt: „Die Mischung mag gewagt sein, sie ist aber auch extrem harmonisch."

Si la modernité appelle un mélange de styles, cet appartement reflète bien l'esprit de son temps. Jacques Garcia a créé pour ses anciens occupants un riche décor néogothique : teintures murales du 19e siècle, couleurs opulentes, placards de cuisine réalisés avec les boiseries d'une ancienne chapelle... Il y a même un trône venu d'un palais de Saint-Pétersbourg et de l'onyx de la Rome antique dans la salle de bains principale. Le nouveau propriétaire n'a pratiquement rien touché, conservant même les rideaux et certains meubles. En revanche, il a apporté avec lui son exceptionnelle collection de design du 20e siècle, dont des pièces de Jean Royère et de Gaetano Pesce. Il a fallu deux ans avant que chaque objet trouve sa place, mais à présent, comme il le dit lui-même : « le mélange est peut-être audacieux mais aussi très harmonieux. »

P.517 A suite of Jean Royère furniture in the entrance hall. It is arranged around a coffee table designed by Charlotte Perriand and Jean Prouvé, the terrier is a work by Jeff Koons. • Im Eingangsbereich wurden Jean-Royère-Möbel um einen Couchtisch von Charlotte Perriand und Jean Prouvé gruppiert. Der Terrier ist ein Multiple von Jeff Koons. • Dans le hall d'entrée, un ensemble de sièges de Jean Royère disposés autour d'une table basse de Charlotte Perriand et de Jean Prouvé. Le terrier est une œuvre de Jeff Koons.

← In the guest room, a George Nelson sofa sits beneath a work by Philippe Perrin titled *La Panoplie*, which incorporates objects used for boxing. • Im Gästezimmer steht ein Sofa von George Nelson unter einer Arbeit von Philippe Perrin mit dem Titel *La Panoplie*, die Boxzubehör enthält. • Dans la chambre d'amis, un canapé de George Nelson sous une œuvre de Philippe Perrin incorporant des objets du monde de la boxe et intitulée *La Panoplie*.

↓ Above the red velvet headboard in the master bedroom hangs a Jean Royère light fixture. The portraits of saints date from the 18th century. • Eine Jean-Royère-Leuchte hängt über dem mit rotem Samt bezogenen Betthaupt im Schlafzimmer. Die Heiligenbilder stammen aus dem 18. Jahrhundert. • Dans la chambre principale, un luminaire de Jean Royère est accroché au-dessus de la tête de lit en velours rouge. Les peintures religieuses datent du 18ᵉ siècle.

P. 520 The kitchen units were fronted with wood panelings from a chapel. The range is from La Cornue. • Die Front der Küchenschränke besteht aus den Holzvertäfelungen einer Kapelle. Der Herd ist von La Cornue. • Les placards de la cuisine ont été réalisés avec des boiseries récupérées dans une chapelle. La cuisinière vient de chez La Cornue.

P. 521 A throne from a St. Petersburg palace in the master bathroom. • Im Bad gibt es einen Thronrahmen aus einem Palast in St. Petersburg. • Dans la salle de bains principale, un trône provenant d'un palais de Saint-Pétersbourg.

← A Didier Marcel sculpture of a chocolate grinder stands on the stone coffee table in the dining room. The curvaceous chaise longue in front of it is a creation by Martin Szekely. • Auf dem Couchtisch mit Steinplatte im Esszimmer steht die Skulptur einer Schokoladenmühle von Didier Marcel. Die schnittige Chaiselongue im Vordergrund stammt von Martin Szekely. • Sur la table basse en pierre de la salle à manger, une sculpture de Didier Marcel représentant une broyeuse de chocolat. Devant, une chaise longue arrondie de Martin Szekely.

→ Painted a vivid green, the guest room features a chair by Gaetano Pesce in one corner. • Das Gästezimmer ist in einem kräftigen Grün gestrichen. In der Ecke steht ein Stuhl von Gaetano Pesce. • La chambre d'amis est peinte d'un vert vif, dans le coin, un siège de Gaetano Pesce.

→ The units beneath the desk feature inscriptions in the style of French artist Ben (Benjamin Vautier). • Die Schreibtischunterschränke sind im Stil des französischen Künstlers Ben (Benjamin Vautier) beschriftet. • Les meubles sous le bureau portent des inscriptions dans le style de l'artiste français Ben (Benjamin Vautier).

→ → The Neo-Gothic breakfast room harmonizes perfectly with the atmosphere of the apartment. • Der neugotische Frühstücksraum passt hervorragend zur Atmosphäre der Wohnung. • La « breakfast room » néogothique s'harmonise parfaitement avec l'esprit de l'appartement.

PARIS
FRANCE

Workshop of Wonders

When Isabelle Puech and Benoît Jamin first visited this former restoration workshop for fairground rides, it hadn't been occupied for some 35 years. "Everything was covered in plastic sheeting and it was pitch-black," recalls Jamin. Their goal, they recall, was to make it into something homey. They reconfigured the space around an internal patio and kept a wooden mezzanine and some old doors. Today, it is filled with almost as much poetry as the handbags that the pair create under the Jamin Puech label. There are chairs by Eames, Marcel Breuer, and Hans Wegner, as well as the skeleton of an ostrich, a stuffed crocodile, a collection of antlers, and an enormous Montblanc pen (no doubt a former publicity gadget). As they say, "It's at once a cabinet of curiosities and an industrial space, and somehow that's very cozy."

Als Isabelle Puech und Benoît Jamin die frühere Restaurierwerkstatt für Vergnügungspark-Attraktionen das erste Mal besichtigten, lag sie bereits seit mehr als 35 Jahren verlassen da. „Alles war mit Plastikfolie abgedeckt, und es war stockfinster", erinnert sich Jamin. Ihr Ziel war es, hier ein Zuhause zu schaffen. Als Zentrum des neuen Raumlayouts nahmen sie den alten Innenhof und behielten nur die Holzplanken der Galerie sowie einige alte Türen bei. Heute verfügen die Räumlichkeiten über fast so viel Poesie wie die Handtaschen, die das Paar unter dem Label Jamin Puech kreiert. Es gibt Stühle von Eames, Marcel Breuer und Hans Wegner, aber auch das Skelett eines Straußvogels, ein ausgestopftes Krokodil, eine Geweihsammlung und einen riesigen Montblanc-Füller (zweifellos ein einstiger Werbegag). Beide sagen über ihr Heim: „Es ist zugleich Kuriositätenkabinett, Industrieloft und ein gemütliches Zuhause."

Quand Isabelle Puech et Benoît Jamin ont découvert cet ancien atelier de restauration de manèges, il était abandonné depuis 35 ans. « Il était tapissé de bâches en plastique et il y faisait noir comme dans un four », se souvient Jamin. Pour le rendre chaleureux, ils ont reconfiguré l'espace autour d'un patio tout en conservant la mezzanine en bois et quelques vieilles portes. Aujourd'hui, le décor est aussi poétique que les sacs à main que le couple crée pour la marque Jamin Puech. Des sièges d'Eames, de Marcel Breuer et de Hans Wegner côtoient un squelette d'autruche, un crocodile empaillé, une collection de massacres et un énorme stylo Montblanc (sans doute un gadget publicitaire). « C'est à la fois un cabinet de curiosités, un espace industriel et un nid douillet », déclarent-ils.

← The staircase to the upper level of the library was discovered at an antique market. • Von einem Antikmarkt stammt diese Treppe, die den oberen Teil der Buchsammlung erschließt. • L'escalier qui permet d'accéder à la partie supérieure de la bibliothèque a été trouvé sur un marché des antiquaires.

→ The bathroom features old coat closets from the property's days as a workshop. • Das Bad wurde mit Garderobenschränken aus der Restaurierwerkstatt möbliert. • D'anciennes armoires de vestiaires trouvées dans l'atelier de restauration meublent la salle de bains.

↓ In the corridor, a 19th-century plaster bust stands next to an antique magnifying glass. • Im Korridor steht eine Gipsbüste aus dem 19. Jahrhundert neben einem alten Vergrößerungsglas. • Dans le corridor, ce buste en plâtre du 19ᵉ siècle côtoie une loupe ancienne.

↙ On the way from the dining room to the library you pass a plywood chair from the 1950s. • Auf dem Weg vom Esszimmer in die Bibliothek begegnet man einem Schichtholzstuhl aus den 1950ern. • Dans la galerie qui mène de la salle à manger à la bibliothèque, une chaise en bois lamellé des années 1950.

P. 525 A covered courtyard contains the library—and a 16-foot-long Montblanc pen that gives a surreal pop touch. • Ein überdachter Innenhof birgt die Bibliothek, in der als poppig surreales Dekor der fast fünf Meter lange Montblanc-Füller steht. • Une cour intérieure à toit vitré abrite la bibliothèque et – telle une sculpture pop-surréaliste – un stylo-plume Montblanc de presque cinq mètres de haut.

↑ The dining room was given a new staircase and is furnished with Eames chairs from a 1950s Herman Miller edition. • Eames-Stühle aus einer Herman-Miller-Edition der 1950er Jahre stehen in dem mit neuen Treppen versehenen Esszimmer. • Dans la salle à manger dotée d'un nouvel escalier, des chaises Eames d'une édition Herman Miller des années 1950.

→ Glass-paneled partition walls from the old workshop were reused to separate off the kitchen. • Verglaste Trennwände aus der einstigen Werkstatt separieren die Küche vom Essbereich. • Des cloisons vitrées de l'ancien atelier ont été réutilisées dans la cuisine.

P.530 Portraits from the 18th and 19th centuries are propped up on the gallery; the two lampshades above the dining table were designed by Jamin and Puech. • Porträtgemälde aus dem 18. und 19. Jahrhundert säumen die Galerie, die beiden Lampenschirme über dem Esstisch entwarfen die Besitzer. • Sur la galerie, des portraits à l'huile des 18ᵉ et 19ᵉ siècles, les deux abat-jours au-dessus de la table sont une création des propriétaires.

P.531 In the entrance to the library, an oil painting by Jean-Pierre Pincemin rests on a Jean Prouvé bed. • Auf einem Bett von Jean Prouvé lehnt Jean-Pierre Pincemins Ölgemälde am Eingang zur Bibliothek. • Posé sur un lit de Jean Prouvé, le tableau à l'huile de Jean-Pierre Pincemin à l'entrée de la bibliothèque.

PARIS
FRANCE

Bonjour Glamour

"When I first took this apartment, it was beyond shabby chic," declares designer Hervé Van der Straeten. Twenty years later and it's simply chic. Take the sitting room with its heady but harmonious mix of styles—a Louis XVI sofa, Danish 1960s furniture, a mobile by artist Xavier Veilhan, and many of Van der Straeten's own creations. After starting off designing jewelry for the likes of Thierry Mugler and Christian Lacroix, he ebbed into creating furniture, mirrors and dramatic chandeliers and now counts such top decorators as Peter Marino and Alberto Pinto among his fans. His friends, meanwhile, are often invited round for dinner. Van der Straeten created the large, open kitchen so that he can cook and chat with them at the same time. He also kitted out the bedroom all in red and reupholstered a pair of Le Corbusier armchairs in shocking green satin. As he says, "It makes them more glamorous."

„Als ich mich für diese Wohnung entschied, war sie jenseits von ‚shabby chic'", meint der Designer Hervé Van der Straeten. Zwanzig Jahre später ist sie einfach nur chic. Da ist zum einen das Wohnzimmer mit seinem harmonischen Stil-Mix aus einem Louis-XVI-Sofa, skandinavischen Möbeln aus den 1960er Jahren, einem Mobile des Künstlers Xavier Veilhan und vielen Entwürfen von Van der Straeten selbst. Nachdem er Schmuck für so große Namen wie Thierry Mugler und Christian Lacroix entworfen hatte, verlegte sich der Designer auf das Gestalten von Möbeln, Spiegeln und extravaganten Leuchten. Heute zählt er Top-Interiordesigner wie Peter Marino und Alberto Pinto zu seinen Fans. Gern lädt er seine Freunde zum Abendessen ein und entwarf deshalb eine große, offene Küche, damit er gleichzeitig kochen und sich unterhalten kann. Er kleidete das Schlafzimmer ganz in Rot ein und ließ zwei Le-Corbusier-Sessel mit leuchtend grünem Satin beziehen. „Das macht sie glamouröser", findet Van der Straeten. Und wer wollte ihm widersprechen.

« Quand j'ai pris l'appartement, il était au-delà du ‹ shabby chic › », déclare Hervé Van der Straeten. Vingt ans plus tard, il est simplement chic. Dans son séjour au mélange de styles grisant et harmonieux, un canapé Louis XVI, des meubles danois des années 1960 et un mobile spectaculaire de Xavier Veilhan côtoient les créations du maître de maison. Ce dernier a retapissé une paire de fauteuils de Le Corbusier en satin vert shocking « pour les rendre plus glamour ». Sa chambre est rouge du sol au plafond. Après avoir dessiné des bijoux pour Thierry Mugler et Christian Lacroix, Van der Straeten s'est lancé dans la création de mobilier, de miroirs et de lustres et compte aujourd'hui parmi ses admirateurs de grands décorateurs tels Peter Marino et Alberto Pinto. Comme il aime recevoir ses amis à dîner, il a créé une grande cuisine ouverte pour pouvoir papoter tout en leur mitonnant de petits plats. Il a habillé la chambre à coucher de rouge et a fait recouvrir de satin vert brillant deux fauteuils Le Corbusier. Van der Straeten trouve que cela leur donne du glamour et qui le contredira ?

← Both the Solaire mirror and the Franges cabinet in the entry corridor were created by Van der Straeten. • Sowohl der Solaire-Spiegel als auch der Franges-Schrank im Flur sind Entwürfe Van der Straetens. • Le miroir Solaire et le cabinet Franges dans l'entrée sont des créations de Van der Straeten.

↑ The living-room boasts Xavier Veilhan's Petit Mobile, red plaster column stumps from the 1930s and one of the designer's Mondrian coffee tables. • Im Wohnzimmer sind unterschiedliche Objekte wie Xavier Veilhans *Petit Mobile*, rote Gipssäulen-Stümpfe aus den 1930er Jahren, ein Sofa aus dem 18. Jahrhundert sowie einer der Mondrian-Couchtische des Designers kombiniert. • Un *Petit Mobile* de Xavier Veilhan, des colonnes en plâtre rouge des années 1930, un canapé du 18ᵉ siècle et une des tables basses Mondrian dessinées par le maître de maison.

P. 533 The all-red bedroom features Pierre Paulin's Orange Slice Chair and one of Van der Straeten's Capsule stools. • Im Schlafzimmer stehen Pierre Paulins Orange-Slice-Sessel und einer von Van der Straetens Capsule-Hockern. • Dans la chambre rouge, un fauteuil Orange Slice de Pierre Paulin et un des tabourets Capsule de Van der Straeten.

PP. 536–537 One of Van der Straeten's Dada mirrors hangs above the fireplace. • Über dem Wohnzimmerkamin hängt ein Dada-Spiegel von Van der Straeten. • Un des miroirs Dada de Van der Straeten au-dessus de la cheminée du séjour.

PARIS
FRANCE

Futuristic Fifties

In 2004, Marc Newson, design master and world-class traveler, called his associate architect in Paris, Sébastien Segers, with a mission: "I've seen an extraordinary house," Segers was told. "We've got to find the owner!" The house in question is situated near the Parc des Buttes-Chaumont and was built in 1953 by the French architect Fernand Riehl as his own home and office. It was lying more or less abandoned. "The previous owner," says Segers, "had ripped out almost everything inside." Newson masterminded the restoration as he wanted to ensure that it would be as sympathetic to the original as possible. Outside, the windows and concrete detailing were restored. Inside, the layout was more or less maintained and traditional materials, such as Carrara marble in the bathroom and leather for the upstairs flooring, were employed. A touch of modernity was added with the inclusion of rounded architectural forms and numerous contemporary design classics. "I can't imagine getting rid of this place," states Marc Newson. "It's unique."

Im Jahr 2004 rief der bekannte, international tätige Industriedesigner Marc Newson seinen Pariser Geschäftspartner, den Architekten Sébastien Segers an. „Ich habe ein außergewöhnliches Haus entdeckt", bekam Segers zu hören. „Wir müssen den Eigentümer ausfindig machen." Das fragliche Haus liegt unweit des Parc des Buttes-Chaumont und wurde 1953 von dem französischen Architekten Fernand Riehl als dessen Wohnhaus und Büro gebaut. Inzwischen lag es mehr oder weniger verlassen da. „Der Vorbesitzer", so Segers, „hatte beinahe alles rausgerissen." Newson entwarf das Konzept für die Restaurierung, wobei er dem Original so weit wie möglich nahe kommen wollte. An der Fassade wurden die Fenster und Betondetails wiederhergestellt. Der Grundriss blieb größtenteils erhalten, für neue Features wählten Segers und sein Chef durchwegs traditionelle Materialien wie Carrara-Marmor im Bad und Leder für den Bodenbelag im Obergeschoss. Die Einfügung abgerundeter architektonischer Formen und zahlreiche aktuelle Designklassiker holten die Räume in die Gegenwart. „Ich kann mir nicht vorstellen, das Haus je wieder aufzugeben", so Marc Newson. „Es ist einzigartig."

En 2004, Marc Newson, le designer industriel international bien connu, a appelé son associé à Paris, l'architecte Sébastien Segers : « J'ai vu une maison extraordinaire. Il faut trouver le propriétaire ! ». Située près du parc des Buttes-Chaumont, la maison en question, plus ou moins abandonnée, fut construite en 1953 par l'architecte Fernand Riehl pour y vivre et travailler. « Le précédent occupant avait déjà presque tout détruit à l'intérieur » explique Segers. Le nouveau propriétaire a conçu la restauration qu'il voulait la plus respectueuse possible de l'original. Les fenêtres et les détails en béton de la façade ont été restaurés, à l'intérieur le plan au sol a été plus ou moins conservé en utilisant des matériaux traditionnels tels que le marbre de Carrare pour la salle de bains et le cuir pour le sol à l'étage. Des formes architecturales arrondies et des meubles design apportent à l'ensemble une touche de modernité. « Je ne peux imaginer me défaire de cet endroit. Il est unique » déclare Marc Newson.

P. 539 Both the office desk and tubular-steel chair were designed by Marc Newson. • Büroschreibtisch und Stahlrohrstuhl sind Entwürfe von Marc Newson. • Le bureau et la chaise en tube métallique ont été dessinés par Marc Newson.

← The bathroom looks like a boat cabin in Carrara marble. • Das Bad wirkt wie eine Bootskabine in Carrara-Marmor. • La salle de bains a l'air d'une cabine en marbre de Carrare.

↓ In the dining room, Achille Castiglioni's Arco lamp hovers over a table made from African bubinga wood. • Im Esszimmer überwölbt Achille Castiglionis Arco-Lampe einen Tisch aus afrikanischem Bubinga-Holz. • Dans la salle à manger, un lampadaire Arco d'Achille Castiglioni éclaire une table en bubinga africain.

↑ Newson had the custom-made sheet-metal doors of the kitchen units painted a powder blue, to match the Aga range. • Die Blechtüren seiner Maßküche ließ Newson im pudrigen Blau des Aga-Herds streichen. • Newson a harmonisé les portes en métal de la cuisine sur mesure avec le bleu pastel de la cuisinière Aga.

→ Franco Albini's shelving system was chosen for the office. • An einer Wand des Arbeitszimmers steht ein Regal von Franco Albini. • Dans le bureau, des étagères de Franco Albini.

PP. 542–543 On the second floor, a foldaway blue lacquered screen can be extended in order to enclose the master bed. • Im ersten Stock lässt sich ein blau lackierter Wandschirm ausfalten, um den Bereich des Betts abzugrenzen. • Au premier étage, le paravent en laque bleu se déploie pour préserver l'intimité de la chambre à coucher.

PARIS
FRANCE

Creative Noblesse

"I can't live without color," affirms Michelle Halard. "For me, it's essential." Bright hues certainly dominate the 1,300-square-foot apartment she shares with her husband right by the church of Saint-Sulpice. The dining room is purple, the sitting room green, and the bedroom an orangey-red. The couple have been in the interiors business since 1950 and are best known for the wonderfully *propre* furniture they created under the Yves Halard label, some of which is today available at Pierre Frey. Michelle has also outfitted restaurants and hotels, and created dinnerware for Gien. At home, their decorating approach was free and easy. "It's simply jam-packed with things," admits Michelle. Among them are numerous objects of whimsy—a model of a Danish boat, chairs from a stage set, and a wooden figure from a 19th-century merry-go-round.

„Ich kann nicht ohne Farben leben", erklärt Michelle Halard. „Für mich sind sie essentiell." So wird die 120 Quadratmeter große Wohnung direkt neben der Kirche Saint-Sulpice, die sie gemeinsam mit ihrem Mann bewohnt, von prägnanten Tönen dominiert: Die Wände des Esszimmers sind lila, die im Wohnzimmer grün und das Schlafzimmer leuchtet in Orangerot und Pink. Das Paar ist bereits seit 1950 im Interior-Design tätig und vor allem für seine wunderbar korrekten Möbel, die es unter dem Label Yves Halard entwirft, bekannt (einige davon sind bei Pierre Frey erhältlich). Michelle hat auch Restaurants und Hotels ausgestattet sowie Geschirr für Gien entworfen. Bei sich zu Hause sind die beiden ganz locker und unverkrampft an die Einrichtung herangegangen. „Die Wohnung ist einfach mit allem Möglichen vollgestopft", gibt Michelle zu. Unter anderem mit viel Spleenigem, wie dem Modell eines dänischen Boots, Stühlen aus einem Theaterfundus und einer Holzfigur von einem Karussell aus dem 19. Jahrhundert.

« Je ne peux pas vivre sans couleurs. Elles me sont vitales », affirme Michelle Halard. De fait, les 120 mètres carrés du couple, à deux pas de l'église Saint-Sulpice, sont dominés par les tons vifs : la salle à manger est violette, le salon vert et la chambre rouge orangé. Ils travaillent dans la décoration depuis 1950 et sont surtout connus pour le mobilier qu'ils créent pour la marque Yves Halard (une partie est disponible chez Pierre Frey). Michelle a également décoré des hôtels et des restaurants, et dessiné de la vaisselle pour Gien. Dans leur appartement, ils ont opté pour un décor décontracté et facile à vivre. « Un vrai bric-à-brac », reconnaît-elle. On y trouve de nombreux objets coup de cœur : une maquette de bateau danois, des chaises de théâtre et une figure en bois provenant d'un manège du 19ᵉ siècle.

P. 545 The apartment looks out directly onto the church of Saint-Sulpice. Throughout, the flat is filled with a whole host of unusual objects, such as the wooden Pinocchio on the small cylinder desk. • Von der Wohnung sieht man direkt auf die Kirche Saint-Sulpice. Alle Räume sind voller ungewöhnlicher Objekte – wie dem hölzernen Pinocchio auf dem Rollschreibtisch. • Les fenêtres donnent sur l'église Saint-Sulpice. L'appartement est rempli d'objets inhabituels comme le Pinocchio en bois sur le bureau rouleau.

← The armchair was originally made for a theater production. • Der Sessel wurde ursprünglich für eine Theateraufführung angefertigt. • Ce fauteuil a été conçu pour un décor de théâtre.

↓ Above the bed in pink, a female nude by Bernard Dufour. • Über dem Bett in Pink hängt eine Arbeit von Bernard Dufour, die einen weiblichen Akt zeigt.• Au-dessus du lit rose bonbon, un nu féminin de Bernard Dufour.

→ Two orange Louis XVI armchairs stand in front of the living-room windows. The rug was created by blowing up the pattern of an Yves Halard fabric. • Zwei orangefarben bezogene Louis-XVI-Sessel stehen vor den Wohnzimmerfenstern. Der Teppich entstand durch die Vergrößerung des Musters eines Yves-Halard-Stoffs. • Deux fauteuils Louis XVI orange devant les fenêtres du salon. Le dessin du tapis est un agrandissement d'un motif de tissu Yves Halard.

← The Yves Halard sofa is upholstered in a cotton velvet from Nobilis and the 18th-century prie-dieu in a yellow damask. The photo with a view from the Casa Malaparte in Capri was taken by the Halards' son, François. • Das Yves-Halard-Sofa ist mit Baumwollsamt von Nobilis bezogen und der Betstuhl aus dem 18. Jahrhundert mit gelbem Damast. Das Foto, das einen Ausblick von der Casa Malaparte auf Capri zeigt, wurde von François, dem Sohn der Halards, aufgenommen. • Le canapé Yves Halard est tapissé d'un velours de coton Nobilis et le prie-Dieu du 18ᵉ siècle d'un damas jaune. La vue depuis la maison de Malaparte à Capri est une photo du fils des Halard, François.

↓ A Neo-Gothic cabinet dominates the dining room. The dining chairs are the Clarisse model from Yves Halard. • Ein neugotischer Schrank ist der Blickfang im Esszimmer. Die Stühle sind das Modell Clarisse von Yves Halard. • Un vaisselier néogothique domine la salle à manger. Les chaises Clarisse sont d'Yves Halard.

↑ Michelle often works on her fabric collections at the kitchen table. • Michelle arbeitet oft am Küchentisch an ihrer Kollektion von Bezugsstoffen. • Sur la table de la cuisine, Michelle travaille à sa collection de tissus.

↓ A 1930s vase in hammered silver. • Eine Vase der 1930er-Jahre aus gehämmertem Silber, die die Halards vor etwa 50 Jahren kauften. • Un vase en argent martelé des années 1930.

↓ A yellow armchair from the Yves Halard collection. • Ein gelber Sessel aus der Yves-Halard-Kollektion steht im Wohnzimmer. • Dans le salon, un fauteuil jaune de la collection Yves Halard.

PARIS
FRANCE

Baroque 'n' Roll

This apartment in the 16th arrondissement certainly has a lot going for it: a 1,500-square-foot roof garden, views of the Eiffel Tower, and a spectacular double-height main room. It was originally constructed around a number of pre-existing architectural elements. In the wood-paneled sitting room are a stained-glass window and vintage Versailles parquet. In the atelier-like main room, an imposing oak fireplace carved with lion's heads, a 19th-century balustrade, and 15th-century pillars. Architect Christian Baquiast's mandate was to open up the space. He created an aperture above the fireplace and bestowed the master bedroom with a porthole. He also paid homage to the flat's architectural heritage. "My idea," he says, "was to use industrial materials, but to give them a classical twist." An example? A concrete wall bearing a wood-grain relief that was created by using the silicone mold of an oak plank.

Dieses Apartment im 16. Arrondissement hat wirklich einiges zu bieten, unter anderem einen 140 Quadratmeter gro-ßen Dachgarten mit Blick auf den Eiffelturm und einen spektakulär hohen Raum mit Galerie. Ursprünglich wurde es um mehrere Architekturelemente herumgebaut. Im holzvertäfelten Wohnsalon gibt es ein Butzenscheibenfenster sowie altes Versailles-Parkett. Im atelierartigen Hauptraum befinden sich ein imposanter Kaminrahmen aus Eiche mit geschnitzten Löwenköpfen sowie eine Empore aus dem 19. Jahrhundert. Die zentrale Aufgabe des Architekten Christian Baquiast bestand darin, den Räumen das Klaustrophobische zu nehmen. Er sorgte für einen Durchbruch über dem Kamin und bestückte das Schlafzimmer mit einem Bullauge. Trotzdem respektierte er das architektonische Erbe der Wohnung. „Meine Idee war, Industriematerialien zu benutzen, ihnen aber einen klassischen Dreh zu geben." Ein Beispiel? Die wie Holz gemaserte Betonwand, für die eine Silikonform mit dem Abdruck von altem Eichenholz genutzt wurde.

Cet appartement du 16e arrondissement a tout pour lui : un jardin en terrasse de 140 mètres carrés, des vues sur la Tour Eiffel et un séjour spectaculaire avec double hauteur sous plafond. Il a été construit autour d'éléments architectu-raux. Le salon lambrissé possède un vitrail et un parquet Versailles ; le living, une imposante cheminée en chêne sculp-tée de têtes de lion, une balustrade du 19e siècle et des poutres du 15e. L'architecte Christian Baquiast avait pour consigne d'ouvrir l'espace. Il a créé une ouverture au-dessus de la cheminée et un hublot dans la chambre principale, respectant le patrimoine architectural des lieux. « J'ai voulu utiliser des matériaux industriels en leur donnant une tour-nure classique », explique-t-il. Exemple : un mur en béton texturé imitant le grain du bois, réalisé à l'aide d'une forme en silicone avec les empreintes d'une planche en chêne.

← Baquiast punched a porthole into one wall between master bedroom and main room. • Baquiast ließ ein Bullauge in die Wand zwischen Schlafzimmer und Hauptraum brechen. • Baquiast a percé un hublot dans un mur de la chambre principale.

→ The main room is structured around a 19th-century fireplace. The two black armchairs are by Ignazio Gardella. • Den Fokus des Galerieraums bildet ein Kamin aus dem 19. Jahrhundert. Die beiden schwarzen Sessel entwarf Ignazio Gardella. • La pièce principale s'articule autour d'une cheminée du 19ᵉ siècle. Les deux fauteuils noirs sont d'Ignazio Gardella.

↓ At the window, an icon of 1980s design: the Paris chair in welded sheet steel by André Dubreuil. • Am Fenster steht eine Ikone des Designs der 1980er: André Dubreuils Paris-Stuhl aus Stahlblech. • Près de la fenêtre, une icône du design des années 1980 : la chaise Paris en tôle d'acier d'André Dubreuil.

↙ In the living room is a perfectly preserved leaded glass window. • Im Salon befindet sich ein einwandfrei erhaltenes Bleiglasfenster. • Dans le salon se trouve un vitrail parfaitement conservé.

P. 551 The dining table is by Warren Platner, the copper and glass lantern (one of a pair) is a one-off creation by André Dubreuil. • Der Esstisch ist von Warren Platner. Die Kronleuchter aus Kupfer und Glas sind Unikate von André Dubreuil. • La table de salle à manger est de Warren Platner. Les lustres en cuivre et verre sont des pièces uniques signées André Dubreuil.

← The wooden balustrade that frames the gallery dates from the 19th century. • Das Holzgeländer der Galerie stammt aus dem 19. Jahrhundert. • La balustrade en bois de la galerie date du 19ᵉ siècle.

↑ In the wood-paneled sitting room, Jean Royère's Œuf sofa and chairs still have their original 1950s fabric. The coffee table is by Olivier Mourgue and the photo a collaboration between Bruno Bressolin and Bruno Juminer. • Das Œuf-Sofa und die dazugehörigen Sessel von Jean Royère haben immer noch ihren Originalbezug aus den 1950er Jahren. Der Couchtisch ist von Olivier Mourgue und das Foto eine Gemeinschaftsarbeit von Bruno Bressolin und Bruno Juminer. • Dans le salon lambrissé, le canapé et les fauteuils Œuf de Jean Royère possèdent encore leur tissu floral imprimé d'origine. La table basse est d'Olivier Mourgue. La photo est une œuvre conjointe de Bruno Bressolin et de Bruno Juminer.

PARIS
FRANCE

When the Sky Is the Limit

Perched nine floors up on the top of a building on the Right Bank, Sean McEvoy's flat affords spectacular vistas of the cityscape. The bedroom looks out onto Sacré-Cœur and the Eiffel Tower, the sitting room onto the famous Parisian rooftops. When the American architect first saw the space, it was very different—"a series of small rooms with a rusting veranda at the front." As there were no supporting walls, he was able to rip everything out and start all over again. The result is both free-flowing and refreshingly open. The central cube, which contains the bathroom and closets, does not touch the ceiling. The kitchen is defined simply by a 16-foot-long Corian bar and there are no curtains or blinds on the windows. The decoration is also deliberately simple. "What's important here is Paris," states McEvoy. "I didn't want anything to compete with that view."

Das Apartment von Sean McEvoy sitzt als neunte Etage auf dem Dach eines Hauses am rechten Seine-Ufer und bietet einen spektakulären Ausblick auf die Stadt. Vom Schlafzimmer schaut man auf die Kirche Sacré-Cœur und den Eiffelturm, vom Wohnzimmer über die berühmten Pariser Dächer. Als der amerikanische Architekt das erste Mal in der Wohnung stand, sah sie ganz anders aus – „mehrere kleine Zimmer mit einer rostigen Veranda davor". Da es sich nicht um tragende Wände handelte, konnte er alle abtragen und ganz von vorn beginnen. Das Ergebnis sind ineinanderfließende, erfrischend offene Räume. Der Kubus, der das Bad und Einbauschränke enthält, berührt die Decke nicht. Die Küche wird einfach nur durch eine fünf Meter lange Theke aus Corian abgetrennt, und die Fenster besitzen weder Vorhänge noch Rollos. Auch die Einrichtung ist bewusst schlicht gehalten. „Auf Paris kommt es an", erklärt McEvoy. „Nichts sollte mit dieser Aussicht konkurrieren."

Situé au neuvième et dernier étage d'un immeuble de la rive droite, l'appartement de l'architecte américain Sean McEvoy jouit de vues spectaculaires. La chambre donne sur le Sacré-Cœur et la tour Eiffel, le salon sur les célèbres toits de Paris. Quand il l'a vu la première fois, il n'y avait « qu'une série de petites pièces avec une véranda rouillée sur le devant ». Comme il n'y avait pas de murs porteurs, il a pu tout abattre et repartir de rien. Le résultat est fluide, ouvert et frais. Le cube qui contient la salle de bains et des placards ne touche pas le plafond. La cuisine est définie simplement par un bar en Corian de cinq mètres de long. Il n'y a ni rideaux ni stores aux fenêtres. La décoration est délibérément dépouillée. « L'important ici, c'est Paris », explique-t-il. « Je ne voulais rien qui puisse détourner l'attention de cette vue. »

P. 557 The birch plywood desk was designed by McEvoy. The title of the Wout Berger photo is *Ruigoord II*. • Der Tisch aus Birkensperrholz wurde von McEvoy entworfen. Die Fotoarbeit *Ruigoord II* ist von Wout Berger. • Le bureau en contreplaqué de bouleau a été dessiné par McEvoy. La photo de Wout Berger s'intitule *Ruigoord II*.

← A view from the sitting area into the kitchen. The stools are the Hi-Pad model, designed by Jasper Morrison for Cappellini. • Ein Blick aus dem Wohnzimmerbereich auf die Küche. Die Barhocker sind das Modell Hi-Pad von Jasper Morrison für Cappellini. • La cuisine vue du séjour. Les tabourets Hi-Pad ont été dessinés par Jasper Morrison pour Cappellini.

↑ Architect Sean McEvoy designed the modular chaise longue for his home himself. • Die modulare Chaiselonge entwarf der Architekt Sean McEvoy selbst. • La chaise-longue modulaire a été conçue par l'architecte Sean McEvoy.

↓ Jenny, the dog, lies in front of a block that houses both the bathroom and closets. • Hündin Jenny entspannt vor einem Quader, in dem das Bad und Einbauschränke untergebracht sind. • La chienne Jenny est couchée devant le cube qui accueille la salle de bains et des placards.

PP. 560–561 The sitting room offers breathtaking views over the rooftops of Paris. The 1950s Pierre Paulin chairs are upholstered in Leatherette and the 1949 Max Bill coffee table is made from birch and linoleum. • Das Wohnzimmer bietet einen atemberaubenden Blick über die Dächer von Paris. Die Pierre-Paulin-Sessel sind mit Kunstleder bezogen, Max Bills Couchtisch von 1949 besteht aus Birkenholz und Linoleum. • Le séjour offre des vues superbes sur les toits de Paris. Les chaises de Pierre Paulin sont tapissées en skaï, et la table basse de Max Bill datée de 1949 est en bois de bouleau et linoléum.

↑ McEvoy created the base of the bed himself. The 1950s fiberglass and steel chair was designed by Gabriel Vacher and the articulated lamp bought at the Montreuil flea market. • McEvoy designte sein Bettpodest selbst. Der Sessel aus Fiberglas und Stahl ist ein Entwurf von Gabriel Vacher und die kippbare Lampe ein Fund vom Flohmarkt in Montreuil. • McEvoy a dessiné la base du lit. La chaise en acier et fibre de verre est de Gabriel Vacher. La lampe articulée a été trouvée aux Puces de Montreuil.

→ The kitchen counter in Corian fits perfectly into the strict geometry of the space. • Die Küchentheke aus Corian fügt sich perfekt in die strikte Geometrie des Raums. • Le comptoir de la cuisine en Corian s'intègre parfaitement dans la stricte géométrie blanche de la pièce.

PARIS
FRANCE

More Would Be a Bore

Simon de Pury's Parisian pied-à-terre is housed in an 18th-century town mansion in the Marais, built by Claude-Nicolas Ledoux. Author Madame de Staël was born here in 1766. More recently, de Pury's duplex belonged to German artist Anselm Kiefer. De Pury is chairman of the auction house Phillips de Pury & Company and, today, the apartment doubles as offices for the firm's three Parisian employees. The decor is distinctly purist which makes the furniture by artists stand out even more. Objects may be few and far between, but each has an interesting provenance: There are several pieces by Ron Arad, a desk by Martin Szekely, as well as chairs and a sofa by the Campana brothers. There is also an immense dining table and chairs specially commissioned from the Austrian artist Franz West. The former proved so huge that a special crane had to be hired to lift it into the building!

Simon de Purys Pariser Pied-à-terre befindet sich im Marais, in einem Stadtpalais aus dem 18. Jahrhundert, das von Claude-Nicolas Ledoux erbaut wurde. Die Schriftstellerin Madame de Staël kam hier 1766 zur Welt, zuletzt gehörte de Purys Duplex dem deutschen Künstler Anselm Kiefer. De Pury ist Präsident des Auktionshauses Phillips de Pury & Company, seine Wohnung dient gleichzeitig als Büro für die drei Pariser Angestellten der Firma. Die Möblierung ist bewusst puristisch. Es gibt nur wenige, locker verteilte Einrichtungsgegenstände, aber jedes Stück hat eine interessante Herkunft. Da sind verschiedene Entwürfe von Ron Arad, ein Tisch von Martin Szekely sowie Stühle und ein Sofa der Campana-Brüder. Der riesige Esstisch ist eine Sonderanfertigung des Künstlers Franz West, von dem auch die Stühle sind. Dieser Tisch musste mit einem Spezialkran in das Gebäude gehievt werden!

Le pied-à-terre de Simon de Pury est situé dans un hôtel particulier du Marais, bâti au 18ᵉ siècle par Claude-Nicolas Ledoux. Madame de Staël y est née en 1766. Plus récemment, ce duplex appartenait à l'artiste allemand Anselm Kiefer. Président de la maison de ventes Phillips de Pury & Company, Pury accueille également chez lui les bureaux des trois employés de sa branche parisienne. Le décor est puriste. Les objets sont rares mais chacun a son histoire. Il y a plusieurs pièces de Ron Arad, un bureau de Martin Szekely, des fauteuils et un canapé des frères Campana. La table immense et les chaises qui l'entourent ont été commandées spécialement à l'artiste Franz West. Il a fallu louer une grue pour les hisser dans l'appartement !

P. 565 The dining table and chairs were specially commissioned from Franz West. The tabletop was made from part of the floor of the Austrian artist's studio. • Der Esstisch und die Stühle sind eine Spezialanfertigung von Franz West. Die Tischplatte besteht aus einem Teil des Bodens im Atelier des österreichischen Künstlers. • La table et les chaises de la salle à manger ont été commandées spécialement à Franz West. Le plateau de table a été réalisé avec une partie du sol de l'atelier de l'artiste autrichien.

↑ A series of Mario Testino photos hangs —temporarily—above de Pury's bed on the upper floor of the duplex. To the left is a 16th-century stone skull and a wooden sculpture of the Madonna and Child. To the right, Axel Salto's Sprouting Vase and a ceramic lamp base by Georges Jouve. • Eine Fotoserie von Mario Testino hängt vorübergehend über de Purys Bett im oberen Geschoss des Duplex. Links davon sieht man einen steinernen Totenkopf aus dem 16. Jahrhundert und eine Holzskulptur der Jungfrau Maria mit Kind. Rechts stehen Axel Saltos „Sprouting-Vase" und ein Keramiklampenfuß von Georges Jouve. • Une série de photos de Mario Testino est temporairement au-dessus du lit à l'étage supérieur du duplex.

À gauche, un crâne en pierre du 16e siècle et une sculpture en bois d'une Vierge à l'Enfant. À droite, le Sprouting Vase d'Axel Salto et un pied de lampe en céramique créé par Georges Jouve.

→ Also in de Pury's bedroom, the A.K. desk by Martin Szekely, the Little Heavy Chair by Ron Arad and the steel-wire Corallo armchair by the Campana brothers. • In de Purys Schlafzimmer stehen auch der A.K.-Schreibtisch von Martin Szekely, der Little Heavy Chair von Ron Arad sowie der Stahldrahtsessel Corallo der Campana-Brüder. • Aussi dans de Pury's chambre : le bureau A.K. de Martin Szekely, la Little Heavy Chair de Ron Arad et le fauteuil en fil d'acier Corallo des frères Campana.

←→ The minimalistic kitchen and bathroom reflect de Pury's preference for
pared-down spaces with a certain sensual rigor. • Die minimalistische Küche
und das Bad verraten de Purys Vorliebe
für puristische Räume voll sinnlicher
Strenge. • La cuisine et la salle de bains
minimalistes reflètent le goût de Pury
pour les espaces épurés avec une
rigueur sensuelle.

"I wanted the rooms to be at once simple and grand.
I like it spartan if it's sensual at the same time." SIMON DE PURY

„Ich wollte, dass die Räume schlicht und zugleich eindrucksvoll sind.
Ich mag das Spartanische, wenn es zugleich sinnlich ist."
« Je voulais des espaces à la fois sobres et impressionnants.
J'aime le côté spartiate s'il est en même temps sensuel. »

PARIS
FRANCE

Living with True Treasures

Swiss-born attorney-at-law Martin Hatebur bought his first work of art (an untitled piece by Christopher Wool) in 1996. Today, it hangs in his Paris living room. The front of the two-floor flat looks directly over the Seine. At the back, the kitchen is housed in what was originally a winter garden built by Gustave Eiffel. Hatebur says it took him about ten years to furnish the place. Over that time, he has accumulated every light created by his designer friend, Arik Levy, as well as numerous pieces by Charlotte Perriand, Jean Prouvé, and Pierre Jeanneret. Still, his main passion remains art. He talks about discovering Polish painter Wilhelm Sasnal on a trip to Warsaw and admits to having some one hundred works divided between Paris and his home in Basel.

Der in der Schweiz geborene Rechtsanwalt Martin Hatebur erwarb sein erstes Kunstwerk 1996 (eine Arbeit von Christopher Wool ohne Titel). Heute hängt es in seinem Pariser Wohnzimmer. Der Blick aus der über zwei Geschosse reichenden Wohnung geht direkt auf die Seine hinaus. Die auf der Hofseite liegende Küche befindet sich in einem früheren Wintergarten, der von Gustave Eiffel gebaut wurde. Hatebur meint, er habe gut zehn Jahre zum Einrichten gebraucht. In dieser Zeit sammelte er jede Lampe des Designers Arik Levy, ein Freund Hateburs, sowie zahlreiche Möbel von Charlotte Perriand, Jean Prouvé und Pierre Jeanneret. Trotzdem gilt seine größte Liebe der Kunst. Er erzählt davon, wie er auf einer Warschaureise den polnischen Künstler Wilhelm Sasnal entdeckte, und gesteht, dass es in seinen Wohnungen in Paris und Basel zusammen bestimmt einhundert Kunstwerke gibt.

L'avocat suisse Martin Hatebur a acheté sa première œuvre d'art en 1996 (un Christopher Wool sans titre). Aujourd'hui, elle est accrochée dans son séjour parisien. La façade du duplex donne sur la Seine ; à l'arrière, sa cuisine est située dans un ancien jardin d'hiver construit par Gustave Eiffel. Hatebur a mis dix ans à le meubler. Durant cette période, il a accumulé tous les luminaires créés par son ami Arik Levy ainsi que de nombreuses pièces de Charlotte Perriand, Jean Prouvé et Pierre Jeanneret. Mais l'art demeure sa vraie passion. Il raconte comment il a découvert le peintre polonais Wilhelm Sasnal lors d'un séjour à Varsovie et avoue posséder près de cent œuvres réparties entre Paris et sa demeure à Bâle.

P. 571 Verner Panton's Flower Pot light fixture hangs above a monastery table in the dining room. The light box is by Chen Zhen. • Verner Pantons Flower-Pot-Lampen hängen über dem Refektoriumstisch im Esszimmer. Der Leuchtkasten ist von Chen Zhen. • Dans la salle à manger, un lustre Flower Pot de Verner Panton est suspendu au-dessus d'une table de monastère, à côté d'une boîte lumineuse de Chen Zhen.

← The kitchen features a Piet Hein and Bruno Mathsson table, Jean Prouvé Standard chairs, Arik Levy's Flexible Flyer ceiling light, and artworks by Wilhelm Sasnal (left) and Georgine Ingold (right). • In der Küche kann man einen Tisch von Piet Hein und Bruno Mathsson, Standard-Stühle von Jean Prouvé, Arik Levys Flexible-Flyer-Deckenleuchte sowie Kunst von Wilhelm Sasnal (links) und Georgine Ingold (rechts) bewundern. • Dans la cuisine, une table de Piet Hein et Bruno Mathsson, des chaises Standard de Jean Prouvé, un plafonnier

Flexible Flyer d'Arik Levy et des œuvres d'art de Wilhelm Sasnal (à gauche) et de Georgine Ingold (à droite).

↑ The master bedroom is situated on the top floor of the duplex and affords a spectacular view over Paris. • Das Schlafzimmer befindet sich im oberen Geschoss der Duplexwohnung und hat einen spektakulären Ausblick. • La chambre principale est au deuxième étage du duplex et offre une vue sensationnelle sur Paris.

↓ In the bathroom, large slabs of granite cover the walls and the bath; in the background is a fitted cupboard unit. • Große Granitplatten verkleiden die Wände und Wanne im Bad, im Hintergrund ein Einbauschrank. • Dans la salle de bains, de grandes plaques de granit recouvrent les murs et le tour de la baignoire ; à l'arrière-plan un placard intégré.

← The mass of closely hung drawings in the study is an artistic composition in its own right. • Im Arbeitszimmer wirken die gesammelten Zeichnungen durch ihre dichte Hängung selbst wie eine Installation. • Dans le bureau, les dessins suspendus très près l'un de l'autre forment une nouvelle œuvre d'installation.

PP. 576–577 In the living room, a work by Christopher Wool and two photos by Ryan Gander hang behind a sofa from the store Caravane in Paris. • Im Wohnzimmer hängen eine Arbeit von Christopher Wool sowie zwei Fotografien von Ryan Gander hinter einem Sofa aus dem Geschäft Caravane in Paris. • Dans le séjour, une œuvre de Christopher Wool ainsi que deux photos de Ryan Gander sont accrochées derrière un canapé provenant de la boutique Caravane à Paris.

POSITANO
ITALY

Trail of Tiles

When architects Claudio Lazzarini and Carl Pickering first saw this 18th-century villa, it was "incredibly rundown." The house had suffered a structural collapse in the 1920s, was letting in water, and had been uninhabited for many decades. For the new owners, a 50-something Australian couple, they transformed the former conservatory into a 20-foot-high living room, inserted huge gunmetal doors into the Neoclassical arches, and created a Moroccan-style pool by enlarging a cistern. The most striking features, however, are four steel-framed elements, covered in some 3,000 historic Vietri tiles. A collection of antique Suzanis on the walls adds yet more visual drama. The idea, asserts Pickering, was to create a touch of 1960s glamour. "It's the image of what the Amalfi coast was like then, when visitors included people like Lee Radziwill and Jackie Onassis."

Als die Architekten Claudio Lazzarini und Carl Pickering zum ersten Mal diese Villa aus dem 18. Jahrhundert sahen, war sie „unglaublich heruntergekommen". In den 1920er Jahren waren tragende Teile eingestürzt, sodass der Bau nicht mehr regengeschützt war. Seit mehreren Dekaden war das Haus unbewohnt. Für ein australisches Ehepaar in den Fünfzigern verwandelten sie den ehemaligen Wintergarten in einen Wohnraum mit sechs Meter hoher Decke, setzten riesige Metalltüren in die klassizistischen Bögen und erweiterten eine Zisterne zu einem Pool im marokkanischen Stil. Der faszinierendste Blickfang aber sind die vier Konstruktionen aus stahlgerahmten Flächen, die mit über 3000 historischen Vietri-Fliesen gekachelt sind. Eine Sammlung von Suzanis aus dem 19. Jahrhundert an den Wänden setzt zusätzliche dramatische Akzente. Laut Pickering galt es, die 1960er Jahre anklingen zu lassen: „Das glamouröse Flair der Küste von Amalfi, als Lee Radziwill und Jackie Onassis hier Ferien machten".

Quand les architectes Claudio Lazzarini et Carl Pickering ont vu pour la première fois cette villa du 18ᵉ siècle, elle était « incroyablement délabrée ». En partie effondrée dans les années 1920, elle prenait l'eau et n'était plus habitée depuis plus d'un demi-siècle. Pour un couple de quinquagénaires australiens, ils ont aménagé un séjour dans l'orangerie avec ses six mètres sous plafond, inséré des portes en bronze à canon sous les arches néoclassiques et converti la citerne en piscine marocaine. Toutefois, le plus saisissant, ce sont les quatre structures en acier couvertes de 3000 carreaux anciens de Vietri. Sur les murs, une collection de suzani du 19ᵉ siècle achève le décor. L'idée, selon Pickering, était d'évoquer le glamour des années 1960, « quand la côte amalfitaine attirait des célébrités comme Lee Radziwill et Jackie Onasssis ».

P. 579 Tall gunmetal doors have been fitted with bulletproof glass and inserted into Neoclassical arches. • Hohe Metalltüren wurden mit kugelsicherem Glas versehen und in klassizistische Bögen eingepasst. • Des portes massives en bronze à canon ont été équipées de vitres pare-balles et insérées sous les arches néoclassiques.

↑ In the seating area with "flying sofa" is one of the six 19th-century Suzanis that add a dramatic touch to the decor. • Der „Flying Sofa" genannte Sitzbereich zeigt einen der sechs Suzanis aus dem 19. Jahrhundert, die dem Dekor einen dramatischen Effekt geben. • Dans le coin salon baptisé le canapé volant, un des six suzani du19e siècle ajoute une belle touche de flamboyance au décor.

→ A ribbon of vintage 18th- and 19th-century Vietri tiles extends across the main living room. • Ein Band aus erlesenen Vietri-Fliesen aus dem 18. und 19. Jahrhundert zieht sich über die Wände und durch den zentralen Wohnraum. • Un ruban de carreaux de Vietri des 18e et 19e siècles s'insinue dans le salon principal.

PP. 582–583 Stairs lead up to a master bedroom and the "flying sofa" seating area, which is cantilevered seven feet into the main space. Antonio Citterio's Apta chair is slip-covered in raw linen. • Eine luftige Treppe führt zu einem Schlafzimmer und zum mit Sofaelementen bestückten Sitzbereich, der zwei Meter weit in den Hauptraum vorkragt. Antonio Citterios Apta-Stuhl hat eine Stoffhusse aus grobem, naturbelassenem Leinen. • Des marches mènent à la chambre des maîtres et au canapé volant, un coin salon qui s'avance de deux mètres au-dessus de l'espace principal. Le fauteuil Apta d'Antonio Citterio est tapissé d'une housse en lin brut.

← As the ribbon descends, it is transformed into the dining table. On either side stand Eero Saarinen's Tulip chairs. The kitchen units are from Boffi and the design of the brushed-steel spots was inspired by those fitted in the original 1970s Concorde. • Das von oben kommende Band verwandelt sich unten in den von Eero Saarinens Tulip-Stühlen flankierten Esstisch. Die Kücheneinrichtung stammt von Boffi, und das Design der Spotlights aus poliertem Edelstahl orientiert sich an den Deckenlampen der ersten Concorde aus den 1970er Jahren. • En chemin, le ruban devient table de salle à manger. De part et d'autre, des chaises Tulip d'Eero Saarinen. Les éléments de cuisine viennent de chez Boffi, et les spots en acier brossé s'inspirent de ceux du premier Concorde des années 1970.

↑ An Antonio Citterio-designed bed stands on another steel-framed platform covered with vintage Vietri tiles. The bedspread is made from a Manuel Canovas striped chenille. • Ein Antonio-Citterio-Bett auf einer weiteren stahlgerahmten, mit alten Vietri-Fliesen gekachelten Plattform. Der Bettüberwurf wurde aus einem gestreiften Chenillestoff von Manuel Canovas genäht. • Un lit dessiné par Antonio Citterio est posé sur une autre plateforme tapissée d'anciens carreaux de Vietri. Le dessus-de-lit est en chenille rayée de chez Manuel Canovas.

PRAIA DO FORTE
BRAZIL

A Place for Friends

Architect David Bastos designed and built his own vacation home in Praia do Forte, an old fishing village about 40 miles to the north of Salvador. The red house was built on two plots of land some 700 feet from the beach. It catches the prevailing winds and so enjoys pleasant breezes. It's a house on stilts, which lends it a special charm and consists of four sections, or "modules," so that the social areas are separate from the owner's private quarters. The former include a gazebo, the setting for festivities and leisurely weekend lunches, which the party-loving host enjoys enormously. Between the modules stretch a single-lane swimming pool and a wooden footbridge. The simplicity of the house's design is underscored by its walls, which lack sharp edges (most corners are rounded). The basic flooring is white concrete, and eucalyptus wood predominates throughout. The decidedly unconventional landscaping favors green year-round.

Sein Sommerhaus in Praia do Forte, einem alten Fischerdorf rund 60 Kilometer nördlich von Salvador, hat der Architekt David Bastos selbst entworfen und gebaut. Das rote Haus wurde auf zwei Parzellen errichtet, die 200 Meter vom Strand entfernt und immer der Meeresbrise ausgesetzt sind, was im Haus zu einer angenehmen Belüftung führt. Seine Pfahlbauweise verleiht dem Haus einen ganz besonderen Charme. Die Gesellschaftsräume und der Privatbereich des Besitzers sind auf vier Module verteilt und solchermaßen klar getrennt. Der offene, wie eine Loggia gestaltete Pavillon bietet, ganz dem Geschmack des gastfreundlichen Hausherrn entsprechend, ein stimmungsvolles Szenario für Feste und ausgedehnte Dinners an den Wochenenden. Die vier Module sind zwar durch den Swimmingpool voneinander abgegrenzt, jedoch durch einen Steg miteinander verbunden. Die gewollt fließenden Übergänge spiegeln sich auch in den abgerundeten Kanten der nur angedeuteten Raumbegrenzungen wider. Der Boden ist meist in weißem Beton gehalten, und in der Einrichtung dominiert Eukalyptusholz. Eine unkonventionelle, ganz auf Grünnuancen setzende Gartengestaltung rundet das Bild ab.

C'est à Praia do Forte, une ancienne bourgade de pêcheurs située sur le littoral à 60 kilomètres au nord de Salvador, que l'architecte David Bastos a construit sa maison d'été. De couleur rouge, cette maison a été édifiée sur deux parcelles de terrain situées à 200 mètres de la plage et bénéficiant des vents dominants, ce qui apporte une ventilation très agréable. La construction sur pilotis donne un charme spécial à la maison organisée en quatre modules qui délimitent les espaces ouverts à la vie sociale et ceux réservés à l'intimité du maître de maison. C'est dans cette partie ouverte aux invités que se trouve la terrasse, lieu idéal pour les fêtes et les repas prolongés, particulièrement appréciés de cet hôte amateur de réceptions. Les modules sont séparés par la ligne simple de la piscine et reliés par une passerelle. Le dépouillement du style se remarque sur la maison, avec ses murs sans arêtes (les angles sont arrondis), son sol en ciment blanc et la prédominance du bois d'eucalyptus. L'agencement du paysage, en rien conventionnel, valorise la verdure à toutes les hauteurs.

P. 587 The rustic roof in eucalyptus wood, precision-built by Praia do Forte carpenters, contrasts with the straight, sophisticated lines of the furniture. • Die rustikale Zimmerdecke aus Eukalyptusholz, von Schreinern in Praia do Forte angefertigt, kontrastiert mit den klaren, urbanen Linien des Mobiliars. • Le plafond charpenté en bois d'eucalyptus, fabriqué méticuleusement par des menuisiers de Praia do Forte, contraste avec les lignes droites et sophistiquées du mobilier.

← A *faux-naïve* painting by contemporary artist Iuri Sarmento as a bedstead. • Ein naiv anmutende Werk des zeitgenössischen Künstlers Iuri Sarmento schmückt das Kopfende des Bettes. • Un tableau faux-naïf de l'artiste contemporain Iuri Sarmento sert de tête de lit.

→ The contrast between modern and rustic permeates the decor throughout the entire house. • Der Kontrast zwischen rustikaler und moderner Gestaltung bestimmt die gesamte Hauseinrichtung. • Le contraste entre moderne et rustique imprègne toute la décoration.

"The basic idea of the design was to create open spaces surrounded by the green." DAVID BASTOS

„Ich wollte offene Räume schaffen, die von Grün umgeben sind."
« Je voulais des espaces ouverts entourés de verdure. »

← The living room's dark wooden floorboards and eucalyptus roof set it apart from the other, lighter-hued interiors. • Das Wohnzimmer setzt sich durch dunkle Dielen und eine Dachkonstruktion aus Eukalyptus von den hellen Interieurs der anderen Räume ab. • Le séjour se démarque des pièces claires par un plancher sombre et un plafond en eucalyptus.

↖ Like the floors, the staircase, which has gently rounded edges, is made of white concrete. • Die Treppe mit ihren leicht abgerundeten Kanten wurde, wie alle Böden, in weißem Beton ausgeführt. • L'escalier aux arêtes légèrement arrondies est en béton blanc comme tous les sols dans la maison.

↓ The social area of the house has round tables, where there is always room for another guest. • Im für alle offenen Bereich stehen runde Tische, an denen sich immer ein Platz für einen weiteren Gast findet. • Des tables rondes sont installées dans les parties ouvertes de la maison, il y a toujours de la place pour un nouvel invité.

RUNGSTED KYST
DENMARK

The Legacy of Style

Hanne Kjærholm was one of Denmark's most distinguished architects. Together with her husband, Poul, one of the 20th century's greatest furniture designers, she bought in 1959 a plot of land on the Øresund—the stretch of water between Denmark and Sweden. On it, Hanne built a four-bedroom house with under-floor heating (a novelty at the time) and a portico of whitewashed pillars. "I put in a portico because the horizon is so large, it could easily become overwhelming," she explained. Poul, meanwhile, dealt with the interiors. He employed natural materials and would often test out new furniture designs before putting them into production. The house acted as a showcase for his elegant creations. His favorite spot, apparently, was the desk in the immense main room. "It was there," recalled Hanne, who passed away in 2009, "that we used to sit face-to-face."

Hanne Kjærholm war einer der bedeutendsten Architekten Dänemarks, während ihr Mann Poul zu den größten Möbeldesignern des 20. Jahrhunderts gehörte. 1959 kaufte das Paar ein Grundstück am Øresund, der Meerenge zwischen Dänemark und Schweden. Hier errichtete Hanne ein Haus mit vier Schlafzimmern und Fußbodenheizung (damals eine Neuheit) sowie einem Portikus mit weiß gestrichenen Säulen. „Ich habe einen Portikus hinzugefügt, weil der Horizont so weit ist, dass er einen leicht überwältigen könnte", erkärte sie die Entscheidung. Währenddessen befasste sich Poul mit der Inneneinrichtung. Dabei verwendete er natürliche Materialien und pflegte häufig neue Möbelentwürfe auszutesten, bevor er sie zur Produktion freigab. Das Haus fungierte dabei als ein idealer Rahmen für seine eleganten Kreationen. Sein Lieblingsplatz war augenscheinlich sein Arbeitstisch in dem riesigen Hauptraum. „Hier saßen wir einander gewöhnlich gegenüber", erinnerte sich Hanne, die 2009 ebenfalls gestorben ist.

Hanne Kjærholm a été l'une des plus éminentes architectes du Danemark. Son mari Poul, lui aussi disparu, fut l'un des plus grands créateurs de meubles du 20ᵉ siècle. En 1959, le couple avait acheté un terrain au bord du Øresund, le bras de mer entre le Danemark et la Suède. Hanne y a construit une maison de 4 chambres avec le chauffage par le sol (une nouveauté à l'époque) et un portique blanchi à la chaux « parce que l'horizon est tellement vaste qu'il risquait d'être écrasant ». Poul, lui, a aménagé l'intérieur en utilisant des matériaux naturels. Il y testait souvent ses prototypes avant de les mettre en production. La maison était une vitrine pour ses élégantes créations. Son endroit favori était le bureau dans l'immense pièce principale. « C'est là qu'on s'asseyait tous les deux face à face », se souvenait Hanne Kjærholm qui nous a quittés en 2009.

P. 593 A work by Arne Haugen Sørensen hangs above Poul Kjærholm's black-painted plywood PK0 chair in the entrance hall. • Im Eingangsbereich hängt ein Werk von Arne Haugen Sørensen über einem schwarz lackierten PK0-Schichtholzstuhl von Poul Kjærholm. • Dans l'entrée, une œuvre d'Arne Haugen Sørensen au-dessus d'un siège PK0 de Poul Kjærholm en contreplaqué peint en noir.

↑ The bedspread in the bedroom was made in Mexico. • Der Bettüberwurf im Schlafzimmer ist eine Handarbeit aus Mexiko. • Le dessus-de-lit dans la chambre à coucher vient du Mexique.

→ Poul Kjærholm's PK9 tulip chairs and a PK54 table in the dining room. The painting is again by Danish artist Arne Haugen Sørensen. • Poul Kjærholms PK9-Stühle und ein PK54-Tisch im Esszimmer. Das Gemälde ist ebenfalls ein Werk des dänischen Malers Arne Haugen Sørensen. • Dans la salle à manger, des chaises tulipes PK9 et une table PK54 de Poul Kjærholm. Au mur, une autre œuvre de l'artiste danois Arne Haugen Sørensen.

PP. 596–597 On the left is perhaps Poul Kjærholm's most iconic piece—the PK24 rattan chaise longue, which dates from 1965. • Links ist das Kjærholm-Möbelstück zu sehen, das vielleicht den größten Kultstatus hat – der PK24-Rattananliegestuhl aus dem Jahr 1965. • À gauche, la chaise longue en rotin PK24, sans doute la pièce la plus célèbre de Poul Kjærholm. Il l'a créée en 1965.

← Sisal flooring made in Haiti was used in the hallway, as elsewhere in the house. • Der in Haiti hergestellte Sisal-Boden-belag wurde nicht nur für den Eingangs-bereich und Flur, sondern auch für an-dere Räume im Haus verwendet. • Dans le couloir comme dans le reste de la mai-son, un revêtement de sol en sisal réalisé à Haïti.

↓ A view of the terrace from the main living room. • Der Blick vom großen Wohnzimmer hinaus auf die Terrasse. • La terrasse vue du séjour.

SAN ISIDRO
ARGENTINA

Nature Tamed

A large green space to the north of Buenos Aires, the dreams of a photographer and a fashion designer, and the expertise of Argentinian firm PAC (Producción de Arquitectura Contemporánea) are the foundations on which this timeless, two-story dwelling was constructed. "The first thought we had was that it should be possible to see right through the house and that it should be at one with its surroundings," explains architect Martín Olabarrieta. "From that came the decision not to interrupt the glazing with frames and bars," he goes on. Achieving privacy in each environment without losing a sense of continuity was another of the challenges that the architects set themselves, achieving this by varying the materials—glass, wood, plant screens, and stone walls—but also by using dividers like the floating staircase, the metal kitchen island, and simple variations in floor level. "This work may be futuristic, modern, or classical, but the materials and the particular way they are used make it Argentinian through and through," Olabarrieta concludes.

Auf einer großen Grünfläche im Norden von Buenos Aires errichteten ein Fotograf, eine Modedesignerin und das argentinische Architekturbüro PAC (Producción de Arquitectura Contemporánea) eine zeitlose zweigeschossige Villa. „Wir wollten ein Haus bauen, das Durchblicke erlaubt und eine Einheit mit der Umgebung bildet", erzählt der Architekt Martín Olabarrieta. „Daraus folgte die Entscheidung, die Verglasungen nicht zu unterbrechen." Eine weitere Herausforderung, der sich die Architekten stellten, lag darin, jedem Raum Intimität zu geben, ohne das Gefühl von Kontinuität zu verlieren. Sie lösten diese Aufgabe durch Verwendung unterschiedlicher Materialien (Glas, Holz, durch Pflanzen betonte Wände oder Steinmauerwerk) und mit Kontrapunkten wie einer schwebenden Treppe, einem großen Küchenmöbel aus Stahl oder einfach durch Höhenunterschiede. „Dieses Haus könnte futuristisch, modern oder klassisch genannt werden", bekräftigt Martín, „aber seine Materialien und deren besonderer Einsatz kennzeichnen es als argentinisch."

Un grand espace vert au nord de Buenos Aires, les rêves d'un photographe et d'une styliste de mode, et le savoir du cabinet d'architecture argentin PAC (Producción de Arquitectura Contemporánea), voilà les bases de cette structure atemporelle d'un étage. « Nous sommes partis de l'idée qu'on puisse voir à travers toute la maison et que celle-ci se fonde dans son environnement », explique l'architecte Martín Olabarrieta. « À partir de là, la décision d'éviter la menuiserie qui interrompait les vitres s'est imposée d'elle-même. » L'autre défi consistait à conférer de l'intimité à chaque pièce sans rompre l'impression de continuité. La solution : des changements de matières – vitre, bois, murs végétaux ou en pierre – ainsi que des divisions subtiles tels qu'un escalier flottant, le meuble en métal de la cuisine ou de simples différences de niveau. « Ce pourrait être une œuvre futuriste, moderne, classique mais, par ses matériaux et l'usage qu'il en est fait, elle est par essence argentine », conclut Olabarrieta.

P. 601 A "floating" concrete staircase is dressed in lapacho hardwood. The wood sculptures are by Ricardo Marcenaro. • Eine wie schwebende Betontreppe ist mit Lapacho-Holz verkleidet. Die Holzskulpturen sind von Ricardo Marcenaro. • L'escalier flottant en béton est revêtu d'un placage en lapacho. À gauche, des sculptures en bois de Ricardo Marcenaro.

← The living room with solid plate-glass wall facing the front. Table and stools are carved in eucalyptus wood from a tree that had to be felled to provide the best site for the house; most of the furniture was made from this tree. • Das Wohnzimmer hat eine durchgehende Außenfront aus Glas. Tisch und Hocker sind aus dem Holz eines Eukalyptusbaums, der einst auf dem Grundstück stand und bei Baubeginn gefällt werden musste. Ein Großteil der Möbel wurde aus dem Holz dieses Baums gefertigt. • Le séjour avec un grand mur de verre donnant sur l'extérieur. La table et les bancs ont été sculptés dans un eucalyptus qu'il a fallu abattre pour construire la maison et qui a fourni la matière première de la plupart des meubles.

→ The house was built with gabions, wire cages filled with loose stones. Normally used in landscape design or for sound barriers, they make for unusual interiors (pictured here is a bathroom) that appear both high tech and elemental. • Für den Bau des Hauses wurden Gabionen, mit losen Steinen gefüllte Drahtkörbe, verwendet. Normalerweise werden sie in der Landschaftsarchitektur oder als Lärmschutzmauer eingesetzt. In Innenräumen, wie hier im Bad, erzeugen sie eine ungewöhnliche Raumatmosphäre zwischen Urwüchsigkeit und Hightech. • Pour construire la maison, on a utilisé des gabions, des casiers en treillis métallique remplis de pierres. On y a normalement recours pour aménager les paysages ou comme écran phonique. À l'intérieur, comme ici dans la salle de bains, ils créent une ambiance inhabituelle, à mi-chemin entre le primitif et le high-tech.

↑ The master bedroom is a large box lined with lapacho wood, interrupted only by the windows. • Das Schlafzimmer der Hausbesitzer ist mit Lapacho-Holz ausgekleidet, in dessen einheitlicher Fläche die Fenster wie ausgeschnitten wirken. • Les murs de la chambre principale sont revêtus d'un placage en lapacho.

→ In the kitchen—a rectangle of glass and stone—stretches a steel island, designed as a single, visual block. • Die Küche, ein Rechteck aus Glas und Stein, wird nur durch eine Insel aus Stahl unterbrochen, die optisch einen geschlossenen Block bildet. • La cuisine, rectangle de vitre et de pierre interrompu par un îlot construit comme un seul bloc visuel.

PP. 606–607 The kitchen wall consists of three successive planes: dry stone walling, glass, and concrete. • Die Küchenfassade besteht aus drei gestaffelten Flächen: einer Mauer aus Gabionen, einer Glaswand und einer Betonwand. • Le mur de la cuisine est composé de trois plans successifs : pierres sèches, vitre et mur en béton.

SANTIAGO DE CUBA
CUBA

With a French Accent

Étienne Sulpice Hallet, a French architect known for the original, unused designs for the US Capitol building he drafted in 1792, was living in Havana by 1800. He introduced Neoclassical architecture to Cuba. In 1828, Antonio María de la Torre built a pavilion—the "Templete," shaped like a classical temple—on the Plaza de Armas, so furthering the influence of Neoclassicism on the island. At around the same time, French sugar and coffee planters who had migrated to Cuba after the 1791 Haitian Revolution, brought with them the spirit of enlightenment as well as economic growth. Their cultural imprint can certainly be seen in the Cuban appreciation of French music and painting, but perhaps more so in the practice of coffee-drinking. Those who settled in Santiago de Cuba brought these new ideas and habits with them, as well as their fondness for Neoclassicism in their homes. Although the traditional arrangement of a house around a central courtyard was retained, the style of interior decoration was updated. In the Quesada house, the arches facing the patio were enclosed with French louvered doors, or *persiennes*, while colored glass windows filtered the sunlight. Terracotta floors were replaced by marble, and friezes were added to the interior paneling.

Der französische Architekt Étienne Sulpice Hallet entwarf 1792 Pläne für das Kapitol in Washington, die jedoch nie umgesetzt wurden. Um 1800 ließ er sich in Havanna nieder und brachte die klassizistische Architektur nach Kuba. Die Strömung gewann an Einfluss, als Antonio María de la Torre 1828 den Pavillon Templete auf der Plaza de Armas nach dem Vorbild eines klassischen Tempels baute. Französische Zucker- und Kaffeeplantagenbesitzer, die 1791 vor der Revolution in Haiti nach Kuba geflüchtet waren, brachten schon damals den Geist der Aufklärung ins Land. Ihr Einfluss ist immer noch spürbar: Die Kubaner haben bis heute eine besondere Vorliebe für französische Musik und Malerei. Auch die Kaffeekultur wurde von den französischen Einwanderern eingeführt. Die Häuser wurden damals zwar in alter Tradition rund um einen Innenhof gebaut, doch bei der Einrichtung ließ man sich von den neuen Ideen inspirieren. So auch die Familie Quesada in Santiago de Cuba: In ihrem Haus ließen sie französische Lamellentüren, *persiennes*, in die Torbögen zum Innenhof einbauen und in die Oberlichter farbiges Glas einsetzen. Die Terrakottaböden haben sie durch Marmor ersetzen lassen und die Wandpaneele mit Friesdekor versehen.

Étienne Sulpice Hallet, un architecte français connu pour ses plans non retenus pour le Capitol de Washington en 1792, s'installa à la Havane vers 1800. Il y introduisit l'architecture néoclassique en dessinant le premier cimetière municipal. En 1828, Antonio María de la Torre érigea un pastiche de temple antique, le Templete, sur la Plaza de Armas, renforçant l'influence de ce style. Vers la même époque, les planteurs français de tabac et de sucre, émigrés à Cuba après la révolution haïtienne de 1791, apportèrent, outre la croissance économique, l'esprit des Lumières. Le goût des Cubains pour la musique et la peinture françaises imprégna la culture locale, mais pas autant que la consommation de café. Ceux qui s'établirent à Santiago de Cuba importèrent leurs idées et pratiques, ainsi que leur attachement au néoclassicisme. Tout en conservant la disposition traditionnelle des pièces autour d'un patio central, ils modernisèrent la décoration. Dans la maison de la famille Quesada, des persiennes protègent les arcades du patio, les arcs en plein cintre sont dotés de vitraux. Sur les sols, les carreaux de terre cuite ont été remplacés par du marbre et les boiseries enrichies de frises.

P. 609 On the salon's rococo-style console table is a female bust flanked by two vases. Reflected in the mirror are the double doors leading to the courtyard. • Im Salon steht auf der Spiegelkonsole im Stil des Rokoko eine Frauenbüste, die von zwei Vasen flankiert wird. Im Spiegel sieht man eine Flügeltür, die in den Hof führt. • Dans le salon, sur la console à miroir de style rococo, un buste féminin est flanqué de deux vases. Une porte à battants qui s'ouvre sur la cour est reflétée dans le miroir.

↑ The pleasant dining room is bedecked with fine Cuban wooden furniture, and occupies a key location near the courtyard. The semicircular colored glass windows filter the strong outdoor light. • Das Esszimmer ist im klassizisti-schen Stil und mit Möbeln aus kubanischem Edelholz eingerichtet und hat eine zentrale Lage direkt am Innenhof. Die Fenster aus Buntglas filtern das harsche Sommerlicht. • La salle à manger de style néoclassique dégage une atmosphère agréable avec ses meubles cubains en bois précieux. Elle occupe une place de choix devant le patio. Les vitraux filtrent la lumière extérieure.

→ Marble floor tiles were laid in most of the rooms when the house was being renovated; here, though, the original flooring of hexagonal terra-cotta tiles has been preserved. • Während bei einem Umbau die meisten Böden im Haus mit Marmorplatten ausgelegt wurden, blieb im Salon der originale Bodenbelag mit sechseckigen Terrakottafliesen erhalten.

• Si la plupart des sols de la maison ont été recouverts de marbre pendant les travaux, cette pièce a gardé ses carreaux de terre cuite hexagonaux d'origine.

P. 612 The kitchen at the back of the house. • Die Küche im hinteren Teil des Hauses. • La cuisine est généralement placée au fond de la maison.

P. 613 French *persiennes*, or louvered doors, are set into the bays, and the semicircular arches are surmounted by lovely colored glass windows. • Die Bogennischen werden mit Lamellenläden verschlossen, über denen Halbkreisfenster aus Buntglas leuchten. • Les portes-fenêtres sont protégées par des persiennes et surmontées d'arcs en plein cintre ornés de beaux vitraux.

← A crystal chandelier is suspended from the living room with wooden trussing. The English furniture is crafted of rosewood. • Im Wohnzimmer hängt ein Leuchter aus Kristallglas. Die englischen Möbel sind aus Palisanderholz geschreinert. • Le vaste salon, avec son lustre en cristal très raffiné et des meubles en palissandre.

↑ Colored glass fanlights were inserted into the arches above the doors. A sculpture stands at the entrance to the paved courtyard. • In die Torbögen ließ man Oberlichter aus farbigem Glas einsetzen. Eine kleine Skulptur bewacht den Zugang zum gepflasterten Hof. • Des impostes en verre coloré ont été intégrées dans les portes voûtées. Une petite sculpture borde l'accès à la cour carrelée.

↗ The shady courtyard with its cast-iron bench and fountain provides outdoor living space. • Durch den schattigen Innenhof mit gusseiserner Bank und einem Brunnen erweitert sich der Wohnraum nach außen. • La salle de séjour est agrandie par la cour intérieure ombragée, avec son banc en fer forgé et sa fontaine.

SÃO PAULO
BRAZIL

Parallel Universe

A client walking into their practice clutching sketches of his own was not something Marcio Kogan and Renata Furlanetto of Studio mk27 had ever experienced before. But it merely heightened the architects' enthusiasm for this design-loving lawyer's plans: to build a villa in the Brazilian modernist tradition of Lúcio Costa or Oscar Niemeyer for himself, his wife, and their two children. Completed in 2006, the three-story property is situated next to Ibirapuera Park, in one of the few green urban areas of São Paulo, and boasts generously furnished interiors by Diana Radomysler. Wide picture windows, stone facings, and wooden paneling provide a refined backdrop for furnishings that combine local vintage pieces with an elegant international style.

Dass ein Bauherr mit eigenen Skizzen ihr Büro betritt, war den Architekten von Studio mk27, Marcio Kogan und Renata Furlanetto, noch nie passiert. Umso enthusiastischer entwarfen sie für den designbegeisterten Anwalt, seine Frau und die zwei Kinder eine Villa in der Tradition der brasilianischen Moderne à la Lúcio Costa oder Oscar Niemeyer. Das 2006 fertiggestellte Anwesen liegt am Ibirapuera-Park, in einem der raren grünen Stadtviertel von São Paulo. Auf drei Wohnebenen dehnen sich die von Diana Radomysler gestalteten Räume generös fließend aus. Extrabreite Fenster, Naturstein und Holzpaneele bilden die noble Grundlage, vor der die Ausstattung aus lokalem Vintage-Mobiliar und internationaler Eleganz hervorragend zur Wirkung kommt.

Les architectes du Studio mk27, Marcio Kogan et Renata Furlanetto n'avaient jamais vu un client entrer chez eux avec ses propres croquis. Ils n'en ont conçu qu'avec plus d'enthousiasme pour l'avocat passionné de design, sa femme et ses deux enfants, une villa dans la tradition de l'ère moderne brésilienne à la manière de Lúcio Costa ou Oscar Niemeyer. La propriété achevée en 2006 est située près du parc Ibirapuera, dans l'un des rares quartiers verts de São Paulo. Les espaces dessinés par Diana Radomysler s'étirent avec fluidité sur trois niveaux. Des fenêtres allongées, de la pierre naturelle et des panneaux de bois forment la base noble sur laquelle le mobilier vintage régional et l'élégance internationale peuvent faire leur effet.

P. 617 The patio acts as an extension of the living room; thanks to the Brazilian climate, it can be used all year round. • Der Patio erweitert das dahinter liegende Wohnzimmer und kann im brasilianischen Klima ganzjährig genutzt werden. • Le patio agrandit le séjour et peut être utilisé toute l'année grâce au climat tropical.

← A narrow staircase leads from the basement garage up to the first and second floors. • Ein schmales Treppenhaus führt von der Garage im Keller über das Erdgeschoss hoch ins Obergeschoss. • Un escalier étroit, qui passe au-dessus du rez-de-chaussée, mène du garage situé dans la cave jusqu'au premier étage.

→ Brazilian Moledo stone, a natural quarrystone, covers the living room's end wall. • Für die Stirnwand im Wohnbereich wurde brasilianischer Moledo, ein natürlicher Bruchstein, verwendet. • Le mur du séjour a été réalisé en pierre de Moledo brésilienne, une pierre de taille naturelle.

← From their Hans Wegner chairs, diners can look through the picture window to the pool. • Von den Hans-Wegner-Esstischstühlen haben Dinnergäste durch das Panoramafenster Blick auf den Pool. • Assis à la table sur les chaises Hans Wegner, on peut voir la piscine derrière la fenêtre panoramique.

→ Like all the first-floor interiors, the space between the main entrance and dining room has travertine flooring. • Der Boden zwischen Haupteingang und Esszimmer ist wie im gesamten Erdgeschoss aus Travertin. • Entre l'entrée principale et la salle à manger, le sol est en travertin comme dans tout le rez-de-chaussée.

← Eames swivel chairs grace the home office, into which daylight floods via skylights. • Eames-Bürostühle stehen im Home-Office, das durch Oberlichter viel Tageslicht erhält. • Des chaises de bureau Eames dans le home office très bien éclairé grâce aux lanterneaux.

↑ An upholstered window bay acts as a sofa with panoramic views. • Eine gepolsterte Fensterbucht wird zum Sofa mit Ausblick nach draußen. • Un appui de fenêtre rembourré se transforme en divan avec vue sur l'extérieur.

↓ The family living room is on the third floor and features a generous couch by Marcus Ferreira. • Im zweiten Obergeschoss liegt das Familienwohnzimmer mit einer Couch von Marcus Ferreira. • Au second étage, la salle de séjour familiale abrite un canapé de Marcus Ferreira.

"Our houses take their cue from great 20th-century Brazilian architects such as Lúcio Costa." THE ARCHITECTS

„Unsere Häuser folgen dem Vorbild großer brasilianischer Architekten des vergangenen Jahrhunderts wie Lúcio Costa."
« Nos projets suivent le modèle des grands architectes brésiliens du siècle dernier, tel Lúcio Costa. »

SEMINYAK
INDONESIA

Rustic Refinement

The owner of this villa is internationally acclaimed in the field of fashion and design. This is reflected in the house, which occupies less than half of the 11,000-square-foot property. It is built around a garden courtyard where blooming frangipani trees cast soft shadows. The rectangular spaces defined by the colonnaded concrete walkways and verandas feature carefully arranged tables with thick wooden tops, sturdy stools, and benches with an antique patina reflected in the luminous floors. Works by artists who have visited the house hang in the living areas furnished minimalistically with cushions and a mixture of Chinese and Indonesian pieces. The prevailing influence is rustic, with grass-thatched roofs and wooden furniture on the verandas. A quaint and comfortable sitting pavilion overlooks the aquamarine swimming pool, so that indoor and outdoor living are intertwined. This house, with its fluid transitions between unrestricted spaces, is emblematic of modern Bali. Life here seems blissfully unencumbered.

Diese Villa steht auf einem 1000 Quadratmeter großen Grundstück und hat ein grünes Herz: Sie wurde rund um einen Patio gebaut, in dem duftende Jasminbäume wachsen, die für ein faszinierendes Spiel aus Licht und Schatten sorgen. Unter den Kolonnaden und in den Räumen gruppieren sich Tische, Stühle und Bänke aus massivem Holz. Dass die Besitzerin einen internationalen Ruf in der Mode- und Designbranche genießt, erkennt man an den zahlreichen Werken befreundeter Künstler und an den Möbeln aus China sowie Indonesien, die den Wohnbereichen puristisches Flair geben. Traumhafte Terrassen lassen Innen und Außen wie selbstverständlich miteinander verschmelzen – ein Lieblingsplatz ist der grasgedeckte Pavillon, von dem man auf den aquamarinblau leuchtenden Swimmingpool blickt. In dieser Villa zeigt Bali sein modernes Gesicht und besänftigt mit einer ganz besonderen Leichtigkeit des Seins.

Styliste et designer de renommée internationale, la propriétaire a créé une maison caractéristique de la Bali moderne, avec des transitions fluides entre différents environnements dans lesquels on évolue sans entraves. Située sur une propriété de 1000 mètres carrés, la villa occupe moins de la moitié de cette superficie. Elle est construite autour d'une cour-jardin agrémentée de frangipaniers. Les espaces rectangulaires et les vérandas à colonnades sont sobrement meublés de tables à plateau épais, de tabourets et de bancs dont la patine ancienne reflète les sols d'un blanc lumineux. Des œuvres d'art réalisées par des amis artistes lors de séjours à la propriété sont accrochées dans les espaces de vie agrémentés de coussins et de mobiliers chinois et indonésiens minimalistes. Le toit recouvert de chaume d'alang alang et les meubles en bois des vérandas apportent une note rustique, établissant un lien entre l'intérieur et l'extérieur. Un pavillon original douillettement aménagé invite au repos au bord de la piscine.

P. 625 An old wooden wheel from a farmer's cart serves as a decorative symbol on the back wall of the pavilion. • Das alte Holzrad eines Bauernwagens gibt ein dekoratives Element an der Rückwand des Pavillons ab. • La roue en bois ancienne accrochée au mur du fond du pavillon est une décoration chargée de sens. Elle provient d'une charrette paysanne.

← A colonnaded veranda can be seen through an old Balinese door with a patina of aging paint. • Durch eine alte balinesische Tür mit der Patina eines in die Jahre gekommenen Anstrichs blickt man auf eine Veranda mit Kolonnade. • En poussant une porte balinaise ancienne à la peinture passée, on découvre une véranda bordée de colonnes.

↑ The furniture in the center of the room directs the eye towards the French doors and to the next room. • Durch die Möbel in der Mitte des Raumes wird der Blick auf die Flügeltüren und in den nächsten Raum gelenkt. • Les meubles étant disposés au centre de la pièce, le regard est attiré vers la porte à battants et la pièce suivante.

P. 628 A narrow walkway leads from the veranda to a rustic poolside lounger. • Von der Veranda führt ein schmaler Holzsteg zur rustikalen Poolliege. • Un passage étroit mène de la véranda à la chaise longue rustique de la piscine.

P. 629 An old brass, four-poster bed from Holland adds substance to the flowing draperies of gauzy mosquito netting. • Ein altes niederländisches Messinghimmelbett gibt den fließenden Vorhängen aus hauchdünnen Moskitonetzen eine klare Basis. • Un lit ancien à baldaquin provenant de Hollande donne une certaine rigueur aux voilages en moustiquaire vaporeuse.

SÉRIFOS
GREECE

Colors of the Sea

It's been many years since Panos Alexopoulos first discovered the island of Sérifos and laid claim to a group of small houses at the foot of the medieval *kastro*. Undeterred by their dilapidated state, he set about injecting new life into these old stones—with such success that today, what was once a ruin has become a beautiful white house, magnificent in its austerity and simplicity. Under the watchful eye of the architect Vassily Tseghis (an old friend of Alexopoulos), the project emerged as a series of spaces that seem to overlap one into the next with effortless logic. From the living room with its ample sofa bed and cushions covered in geometrical motifs, to the mezzanine where the architect has managed to fit in a bedroom and bathroom, you have the clear impression that you're in a space much larger than is really the case. Furthermore, the windows offer a stunning view of the port, and the ubiquitous blue of the paint marries perfectly with the sunlight of Greece: all of which adds to the charm of this highly original residence.

Etliche Jahre ist es nun her, dass Panos Alexopoulos die Insel Seriphos entdeckte und ein Auge auf eine Gruppe kleiner Häuser am Fuß des mittelalterlichen *kastro*, der Burg, warf. Der Anblick dieser von der Zeit gezeichneten Mauerschale schreckte ihn nicht ab, und er ließ diesen Phönix aus seiner Asche auferstehen. Heute ist nichts mehr von der früheren Ruine zu erkennen: Das steinerne Wrack hat die Gestalt eines schönen weißen Hauses angenommen, schlicht und schnörkellos. Unter dem wachsamen Auge des Architekten Vassily Tseghis (ein Freund seit jeher) sind Räume entstanden, die wie selbstverständlich ineinander verschachtelt sind. Angefangen beim Wohnraum, in dem sich ein großes Bettsofa mit geometrisch gemusterten Kissen befindet, bis hin zum Mezzanin, wo Alexopoulos wundersamerweise ein Schlafzimmer und ein Bad unterbrachte - stets hat man den Eindruck, sich in einem sehr viel weitläufigeren Haus aufzuhalten. Auch die Fenster, die einen fantastischen Blick auf den Hafen freigeben, und das kräftige Blau, das so gut mit dem griechischen Licht harmoniert, verleihen diesem Haus seinen originellen Charme.

Voilà bien des années que Panos Alexopoulos a découvert l'île de Serifos et qu'il a jeté son dévolu sur un groupe de petites maisons au pied du *kastro* médiéval. Alexopoulos ne se laissa pas décourager par la vue d'un tas de pierres rongées par le temps et entama des travaux qui feraient renaître ce phœnix de ses cendres. Aujourd'hui, rien ne subsiste de l'ancienne ruine et l'épave en pierre a pris l'aspect d'une belle maison blanche toute de dépouillement et de simplicité. Sous l'œil vigilant de l'architecte Vassily Tseghis (un ami de toujours) est né un jeu de volumes qui semblent s'imbriquer l'un dans l'autre de manière presque évidente. Du séjour avec son grand canapé-lit et ses coussins aux motifs géométriques, à la mezzanine où l'architecte a réussi à loger une chambre à coucher et une salle de bains, on garde l'impression de se trouver dans un espace beaucoup plus vaste. Et puis, il y a les fenêtres qui donnent une merveilleuse vue sur le port, et la présence du bleu vif en harmonie avec la lumière grecque, qui contribue au charme de cette maison charismatique.

P. 631 A Victorian chair covered with elegant blue fabric heightens the effect of the surrounding simplicity. • Das kräftige Blau des viktorianischen Sessels bringt die Einfachheit des Raums zur vollen Wirkung. • Le bleu très intense du fauteuil victorien met en valeur la simplicité qui l'entoure.

← The kitchen is functional but like everywhere else in this house, there's always room for a charming detail such as a tin lantern or a tray of stones and seashells. • Wie überall im Haus findet sich bei aller Zweckmäßigkeit auch in der Küche ein Plätzchen für reizvolle Details, hier eine Laterne aus Blech und Schalen, die mit Kieseln und Muscheln gefüllt sind. • La cuisine est fonctionnelle mais, comme partout dans cette maison, il y a toujours de la place pour des détails charmants tels cette lanterne en tôle et ces plateaux remplis de galets et de coquillages si décoratifs.

↓ In the bedroom is a four-poster bed made of brass. The shutters are painted blue, as they are throughout the house. • Im Schlafzimmer steht ein Himmelbett aus Messing. Auch hier sind die Fensterläden – wie im ganzen Haus – blau gestrichen. • La chambre à coucher abrite un lit à baldaquin en laiton. Les volets sont peints en bleu ici, comme dans toute la maison.

↑ The toilet is decorated with engravings and stones found on the beach. •
Mit den Stichen und Strandkieseln erhielt selbst die Toilette ein inselgerechtes Dekor. • Les toilettes ont été décorées avec des gravures et des galets trouvés sur la plage.

↗ All Greek-island houses seem to contain some kind of reference to the sea. •
In griechischen Inselhäusern findet man eigentlich immer Verweise auf das Meer.
• Partout dans les maisons des îles, on trouve des références à la mer.

→ The sofa bed and its pile of geometrically patterned cushion were designed by the architect. The 19th-century mirror frame has been painted white to go with the rest of the room. • Auf dem Bettsofa tummeln sich Kissen, deren geometrische Muster der Architekt selbst entworfen hat. Ein Spiegel aus dem 19. Jahrhundert wurde passend zu Mauern, Deckenbalken und Boden kalkweiß gestrichen. • Le canapé-lit et son amoncellement de coussins à motifs géométriques dessinés par l'architecte. Et pour s'harmoniser à la blancheur des murs, des poutres et du sol, le cadre du miroir 19e a été badigeonné de peinture blanche.

SHANGHAI
CHINA

Ascetic Order

Since Taiwan-born architect and artist Teng Kun-Yen moved to Shanghai, he's become the leader of a movement to preserve his adopted city's architectural treasures. In 1997, he rehabilitated a workshop in an abandoned 1920s warehouse on the Suzhou. Dozens of other creative people followed suit and soon the area was being touted as "Shanghai's SoHo." (Teng's careful renovation received an honorable mention by UNESCO.) His apartment on the Bund, where he has lived since 1998, is in a landmark building with a fascinating history: it was built in 1905, by the famous Japanese architect Hirano, to serve as the Japanese consulate in Shanghai. Although the building's name in Chinese means "red mansion," Teng prefers neutral colors for the interior of this open, loft-like space. Minimal furniture and simple decor allow the magnificent features of the structure—ornate ceiling moldings, curved walls, and stately supporting columns—to speak for themselves. "From my window, I can see the famous Pearl Tower, and the ships moving along the Huang Pu River," he enthuses.

Seitdem der aus Taiwan stammende Architekt und Künstler Teng Kun-Yen nach Schanghai gezogen ist, wurde er zu einem aktiven Bewahrer der dortigen Architekturschätze. 1997 mietete er am Suzhou-Fluss eine ehemalige Werkstätte in einem verlassenen Lagerhaus aus den 1920ern und setzte sie instand. Dutzende anderer Kreativer folgten seinem Beispiel und die Gegend wurde bald als SoHo von Schanghai bekannt. Tangs sorgfältige Restaurierung wurde sogar von der UNESCO gewürdigt. In einem anderen außergewöhnlichen Gebäude befindet sich seine Wohnung. Das Haus wurde 1905 vom bekannten japanischen Architekten Hirano als japanisches Konsulat gebaut. Obwohl sein Name „Rote Villa" bedeutet, setzt Teng im loftähnlichen Raum auf weiße und neutrale Töne. Seine minimalistische Einrichtung überlässt den originalen Zierleisten an den Decken, den gewölbten Wänden und tragenden Säulen den großen Auftritt. „Ich habe diese großartige Architektur so gelassen, wie sie ist", sagt Teng. „Durch die Fenster hat man einen Blick auf den berühmten Pearl Tower und die Schiffe, die auf dem Huang Pu auf- und abgleiten."

Depuis que l'architecte et artiste taïwanais Teng Kun-Yen a emménagé à Shanghai il y a dix ans, il a pris la tête du mouvement pour la restauration des trésors architecturaux de la ville. En 1997, il a retapé un atelier dans un entrepôt abandonné des années 1920 au bord du Suzhou. Bientôt, des dizaines d'autres créatifs l'ont suivi, faisant du quartier le « SoHo de Shanghai » (l'UNESCO a salué la restauration soignée de Teng). L'appartement où il vit depuis 1998 se trouve dans un immeuble historique sur le Bund, construit en 1905 par le célèbre architecte japonais Hirano pour être le consulat du Japon. Son nom chinois signifie maison rouge mais, pour son espace ouvert de type loft, Teng a préféré le blanc et les tons neutres. Le décor dépouillé et le mobilier sobre laissent parler la superbe structure originale : les moulures du plafond, les murs incurvés, les colonnes majestueuses. « De ma fenêtre, je vois la célèbre Pearl Tower et les bateaux sur le Huang Pu. Depuis que j'ai emménagé ici, je n'ai rien changé. La belle architecture se suffit à elle-même. »

P. 637 Teng, who has spent time in Japan, has a tatami mat that he spreads out for his daily meditation. • Erinnerung an einen Aufenthalt in Japan: die Tatami-Matte, die Teng täglich zur Meditation ausbreitet. • Teng, qui a passé du temps au Japon, étale un tatami pour ses méditations quotidiennes.

↑ A red wooden staircase leads to Teng's top-floor apartment. He is the only residential tenant in the building, which is owned by the People's Liberation Army. • Eine rot gestrichene Holztreppe führt hinauf zu Tengs Wohnung in das oberste Geschoss. Er ist der einzige private Mieter im Haus, das der Volksbefreiungsarmee gehört. • Un escalier en bois rouge mène au dernier étage où habite Teng. Il est le seul à résider dans l'immeuble qui appartient à l'Armée de libération du peuple.

↗ Teng's desk, graced with traditional Chinese calligraphy brushes. • Traditionelle chinesische Kalligrafiepinsel auf Tengs Schreibtisch. • Une autre vue du bureau de Teng, avec des pinceaux de calligraphie chinois.

→ The plasterwork and wooden pillars are part of the original structure of this former Japanese consulate building. • Der Stuck und die tragenden holzverkleideten Säulen sind originale Bausubstanz des ehemaligen japanischen Konsulats. • Le stuc et les poutres de bois porteuses se trouvaient déjà dans l'ancien consulat japonais.

PP. 640–641 Architect Teng has two desks. This Chinese table, in the corner, is where he keeps his papers. The other desk is where he actually works. • Diesen chinesischen Tisch in der Ecke benutzt Teng allein als Ablage für Papiere. Am zweiten Schreibtisch links arbeitet er. • L'architecte Teng a deux bureaux. Le premier, dans le coin, sert à entreposer ses papiers, le second, à travailler.

SINGAPORE
SINGAPORE

Black and Right

High up on the 15th floor of an early 1960s modernist apartment building in the heart of Singapore, fashion retailer Bernard Teo's flat is a whimsical fusion of old and new. The building sits on a hill, overlooking a green belt dotted with prewar colonial bungalows. Moving in was a pursuit of love: Teo first saw the apartment 20 years ago, when it belonged to a girlfriend. He liked it so much that when it came up for sale six years later, he acquired it—and literally took it apart. One of the bedrooms was sacrificed to extend the dining area and, over the years, he has reworked the place to suit his style. Its ingredients are modern art from Bali, industrial lighting saved from hospitals and schools, eclectic furniture, and, last but not least, a rare flowering cactus in an old Javanese copper basin on the long terrace. Most amusing of all is the 175-piece collection of porcelain figures of Chairman Mao—produced during the Cultural Revolution—which Bernard Teo started because of his father's uncanny resemblance to the Great Helmsman.

Bernard Teos Wohnung liegt hoch oben im 15. Stock eines modernistischen Wohnblocks aus den frühen 1960er Jahren mitten in Singapur. Der Boutiquenbesitzer verbindet in der Einrichtung Alt und Neu auf individuelle Art. Das Gebäude steht auf einem Hügel, der Blick geht auf einen Grüngürtel mit Bungalows im Kolonialstil. Die Wohnung ging Teo nicht mehr aus dem Kopf, seit er sie vor mehr als zwanzig Jahren zum ersten Mal sah. Damals gehörte sie einer Freundin, und als sie sechs Jahre später zum Verkauf stand, griff er sofort zu. Teo mochte die Wohnung sehr und nahm sie dennoch buchstäblich auseinander. Er opferte ein Schlafzimmer zugunsten einer Erweiterung des Esszimmers und gestaltete die Wohnung über die Jahre nach seinem Geschmack um. Moderne Kunst aus Bali kombinierte er mit Lampen, die er aus Schulen oder Krankenhäusern rettete, und Möbelstücken wie dem Sofa im Kolonialstil, das ihm die Bank of China im Zuge einer Renovierung verkaufte. Seine inzwischen 175 Exemplare umfassende Sammlung von Porzellanfiguren aus der Zeit der Kulturrevolution, die den „großen Vorsitzenden Mao" darstellen, begann Bernard Teo wegen der verblüffenden Ähnlichkeit des Politikers mit seinem Vater.

Situé au quinzième étage d'un immeuble construit au début des années 1960 au centre de Singapour, l'appartement de Bernard Teo est un curieux mélange d'ancien et de neuf. L'immeuble est juché sur une colline, d'où il domine une ceinture verte émaillée de pavillons de style colonial remontant à l'avant-guerre. Son propriétaire est tombé amoureux de l'appartement il y a vingt ans, quand il l'a vu pour la première fois. Il appartenait alors à une de ses amies, et lorsqu'il a été mis en vente six ans plus tard, il en a fait l'acquisition parce qu'il l'aimait toujours autant – ce qui ne l'a pas empêché de le mettre littéralement en pièces. Il a sacrifié une des chambres pour agrandir le coin repas et, au fil des ans, il a remodelé le logement à son goût. De l'art moderne balinais et des éclairages industriels récupérés dans des hôpitaux ou des écoles côtoient des meubles hétéroclites. Le plus amusant de la décoration est la collection de 175 présidents Mao en porcelaine produits pendant la Révolution culturelle, collection que Bernard Teo avait commencée à cause de la troublante ressemblance entre son père et le Grand Timonier.

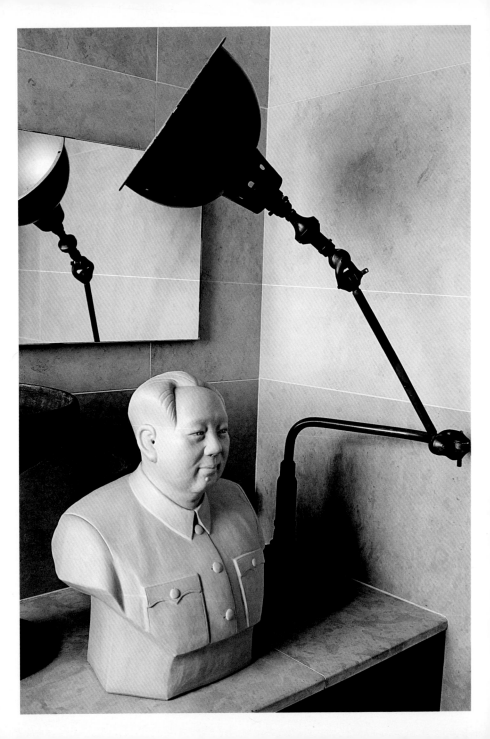

P. 643 In the living area, Jasper Morrison chairs by Cappellini and a sofa are arranged around an Indian table. • Im Wohnbereich stehen ein Sofa und Jasper-Morrison-Sessel von Cappellini um einen indischen Tisch. • Dans le séjour, un canapé et des chaises de Jasper Morrison fabriquées par Cappellini sont disposés autour d'une table indienne.

← Teo collects porcelain sculptures of Mao—because the former chairman of the CPC looks a lot like his father. The old industrial lamp was part of the fittings of a public building. • Porzellanstatuetten von Mao sammelt Teo, weil der „große Vorsitzende" der KP China seinem Vater sehr ähnelt. Die alte Werkslampe gehörte einst zur Ausstattung eines öffentlichen Gebäudes. • Teo collectionne les porcelaines représentant Mao parce que le Grand Timonier ressemblait beaucoup à son père. La vieille lampe industrielle se trouvait autrefois dans un bâtiment public.

↓ The fashion retailer combined modern Balinese art with dark wooden furniture and white porcelain. • Moderne balinesische Kunst kombiniert der Hausherr mit dunklen Holzmöbeln und weißem Porzellan. • Le propriétaire associe l'art moderne balinais à des meubles de bois sombre et des porcelaines blanches.

↑ Terrace doors open to frame the city's skyline. • Durch die Balkontür geht der Blick auf die Skyline der Stadt. • Les portes de la terrasse encadrent la vue de la métropole avec ses gratte-ciel.

→ Photographs of Tibetan children by American photo journalist Phil Borges hang above an Art-Deco style cabinet. • Die Fotos von tibetischen Kindern des amerikanischen Bildjournalisten Phil Borges hängen über einer Anrichte im Art-déco-Stil. • Au-dessus d'un meuble style Art Déco, des photographies d'enfants tibétains prises par le photo-journaliste américain Phil Borges.

ST. PETERSBURG
RUSSIA

Look Back in Color

The intense colors of the early Soviet era inspired these St. Petersburg interiors by Dominique de Roquemaurel-Galitzine. After extensive research, the French jewelry and interior designer devised a boldly hued style russe for the vacation apartment of travel agency Roquemaurel-Galitzine Tourisme. Previously, the flat, which occupies the second floor of a building from 1806 behind the Mariinsky Theater, had housed a kommunalka, a state-owned communal apartment that was divided up into tiny cells for five families. Roquemaurel reopened the spaces and decorated them with folksy antiques. "My interventions were deliberately modest. The floors, doors, and windows are all unchanged and the nostalgic furnishings give the rooms a whimsical charm."

Es waren die Nachklänge der frühen Sowjetzeit mit ihren intensiven Farben, die Dominique de Roquemaurel-Galitzine in Sankt Petersburg inspirierten. Nach eingehenden Recherchen gab die Stylistin und Schmuckdesignerin dem Apartment, das über die französische Reiseagentur Roquemaurel-Galitzine Tourisme gebucht werden kann, Wandanstriche in den intensiven Tönen ihres romantischen style russe. Das erste Stockwerk des 1806 errichteten Gebäudes hinter dem Mariinsky-Theater war, bevor es in den Besitz der Agentur kam, eine „Kommunalka", eine staatliche Wohngemeinschaft, aufgeteilt in winzige Zellen für fünf Familien. Roquemaurel öffnete die Räume und möblierte sie mit folkloristischen Antiquitäten. „Ich hielt mich bewusst zurück. Die Böden, Türen und Fenster blieben alle unverändert, und die Ausstattung verstärkt den nostalgischen Charme der Räume."

Saint-Pétersbourg, le style soviétique à ses débuts, avec ses couleurs intenses a donné des idées à Dominique de Roquemaurel-Galitzine. Après des recherches approfondies, la styliste et créatrice de bijoux a transposé son style russe en peignant de couleurs vives les murs de l'appartement qui peut être loué auprès de l'agence de voyages française Roquemaurel-Galitzine. Situé à deux pas du théâtre Mariinsky, cet ancien appartement communautaire où vivaient cinq familles, est au premier étage d'un beau bâtiment réaménagé en 1806. Roquemaurel a réorganisé les volumes et meublé le tout de ses trouvailles de styles très variés. « J'ai volontairement évité de trop intervenir. Les sols, les portes et les fenêtres sont restés en l'état et le mobilier, les tableaux et objets lui donnent un charme fou. »

P. 649 In accordance with Orthodox traditions, gold-framed icons hang in the eastern corners of both bedrooms. • Nach orthodoxer Tradition hängt in den östlichen Ecken beider Schlafzimmer eine Ikone mit Goldrahmen. • Suivant la tradition orthodoxe, une icône au cadre d'or est suspendue dans le coin oriental des deux chambres.

← Roquemaurel sourced the eclectic collection of pictures and furniture from local antique dealers. • Die eklektische Sammlung von Bildern und Möbeln fand Roquemaurel bei Antiquitäten-händlern vor Ort. • Roquemaurel a chiné les tableaux et les meubles éclec-tiques chez les antiquaires de la ville.

→ For a newspaper feature, Roque-maurel-Galitzine Tourisme allowed a group of St. Petersburg artists to use the bedroom walls as their canvas. • Im Rahmen einer Reportage für eine Zeit-schrift erlaubte die Agentur Roquemau-rel-Galitzine Tourisme einer Gruppe von Sankt Petersburger Künstlern, die Schlafzimmer-wände umzugestalten. • Dans le cadre d'un reportage pour une revue, l'agence Roquemaurel-Galitzine Tourisme a autorisé un groupe d'artis-tes de Saint-Pétersbourg à transformer les murs des chambres.

PP. 652–653 A feast for the eyes. The horse-head benches were made to order by a local carpenter. They take their cue from traditional farmhouse fur-niture. • Ein Fest auch fürs Auge. Die Pferdekopf-Bänke wurden bei einem lokalen Schreiner in Auftrag gegeben, als Vorbild dienten alte Bauernmöbel. • Plaisir des yeux. Les banquettes-têtes de cheval, réalisées sur le modèle de meubles paysans traditionnels, ont été commandées à un menuisier local.

↑ A plush rug covers the table. As in old Russia, others adorn the wall behind the bed. • Ein schwerer Teppich schützt den Tisch. Wie im alten Russland bedecken andere die Wand hinter dem Bett. • Une lourde couverture de velours protège la table. Des tapis habillent le mur derrière le lit, comme autrefois en Russie.

→ "This sofa predates the February Revolution," the stylist notes. The table and chairs were bought from the previous occupants. • „Dieses Sofa gab es schon vor der Februar-Revolution", erläutert die Stylistin. Tisch und Stühle wurden den vorherigen Bewohnern abgekauft. • « Ce canapé existait déjà avant la révolution de Février », explique la styliste. La table et les chaises ont été achetées aux anciens occupants de l'appartement.

STOCKHOLM
SWEDEN

A World of Materials

Filippa Knutsson's work is all about fabrics and colors with day-to-day wearability, and there is a similarly functional yet luxurious feel to her home. For the modernization of the two-story apartment, which occupies the top floors of a Neo-Renaissance building in the heart of Stockholm, the founder of Swedish fashion label Filippa K brought in architects Björn and Marianne Aaro. The interiors were thoroughly transformed and now feature subtle shades and high-end materials such as oak, hand-finished tiles, und pure wool carpets. Completed in 2011, this family duplex with great entertaining potential is perfect for everyday contemporary living. "It's a kind of cocoon," says Knutsson, "an inspiring refuge."

In der Arbeit der schwedischen Modemacherin Filippa Knutsson, der Gründerin des Labels Filippa K, dreht sich alles um den eigentlichen Luxus: die mühelose Alltagstauglichkeit von Stoffen und Farben. Ebenso sinnlich-funktionale Maßstäbe galten bei der Transformation dieses zweistöckigen Apartments zum Zuhause ihrer Familie, mit dem sie die Architekten Björn und Marianne Aaro beauftragte. In den oberen Etagen eines Neorenaissance-Gebäudes im Herzen Stockholms wurden alle Räume erneuert. Dabei blieben die Töne stets dezent, getragen von hochwertigen Materialien wie Eiche, handgefertigten Fliesen und Teppichen aus reiner Wolle. So wird die Wohnung seit 2011 den Ansprüchen des heutigen Lebens gerecht, sei es morgens beim Familienfrühstück oder abends mit Freunden. Oder wie Filippa Knutsson es beschreibt: „Sie ist wie ein Kokon, ein inspirierender Rückzugsort."

Tout le travail de la styliste de mode suédoise Filippa Knutsson, fondatrice du label Filippa K, se concentre sur les qualités au quotidien des étoffes et des couleurs. Ces critères de sensualité et de fonctionnalité – le vrai luxe – ont été aussi appliqués à la transformation de cet appartement de deux étages en foyer familial, un travail qu'elle a confié aux architectes Björn et Marianne Aaro. Toutes les pièces des étages supérieurs d'un bâtiment néo-Renaissance situé au cœur de Stockholm, ont été rénovées. La palette est restée discrète, portée par des matériaux de qualité comme le chêne, des carreaux de terre cuite faits à la main et des tapis pure laine. Depuis 2011, le logement satisfait aux exigences de la vie moderne, que ce soit le matin pendant le petit-déjeuner familial ou bien le soir avec des amis. Ou, ainsi que le décrit Filippa Knutsson : « On dirait un cocon, un refuge où l'on trouve l'inspiration. »

P. 657 With its Dinesen oak floorboards and modular sofa by Piero Lissoni for Living Divani, the living room feels both cozy and grand. • Eichendielen von Dinesen und Piero Lissonis Modulsofa von Living Divani geben dem Wohnzimmer repräsentative Gemütlichkeit. • Un plancher de chêne de Dinesen et un sofa de Piero Lissoni pour Living Divani donnent au séjour un confort représentatif.

← The kitchen tabletop is Carrara marble and the floor features cement tiles by Emery & Cie. • Der Küchentisch mit einer Platte aus Carrara-Marmor steht auf Zementfliesen von Emery & Cie. • La table de cuisine au plateau en marbre de Carrare se dresse sur des carreaux en ciment d'Emery & Cie.

↑ The central hub of the apartment, the hall, boasts newly tiled walls. • Die Eingangshalle dient als zentraler Zugangsraum, die Wände wurden neu gefliest. • Le hall d'entrée sert d'accès central, les murs ont été carrelés à neuf.

P. 660 Hard and clean: the countertop for the custom-made kitchen units is also made of marble. • Auch die Arbeitsfläche der maßgefertigten Küche besteht aus einer Marmorplatte. • Le plan de travail de la cuisine sur mesure est, lui aussi, recouvert d'une plaque de marbre.

P. 661 New terra-cotta flooring adds vitality to the attic, while the Zanotta sofa is the ideal place for a creative time out. • Neue Terrakotta-Fliesen beleben den Boden im Dachgeschoss, das Sofa von Zanotta lädt zu kreativen Pausen ein. • De nouveaux carreaux de terre cuite égaient le sol de l'étage mansardé, le canapé de Zanotta est réservé aux pauses créatives.

← The irregular hand-finished tiles by Emery & Cie blend harmoniously with the old wooden ceiling. • Die handgefertigten unregelmäßigen Fliesen von Emery & Cie harmonieren mit der geplankten Dachschräge. • Les carreaux faits main et irréguliers d'Emery & Cie s'harmonisent avec le vieux plafond de bois.

↓ A flat-screen TV in a specially made panel hangs from the wall of the pristinely modern bedroom. • Das moderne Schlafzimmer erhielt ein speziell angefertigtes Paneel, das den TV-Screen rahmt. • La chambre à coucher moderne est équipée d'un panneau fabriqué spécialement qui encadre l'écran de télévision.

TIELRODE
BELGIUM

The Milky Way of Decoration

In a village 16 miles from Antwerp, artists Sofie Lachaert and Luc d'Hanis have turned a former shipyard building into a gallery for contemporary art, setting up their own living quarters and a bed-and-breakfast next door. As their work revolves around singular objects, the couple wanted the architecture to act as a kind of passe-partout, framing the furniture and artifacts as harmoniously as possible. They thus chose a soft shade of white for all the walls. "The light moves through the bright rooms very gently," Lachaert says. "Lots of our visitors remark how calm the atmosphere makes them feel."

Das Dorf, in dem früher Schiffe gebaut wurden, liegt 26 Kilometer von Antwerpen entfernt. Das Künstlerpaar Sofie Lachaert und Luc d'Hanis kaufte sich dort eine alte Werfthalle und machte daraus seine Galerie für zeitgenössische Kunst. Angeschlossen sind Wohnräume und ein Bed & Breakfast-Gästehaus. Weil sich in den Arbeiten von Lachaert und d'Hanis alles um spezifische Einzelobjekte dreht, sollte die Architektur wie ein Passepartout wirken und Möbel wie Artefakte möglichst harmonisch rahmen. So wurde alles in ein sanftes Weiß getaucht. „Das Licht bewegt sich ganz weich durch die hellen Räume", beschreibt es Lachaert. „Viele unserer Besucher sagen uns, wie friedlich sie diese Atmosphäre stimmt."

Le village, un ancien chantier naval, est situé à 26 kilomètres d'Anvers. Les artistes Sofie Lachaert et Luc d'Hanis ont acheté ici un ancien hall de construction et l'ont transformé en galerie d'art contemporain. Des espaces d'habitation et un pavillon pour invités avec Bed & Breakfast y sont rattachés. Tout, dans les travaux de Lachaert et d'Hanis, se rapportant aux objets particuliers, l'architecture devait servir de passe-partout et offrir le cadre le plus harmonieux possible aux meubles et aux objets exposés. Ainsi tout baigne dans un blanc caressant. Selon la propriétaire : « La lumière se déplace avec légèreté dans les pièces claires. Nos visiteurs sont nombreux à remarquer combien cette atmosphère les apaise. »

P. 665 Set against one of the gallery walls, is an unrestored hospital cupboard—it now contains bed linen. • In der Galerie steht ein alter Krankenhausschrank (nun beherbergt er Bettwäsche) im Originalzustand. • Dans la galerie, une ancienne armoire d'hôpital dans son état d'origine – elle abrite maintenant la literie.

← One of the exhibits is a giant ceramic lamp by Jos Devriendt that blurs the line between art and design. • Teil der Ausstellung ist die Keramiklampe zwischen Kunst und Design von Jos Devriendt. • La lampe en céramique, entre art et design, de Jos Devriendt fait partie de l'exposition de la galerie.

↓ In the guesthouse bedroom is a leather chaise longue by Maarten Van Severen. • Eine lederbezogene Chaiselounge von Maarten Van Severen steht im Schlafzimmer des Gästehauses. • Une chaise longue en cuir de Maarten Van Severen dans la chambre du Bed & Breakfast.

→ The Jasper Morrison chair was the first design object the couple ever bought. • Der Stuhl von Jasper Morrison war das erste Designoriginal, das sich die Eigentümer leisteten. • La chaise de Jasper Morrison a été le premier objet design qu'ont pu s'offrir les propriétaires.

P. 668 On the right beneath the Marlene Dumas print is an upholstered chair inherited from one of the couple's grandmothers. • Unter der Grafik von Marlene Dumas steht rechts ein von der Großmutter geerbter Polstersessel. • À droite, sous le dessin de Marlene Dumas, un fauteuil rembourré qui appartenait à la grand-mère.

P. 669 Panton dining chairs are gathered around the farmhouse table, the silver étagère was made by Lachaert herself. • Zum Bauerntisch gesellen sich Panton-Stühle, die silberne Etagere schmiedete die Besitzerin selbst. • La table rustique est mariée à des chaises Panton, la propriétaire a forgé le présentoir à étages argenté.

← The bathtub is a bespoke item, while a white-painted shopping trolley acts as a towel rail. • Der Badetrog ist eine Maßanfertigung, ein weiß lackierter Einkaufswagen dient als Handtuchhalter. • La cuve de bois a été fabriquée sur mesure, un caddie peint en blanc sert de porte-serviettes.

↖ The furniture objects—a high chair and table-cum-seat—are by Bram Boo. • Die Möbelobjekte – ein hoher Sessel und ein Tisch-Stuhl – sind von Bram Boo. • Les meubles-objets, combinaisons de table et de chaise, sont signés Bram Boo.

↑ Breakfast at the white farmhouse table, whose legs have been lengthened. • Frühstücksszene am weiß gestrichenen Bauerntisch mit nachträglich ver

längerten Beinen. • Le petit-déjeuner est servi sur la table rustique peinte en blanc dont les pieds ont été rallongés.

↓ The white background highlights every object, just as the artists intended. • Das Konzept geht auf: Durch den weißen Hintergrund wird jedes Objekt hervorgehoben. • La stratégie porte ses fruits : le fond blanc met chaque objet en valeur.

TOKYO
JAPAN

Plastic Fantastic

Japan's modern architects' first love in the 1960s was concrete. But at the beginning of the 21st century, they fell into the arms of a new mistress: plastic. The very opposite of concrete, plastic is lightweight, thin-walled, translucent, and malleable—ideal for working with very small spaces. And even wealthy people in Tokyo today must build their homes in very small spaces. Kengo Kuma's Plastic House is an experiment in the use of FRP (fiberglass-reinforced polymer). Built for photographer Rowland Kirishima, the residence, squeezed into a narrow rectangular lot, consists of two stories for Rowland and his wife, with a basement apartment for his mother. FRP forms walls, doors, and stairs, letting light filter in and through the house during the day rather like paper shoji doors did in Japanese houses of old. At the rear is a louvered deck that serves as a tea ceremony platform, and also as a skylight for the mother's apartment below.

Ab den 1960er Jahren galt die große Liebe japanischer Architekten dem Beton. Doch zu Beginn des 21. Jahrhunderts warfen sie sich in die Arme einer neuen Geliebten – des Kunststoffs. Plastik ist das genaue Gegenteil von Beton: Es ist leicht, dünn, durchscheinend und biegsam – und somit ein ideales Arbeitsmaterial für extrem kleine Räume. Und in Tokyo müssen selbst wohlhabende Leute ihre Häuser oft auf sehr kleinen Grundstücken errichten. Kengo Kumas Plastic House ist ein einziges FRP-(fiberglasverstärktes Polymer-)Experiment. Das für den Fotografen Rowland Kirishima errichtete Haus, das sich in eine schmale, rechteckige Baulücke zwängt, besteht aus zwei Stockwerken für Rowland und seine Frau sowie einer separaten Souterrainwohnung für seine Mutter. Aus FRP sind Wände, Türen und Treppen, die tagsüber das Licht herein und von Zimmer zu Zimmer scheinen lassen – genau wie es früher die papierenen shoji-Türen taten. Auf der Rückseite befindet sich ein Lamellendeck, das als Oberlicht für die darunterliegende Wohnung der Mutter dient.

Dans les années 1960, les architectes modernes japonais sont tombés amoureux du béton. Puis, au début du 21ᵉ siècle, ils se sont découverts une nouvelle idylle : le plastique. À l'opposé du béton, celui-ci est léger, fin, translucide et malléable, idéal pour les espaces minuscules. À Tokyo aujourd'hui, même les riches vivent à l'étroit. Dans la maison en plastique, Kengo Kuma a expérimenté le FRP (polymère renforcé de fibre de verre). Construite pour le photographe Rowland Kirishima, elle est coincée sur un mince terrain rectangulaire et comporte, outre un duplex pour Rowland et sa femme, un appartement en sous-sol pour la mère de ce dernier. Le FRP permet de façonner des murs, des portes, des escaliers, tout en laissant filtrer la lumière, un peu à la manière des portes en papier shoji autrefois. À l'arrière, une plateforme à claire-voie accueille la cérémonie du thé et éclaire l'appartement de la mère en contrebas.

P. 673 The kitchen and dining room on the ground floor, with glass wall and high ceiling. • Der Küchen- und Essbereich mit Glaswand im Erdgeschoss. • La cuisine/salle à manger du rez-de-chaussée, avec un mur de verre.

← Plastic mesh covers the treads of the staircase leading from the second floor to the roof terrace. • Kunststoffgitter bilden die Trittflächen der Treppe, die vom zweiten Stock hinauf zur Dachterrasse führt. • Des grilles de plastique forment les marches de l'escalier qui mène du second étage à la terrasse.

↑ The ground-floor living space, open to the kitchen and dining area, features an abundance of closet and cabinet space. • Das Wohnzimmer im Erdgeschoss ist zum Küchen- und Essbereich hin offen und verfügt dank der Einbauschränke über jede Menge Stauraum. • Le séjour du rez-de-chaussée, ouvert sur la cuisine/salle à manger, dispose de nombreux espaces de rangement.

PP. 676–677 The raised louvered deck in the rear garden feeds natural light to the basement apartment below. The deck also serves as a stage for performing tea ceremonies. • Das erhöhte Lamellenpodest geht auf den rückwärtigen Garten hinaus und ermöglicht, dass genügend Licht in die Souterrainwohnung fällt. Hier findet auch die Teezeremonie statt. • La plateforme en console dans le jardin arrière laisse passer la lumière dans l'appartement du dessous. Elle accueille également la cérémonie du thé.

← In the basement are the bedroom and living area of Rowland Kirishima's mother. • Im Souterrain befinden sich die Schlaf- und Wohnräume der Mutter. • Au sous-sol, la chambre à coucher et les pièces d'habitation de la mère.

→ The elliptic curve of the tub stands in sculptural counterpoint to the stark geometry of the house. • Die ovale Wanne bildet einen interessanten Gegensatz zur strengen Rechtwinkeligkeit des Hauses. • La vasque elliptique de la baignoire forme un contraste sculptural avec la géométrie rigoureuse de la maison.

"I chose fiberglass-reinforced plastic because I wanted a material that would be urban and yet warm." KENGO KUMA

„Weil ich ein Material wollte, das urban und trotzdem warm wirkt, fiel meine Wahl auf faserverstärkten Kunststoff."
« J'ai choisi le plastique renforcé de fibres parce que je voulais un matériau qui soit à la fois urbain et chaud. »

TOKYO
JAPAN

House of Study

When Yoshifumi Nakamura acquired his new residence, he was faced with an empty shell. With a footprint of 530 square feet and 20-foot-high outer walls, the house was a "skeleton and infill" arrangement—up to the architect to create his own space. Exceptional among contemporary architects, Nakamura's aim for his wife and himself was "comfort." To this end, he designed a two-floor dwelling with the soft colors of wood, and many a niche to relax, read a book, or lie down for a nap. Completed in 2003, Nakamura's house belongs to no identifiable style. Its appeal lies in the details. Nakamura, also a furniture designer, used the textures of many woods—chestnut and pine floors, paulownia ceilings, walnut railings, teak counters—to conjure a warm and "touchable" environment. In the process, he has created a Tokyo version of the old literati retreat of China or Japan: practical, low-key, fitted with simple but high-quality items.

Als Yoshifumi Nakamura sein neues Zuhause erwarb, stand er vor einer leeren Hülle. Bei den von sechs Meter hohen Wänden umgebenen 7 x 7 Metern Grundfläche handelte es sich um ein sogenanntes Skelettarrangement, sodass sein Inneres vom Architekten selbst zu gestalten war. Im Gegensatz zu vielen anderen zeitgenössischen Architekten wollte Nakamura für sich und seine Frau vor allem eines: Behaglichkeit. Deshalb entwarf er ein zweigeschossiges Haus in verschiedenen Holzschattierungen und mit vielen Nischen, in denen man sich entspannen, ein Buch lesen oder ein Schläfchen machen kann. Das 2003 fertiggestellte Nakamura House ist auf keinen bestimmten Stil festgelegt, sein Reiz liegt im Detail. Nakamura, der auch Möbel entwirft, nutzte die Maserung verschiedener Hölzer – Eiche und Kiefer für die Böden, Paulownie für die Decken, Nussbaum für die Geländer und Teak für die Arbeitsflächen –, um eine warme, „haptische" Atmosphäre zu schaffen. Das Ergebnis ist die Großstadtversion der alten, chinesischen oder japanischen Literatenklausen: praktisch, völlig unaufdringlich und mit schlichter, dabei qualitätvoller Einrichtung.

Quand Yoshifumi Nakamura acheta sa future résidence, ce n'était qu'une coquille vide : un sol de 7 x 7 mètres, entouré de murs de 6 mètres de haut. C'était un squelette sans chair. Il ne lui restait plus qu'à créer son propre espace. Fait exceptionnel pour un architecte contemporain, son mot d'ordre pour lui-même et sa femme était « confort ». Il a donc conçu une habitation sur deux niveaux où dominent les tons doux du bois, remplie de recoins où se détendre, lire ou s'allonger pour une sieste. Achevée en 2003, sa maison ne relève d'aucun courant particulier. Son attrait réside dans le soin du détail. Nakamura, qui crée aussi des meubles, a utilisé les textures de nombreux bois (sols en châtaignier et pin, plafonds en paulownia, rampes en noyer, comptoirs en teck) afin de créer un environnement chaleureux et plaisant au toucher. Sa demeure est une version du Tokyo des anciennes retraites des lettrés chinois ou japonais : fonctionnelle, sobre, dépouillée et ornée d'objets de qualité.

P. 681 The reading nook is accessed via steps whose hatch can be removed from the shelf on the side wall. • Die kleine Lesenische erreicht man über Trittflächen, die von dem seitlichen Regal ausgeklappt werden. • On accède à l'alcôve de lecture en abaissant un panneau inférieur de l'étagère latérale.

↑ Nakamura designed all the cabinets, tables, and chairs as well as the black iron wood-burning stove. • Nakamura entwarf alle Schränke, Tische und Stühle sowie den schwarzen gusseisernen Holzofen. • Nakamura a dessiné tous les placards, les tables et les chaises ainsi que le poêle à bois en fonte noire.

→ An oval bath, rinsing buckets, upper walls, and partitioned tub cover were hand-crafted from various types of cedar. • Der ovale Badezuber, die Wascheimer und der obere Wandbereich sind alle handgearbeitet und bestehen aus unterschiedlichen Sorten von Zedernholz. • La baignoire, son couvercle articulé, les seaux et les boiseries hautes ont été réalisés dans différentes essences de cèdre.

PP. 684–685 The upper living space features a recessed black leather daybed and a 250-year-old Yi dynasty Korean vase complementing the room's spare lines. • Im oberen Wohnbereich gibt es eine Einbauliege mit schwarzem Lederbezug sowie eine 250 Jahre alte koreanische Vase aus der Yi-Dynastie – ein schönes Gegengewicht zu dem ansonsten ganz nüchtern gehaltenen Raum. • Dans le séjour à l'étage, un lit de repos encastré en cuir noir et un vase Yi coréen vieux de 250 ans complètent les lignes sobres de la pièce.

← At the foot of the wooden steps up to the library, a Shaker chair has found a new home. • Ein Shaker-Stuhl fand am Fuß der Holztreppe zur Bibliothek eine neue Heimat. • Une chaise Shaker au pied de l'escalier en bois menant à la bibliothèque.

↓ Nakamura used different types of wood for different parts of the house; for the floors, he chose oak and pine planks. • Für die verschiedenen Teile des Hauses setzte Nakamura unterschiedliche Holzarten ein: Eichen- und Kiefernholzdielen bilden die Böden. • Nakamura a utilisé diverses essences de bois selon les pièces de la maison : un parquet de chêne et de pin recouvre les sols.

TRANCOSO
BRAZIL

All in Good Order

Trancoso is considered to be one of the oldest Jesuit villages in the world. The arrival in Brazil of the first members of the Catholic Society of Jesus, founded by St. Ignatius of Loyola, came shortly after the discovery of Brazil in 1500. The humble cluster of houses around the rectangular town square, with the church of St. John the Baptist at one end with its back to the sea, was built by the Jesuits around 1586. Since the 1970s, when the first hippies began to arrive in Trancoso, the Praça de São João Batista (the Square of St. John the Baptist) has been known as the "Quadrado" or "Square." It is the nerve center of everything that happens in the village, so its uniform, colorful houses have become sought-after and prized not only as homes but also as designer shops, restaurants, and inns. One of the privileged few to have a residence in the Quadrado is Fernando Droghetti, a São Paulo interior-decoration entrepreneur who, with the help of architect Sig Bergamin, lent a distinctly Brazilian charm to the decor—from white-washed walls to flashes of tropical blue.

Trancoso gilt als eine der ältesten Jesuitensiedlungen der Welt. Die ersten Jesuiten, deren Orden von Ignatius von Loyola gegründet wurde, gelangten bereits kurz nach der Entdeckung Brasiliens im Jahre 1500 hierher. Um 1586 legten sie rings um einen rechteckigen, grünen Platz einen Häuserkomplex mit einer vom Meer abgewandten Kirche an, die sie Johannes dem Täufer widmeten. Als die ersten Hippies in den 1970er Jahren nach Trancoso kamen, wurde diese Praca de São João Batista von ihnen Quadrado („Quadrat") genannt. Hier laufen alle Stränge des Dorflebens zusammen. Die gleichförmigen, bunten Häuschen rund um den Platz sind heutzutage sehr gefragt. Sie beherbergen nicht nur Privatwohnungen, sondern auch elegante Boutiquen, Restaurants und Hotels. Einer der Privilegierten, der ein Haus am Quadrado besitzt, ist der Einrichtungsexperte Fernando Droghetti aus São Paulo. Mithilfe des Architekten Sig Bergamin hat er ihm brasilianischen Charme verliehen – von den schlicht geweißten Wänden bis zu den Akzenten in tropischem Blau.

Trancoso est considérée comme l'une des plus vieilles bourgades jésuites du monde. L'arrivée au Brésil des premiers religieux de la compagnie de Jésus, fondée par Ignace de Loyola, a eu lieu peu après la découverte du Brésil, en l'an 1500. Un ensemble de maisons simples entourent la place rectangulaire couverte de gazon, au fond de laquelle se dresse l'église São João Batista, édifiée autour de 1586 et qui surplombe la mer. C'est depuis les années 1970, lorsque les premiers hippies sont arrivés à Trancoso, que la place São João Batista est connue sous le nom de « Quadrado ». C'est là le lieu de convergence de la vie du hameau, ce qui a fini par rendre ces petites maisons identiques et colorées très recherchées. Aujourd'hui, elles ont été transformées en résidences, boutiques de marque, restaurants ou auberges. L'entrepreneur en décoration Fernando Droghetti, de São Paulo, est l'un des privilégiés possédant une maison sur le Quadrado. Avec l'aide de l'architecte Sig Bergamin, il a donné à la décoration un charme très brésilien.

P. 689 The dining table came from a ranch in Minas Gerais, and the chairs were purchased in São Paulo. The wooden wall sconce was found in Trancoso. • Der Esstisch stammt von einer Fazenda in Minas Gerais, die Stühle kommen aus São Paulo. Die hölzerne Wandleuchte ist eine Arbeit aus Trancoso. • La table de repas vient d'une ferme du Minas Gerais, et les chaises ont été dénichées à São Paulo. Sur le mur, une applique en bois venant de Trancoso.

↑ In the entrance area of the house is an old wardrobe from Minas Gerais now used as a crockery cupboard. • Im Eingangsbereich steht ein alter Schrank aus Minas Gerais, in dem Geschirr aufbewahrt wird. • Dans l'entrée de la maison, une armoire typique du Minas Gerais.

↗ Old glass-paneled doors form the head of the bed, which, like the rest of the room's furniture, is all in white. • Alte Türen mit Glaseinsätzen bilden das Kopfende des Bettes im Schlafzimmer, in dem alles wie in Weiß getaucht ist. • Dans la chambre à coucher, de vieilles portes vitrées forment la tête du lit, blanc comme tout les meubles dans la pièce.

→ In the living room, the collection of indigenous headdresses was framed and is displayed as works of art. The table in the center is an antique from Sul da Bahia. • Im Wohnzimmer hängt indianischer Federschmuck, gerahmt wie Gemälde präsentiert. Der antike Tisch in der Mitte kommt aus dem Süden Bahias. • Dans la pièce principale, la collection de parures indigènes a été encadrée et présentée comme œuvres d'art. La table ancienne provient du sud de l'État de Bahia.

← A platform covered with cushions acts as a sofa. The wide opening to the hall provides indirect daylight. • Ein gemauertes Podest wird, mit Sitzkissen belegt, zum Sofa. Für indirektes Tageslicht sorgt der breite Wanddurchbruch zum Flur. • Une estrade recouverte de coussins sert de canapé. Derrière, la grande ouverture qui donne sur le couloir laisse passer la lumière.

↑ The twin Saints Cosmas and Damian, seen from the back, are a lamp in painted plaster. • Die Heiligen Kosmas und Damian, hier von hinten, sind aus bemaltem Gips und dienen als Lampe. • Vue ici de dos, la statue des saints jumeaux Côme et Damien, en plâtre peint, est un luminaire.

↗ Patterned floor vases in the style of traditional Marajoara ceramics are the eye-catchers in this arrangement. • Bodenvasen im Stil der traditionellen brasilianischen Marajoara-Keramik werden mit ihrem grafischen Muster zum Blickfang. • Les motifs géométriques des jarres peintes dans le style de la céramique brésilienne traditionnelle Marajoara attirent ici le regard.

VICTORIA
AUSTRALIA

Blessed with Ideas

If it hadn't been for the Australian Gold Rush of the mid-19th century, this family of four would never have found themselves living in a church. Theirs is one of many places of worship erected out of gratitude for the wealth that prospecting brought to the townships around Melbourne. Built in 1860, it was finally put up for sale after having stood empty for 20 years. The new owners invited the entire village to its official deconsecration, then tasked architectural practice Multiplicity with its conversion: "Our interventions didn't alter the actual structure of the building. It could easily be turned back into a church one day if need be."

Ohne den australischen Goldrausch, der Mitte des 19. Jahrhunderts losging, könnte die vierköpfige Familie heute nicht in einem Kirchenschiff leben. Denn der Sturm auf die kostbaren Nuggets machte die Bewohner rund um Melbourne so reich, dass sie zum Dank zahlreiche Gotteshäuser errichteten – darunter auch dieses von 1860. Zwanzig Jahre stand es leer und wurde schließlich zum Verkauf angeboten. Nach einer feierlichen Entweihung, zu der die neuen Besitzer den ganzen Ort einluden, beauftragten sie die Architekten von Multiplicity mit dem Ausbau. „Unsere Eingriffe berühren die Grundstruktur des Bauwerks nicht", erläutern sie. „Wollte man irgendwann wieder eine Kirche daraus machen, wäre das ohne Weiteres möglich."

Sans la ruée vers l'or qu'a connue l'Australie au milieu du 19ᵉ siècle, la famille de quatre personnes ne pourrait pas vivre aujourd'hui dans une église. En effet, les habitants des communes entourant Melbourne étaient devenus si riches qu'ils édifièrent de nombreuses églises pour remercier le Seigneur, dont celle-ci en 1860. Restée inutilisée pendant vingt ans, elle a finalement été mise en vente. Après sa désacralisation et une fête à laquelle les nouveaux propriétaires ont invité tous les habitants, ils ont chargé les architectes de Multiplicity de la réaménager : « Nous n'avons pas touché à la structure de base de l'édifice. Si on voulait un jour la retransformer en église, ce serait possible sans difficultés. »

P. 695 Situated in what was the chancel, the kitchen features a white concrete island and a custom-made cupboard. • Im Altarraum ist heute die Küche untergebracht, mit einem weißen Betonküchenblock und maßgeschreinertem Schrank. • Le sanctuaire abrite aujourd'hui la cuisine avec son bloc de béton blanc et des éléments faits sur mesure.

← The chairs in front of the steel-framed fireplace are by Patricia Urquiola for Moroso; the coffee table was designed by the architects. • Die Sessel vor dem Kamin aus Stahl entwarf Patricia Urquiola für Moroso, der Coffeetable ist ein Entwurf der Architekten. • Les fauteuils, devant la cheminée en acier, sont signés Patricia Urquiola pour Moroso, la table roulante a été dessinée par les architectes.

↑ Suspended between the boxes, a platform serves as a study. Situated around the dining table are reupolstered 1960s original Scape chairs by Australian designer Grant Featherstone. • Zwischen den Boxen ragt eine Plattform hervor, auf der sich ein Arbeitsraum befindet. Um den Esstisch stehen mehrere Exemplare des Stuhls Scape, den der australische Designer Grant Feathers-

tone in den 1960ern entwarf. • Entre les box, une plateforme en saillie sur laquelle se trouve l'espace-travail. Autour de la table, des chaises Scape des années 1960, une création du designer australien Grant Featherstone.

PP. 698–699 To allow more daylight to enter the building, the heavy wooden church doors were replaced with a glass door, with the original timbers having been set into the dining table. • Um mehr Tageslicht einfallen zu lassen, wurden die schweren hölzernen Kirchentüren durch neue aus Glas ersetzt. Das alte Holz der Türen wurde für den Esstisch verwendet. • Les lourdes portes d'église en bois ont été remplacées par du verre qui laisse passer davantage de lumière. Les poutres d'origine y ont été insérées pour former la table des repas.

← The two-story cube containing the children's bedrooms is in close vicinity to the kitchen. • Von der Küche aus hat man den zweistöckigen Kubus der Kinderzimmer im Blick. • De la cuisine, on voit le cube de deux étages qui abrite les chambres d'enfants.

→ The original rose window is now in the master bedroom. • Das original erhaltene Rosettenfenster gehört nun zum Elternschlafzimmer. • Le vitrail d'origine se trouve maintenant dans la chambre des parents.

"The use of modern materials like steel and acrylic enhances the old church building." THE ARCHITECTS

„Durch die Verwendung moderner Materialien wie Stahl und Acryl wird das alte Kirchengebäude visuell hervorgehoben."
« L'utilisation de matériaux modernes comme acier et acrylique met le bâtiment historique en valeur. »

VIENNA
AUSTRIA

Space and Simplicity

"I'm not a person who buys design furniture," asserts artist and photographer Marina Faust. Instead, her apartment in Vienna is furnished mainly with possessions she inherited from her parents. There is part of her father's stunning book collection, a vintage American refrigerator with drawers, and several pieces by Austrian mid-century designer Carl Auböck, who was a family friend. The look today is much sparer than when her parents lived here. "I like whiteness," Faust admits. "I love empty walls. It's a kind of freedom." But not everything is perfectly pristine. "My atelier space in the back is full of stuff. Sometimes I need both chaos and order," she says. Among the things she added are several objects by her friend, the late artist Franz West. In the living room is a monochrome screen that she views and uses as both an artwork and room divider. She also has one of West's centipede wooden sculpture plinths, which acts as a bedside table. On top of it is a simply chic glass lamp made by her mother around 1960. The act of bold, impromptu creation, it would seem, is in the genes.

„Ich war nie jemand, der sich neue Designermöbel kauft." Stattdessen ist das Wiener Apartment der Künstlerin und Fotografin vor allem mit Erbstücken ausgestattet – man entdeckt zahllose wertvolle Bände aus der erstaunlichen Bibliothek ihres Vaters, einen amerikanischen Kühlschrank mit Schubladen und mehrere Objekte des legendären österreichischen Midcentury-Designers Carl Auböck, der ein Freund der Familie war. Der heutige Look ist allerdings viel karger als zu Zeiten ihrer Eltern. „Ich habe es gern weiß", gesteht Faust. „Ich liebe leere Wände. Das ist eine Art Freiheit." Doch das gilt nicht überall. „Mein Atelierbereich ist vollgestopft", erzählt sie. „Irgendwie brauche ich beides, Chaos und Ordnung." Zu den Dingen, die sie zur Einrichtung hinzufügte, gehören mehrere Arbeiten ihres verstorbenen Freunds Franz West, darunter ein monochromer Wandschirm – für Faust Kunstwerk und Raumteiler in einem. Sie besitzt auch eines von Wests vielbeinigen Postamenten, das nun als Nachttisch dient. Die so simple wie schicke Glas-Leuchte darauf baute ihre Mutter um 1960. Das Talent zum kühnen Impromptu steckt offenbar in den Genen.

« Je ne suis pas du genre à acheter du mobilier design », prévient l'artiste et photographe Marina Faust. Effectivement, son appartement viennois est aménagé principalement avec ce que lui ont laissé ses parents. On y trouve l'impressionnante bibliothèque de son père, un vieux réfrigérateur américain à tiroirs et plusieurs pièces des années 1950 du designer autrichien Carl Auböck, un ami de la famille. Le décor y est plus dépouillé que du temps de ses parents. « J'aime le blanc et les murs nus, c'est une forme de liberté », confie Faust. Toutefois, tout chez elle n'est pas immaculé. « Mon atelier à l'arrière est plein à craquer. En fait, j'ai besoin à la fois du chaos et de l'ordre. » Elle a ajouté au décor des œuvres de son ami disparu Franz West. Dans le séjour, l'écran monochrome de ce dernier fait à la fois office de sculpture et de cloison. Un de ses piédestaux « mille-pattes » sert de table de chevet. Dessus, Faust a placé une lampe en verre à l'élégante simplicité réalisée par sa mère vers 1960. À croire que le sens de la création spontanée est un trait de famille !

← Skylights recall the prewar use of the space as a photo studio. • Oberlichter erinnern daran, dass die Wohnung einst ein Fotostudio war • Avant la guerre, l'espace était un studio de photographe, comme le rappelle le puits de lumière.

↑ The 1970s sofa was bought by Faust's mother at auction in Munich. The Franz West floor lamp is made from steel and acrylic glass. • Das Sofa aus den 70ern ersteigerte ihre Mutter in München. Franz Wests Stehleuchte besteht aus Stahl und Acrylglas. • Le canapé des années 1970 provient d'une vente aux enchères à Munich. Le lampadaire de Franz West est en acier et en verre acrylique.

P. 703 A lamp made by Faust's mother from a blown-glass jar stands on one of artist Franz West's sculpture plinths in the master bedroom. • Eine Leuchte, die Fausts Mutter aus einem Einweckglas machte, steht im Schlafzimmer auf einem Postament des Künstlers Franz West. • Dans la chambre principale, une lampe réalisée par la mère de Faust avec un bocal en verre soufflé est posée sur un piédestal de Franz West convertie en table de chevet.

→ In the living room, a Carl Auböck floor lamp is placed next to a screen created by West from rebar steel, wood and acrylic paint. Faust inherited the tables and chairs from her parents. • Die Tische und Stühle im Wohnzimmer erbte Faust von ihren Eltern. Eine Carl-Auböck-Leuchte steht neben einem Paravent von West aus Betonstahl, Holz und Acrylfarbe. • Dans le séjour, un lampadaire de Carl Auböck près d'un paravent de West en acier d'armature, bois et acrylique. Faust a hérité des tables et des chaises de ses parents.

↑ The back terrace is nicknamed Twin Peaks Terrace due to the rustic wooden furniture, which reminds Faust of David Lynch's iconic TV series. "I was crazy about it," she smiles. • Die hintere Terrasse heißt Twin-Peaks-Terrasse, wegen der großen Holzmöbel, die Faust an David Lynchs TV-Serie erinnern. „Ich war verrückt danach", erklärt sie. • À l'arrière de l'appartement, la terrasse « Twin Peaks » avec ses meubles rustiques en bois, baptisée ainsi par Faust en clin d'œil à la célèbre série TV de David Lynch. « J'en étais folle », confie-t-elle.

→ In the guest room, a chair from Franz West's studio stands near an Auböck coat rack. From left, art by Nicolas Jasmin, Clegg & Guttmann, and Pierre Leguillon. • Im Gästezimmer steht ein Stuhl aus Franz Wests Studio, die Garderobe ist von Auböck. Kunst von Nicolas Jasmin, Clegg & Guttmann und Pierre Leguillon. • Dans la chambre d'amis, une chaise de l'atelier de Franz West côtoie un portemanteau d'Auböck. Sur les étagères, des œuvres de Nicolas Jasmin, Clegg & Guttman, et Pierre Leguillon (de gauche à droite).

ZÜRICH
SWITZERLAND

An Eye for Quality

Twenty-two years ago, This Brunner, a film curator and former director of Zurich's Arthouse cinema, discovered via a friend that an apartment in a typical Zürichberg villa from 1910 had become available. He took it and has spent the subsequent years filling its maze of rooms with objects that reflect the various episodes of his life—that is, with art by the likes of Andy Warhol, Francesco Clemente, Wolfgang Tillmans, Walter Pfeiffer, and John Waters. Although he can appreciate the skill of a good decorator, Brunner has always planned the interiors himself. "Your personality only shines through if you make your own choices. I myself was able to do that—the 30,000 films I've watched and the homes of all the great people I was lucky to meet over the years have trained my eye."

Vor 22 Jahren erfuhr der Filmkurator und ehemalige Leiter der Züricher Arthouse-Kinos This Brunner durch einen Freund von dem freien Apartment in einer typischen Zürichberg-Villa von 1910. Die ineinanderfließenden Wohnräume füllt er seitdem mit Episoden aus seinem Leben – also mit Kunst von Andy Warhol, Francesco Clemente, Wolfgang Tillmans und Walter Pfeiffer bis John Waters. Dabei behielt er das Einrichten stets selbst in der Hand. Zwar weiß Brunner durchaus das Können von Interiordesignern zu schätzen, doch „die Persönlichkeit des Bewohners zeigt sich nur, wenn man mit den eigenen Augen auswählt. Ich konnte das – meine sind geschult durch 30 000 Filme und die Häuser all der großartigen Menschen, die ich über die Jahre treffen durfte."

Il y a 22 ans, un de ses amis a informé This Brunner, l'ancien manager du cinéma Arthouse de Zurich, qu'un appartement était libre dans une villa zurichoise typique de 1910. Il l'a pris. Depuis, il remplit les espaces qui se succèdent avec fluidité avec les épisodes de sa vie. C'est-à-dire, entre autres, les œuvres d'Andy Warhol, Francesco Clemente, Wolfgang Tillmans, Walter Pfeiffer et John Waters. Ce faisant, il s'est occupé seul de la décoration. S'il sait estimer à sa juste valeur l'habileté des architectes d'intérieur, il n'en pense pas moins que « la personnalité de l'habitant ne se montre que lorsque l'on choisit soi-même. Je pouvais le faire – mon œil est éduqué par 30 000 films et les maisons de tous les gens formidables que j'ai rencontrés pendant des dizaines d'années ».

← Taken in 2005, the living room's soldier photograph by Wolfgang Tillmans remains highly topical. • Aktuelle Brisanz hat die 2005 entstandene Soldatenfotografie von Wolfgang Tillmans im Wohnraum. • Dans le séjour, la photo représentant des soldats réalisée en 2005 par Wolfgang Tillmans est tout à fait d'actualité.

P. 709 The dining table and chairs are one-offs made in the 1950s to designs by Jean Royère. • Tisch und Stühle im Esszimmer stammen aus den 1950ern und sind eine Einzelanfertigung nach Entwürfen von Jean Royère. • La table et les chaises de la salle à manger datent des années 1950, ce sont des pièces uniques fabriquées d'après des dessins de Jean Royère.

← Upholstered in Le Manach fabric, the reading sofa was designed by This Brunner himself. Next to it is a Jean Royère lamp. • Das Lesesofa entwarf This Brunner selbst und ließ es mit Stoff von Le Manach beziehen. Daneben eine Lampe von Jean Royère. • This Brunner a dessiné lui-même le canapé de lecture qu'il a fait recouvrir d'un tissu de Le Manach. À côté, une lampe de Jean Royère.

→ Above the living-room sofa is a portrait by Francesco Clemente and, on the far wall, a painting by Philip Taaffe. The lamp is by Serge Mouille. • Über dem Wohnzimmersofa hängt links ein Porträt von Francesco Clemente und an der Stirnwand ein Gemälde von Philip Taaffe. Die Lampe ist ein Entwurf von Serge Mouille. • À gauche, au-dessus du canapé du séjour, un portrait de Francesco Clemente et, sur le mur du fond, un tableau de Philip Taaffe. La lampe est signée Serge Mouille.

↓ In the bedroom is a small Jean-Michel Frank table with an original Alberto Giacometti lamp and a chair by Jacques Adnet. • Im Schlafzimmer steht ein kleines Pult von Jean-Michel Frank, die Lampe darauf ist ein Original von Alberto Giacometti. Der Stuhl stammt von Jacques Adnet. • Dans la chambre à coucher, un petit bureau de Jean-Michel Frank, la lampe posée dessus est un original d'Alberto Giacometti. La chaise est de Jacques Adnet.

PP. 712–713 Jean Royère armchairs sit in front of Elaine Sturtevant's acrylic painting *20 Marilyns* and a still from Warhol's *Blue Movie*. • Vor dem Acrylbild *20 Marilyns* von Elaine Sturtevant und einem Filmstill aus Warhols *Blue Movie* stehen Sessel von Jean Royère. • Des fauteuils de Jean Royère devant *20 Marilyns*, un tableau à l'acrylique d'Elaine Sturtevant, et une photo de tournage du *Blue Movie* de Warhol.

1000 Chairs

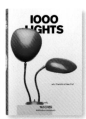

1000 Lights

Decorative Art 50s

Decorative Art 60s

Decorative Art 70s

Design of the
20th Century

domus 1950s

Logo Design

Scandinavian Design

100 All-Time
Favorite Movies

The Stanley Kubrick
Archives

Bookworm's delight:
never bore, always excite!

TASCHEN
Bibliotheca Universalis

20th Century
Photography

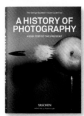

A History of
Photography

Stieglitz.
Camera Work

Curtis. The North
American Indian

Eadweard Muybridge

Karl Blossfeldt

Norman Mailer.
MoonFire

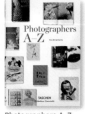

Photographers A–Z

Dalí. The Paintings

Hiroshige

Leonardo.
The Graphic Work

Modern Art

Monet

Alchemy & Mysticism

Braun/Hogenberg.
Cities of the World

Bourgery. Atlas of
Anatomy & Surgery

D'Hancarville.
Antiquities

Encyclopaedia
Anatomica

Martius.
The Book of Palms

Seba. Cabinet of
Natural Curiosities

The World
of Ornament

Fashion. A History from
18th–20th Century

100 Contemporary
Fashion Designers

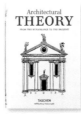
Architectural Theory

The Grand Tour

20th Century
Classic Cars

1000 Record Covers

1000 Tattoos

Funk & Soul Covers

Jazz Covers

Mid-Century Ads

Mailer/Stern.
Marilyn Monroe

Erotica Universalis

Tom of Finland.
Complete Kake Comics

1000 Nudes

Stanton.
Dominant Wives

CREDITS

PHOTO – 148-153, 214-219, 608-615 © Gianni Basso, Vega Mg, TASCHEN GmbH **296-303** © Bill Batten **478-485, 494-501,550-563** © Xavier Béjot, Tripod Agency, Production & Styling: Ian Phillips **486-493, 516-523, 532-537, 570-577** © Xavier Béjot, Tripod Agency, TASCHEN GmbH **236-241** © Ali Bekman, www.alibekman.com **18-25** © Mirjam Bleeker, www.mirjambleeker.nl, Photo Stylist: Frank Visser, www.ijm.nl **304-309** © Ana Paula Carvalho, www.anacarvalhophoto.com, Production: João Carriço **694-701** © Lisa Cohen, www.lisacohenphotography.com **430-437** © Anthony Cotsifas, www.anthonycotsifas.com **190-198** © Pieter Estersohn, www. pieterestersohn.com **564-569, 702-707** © Marina Faust, www.marinafaust.com **234-241** © Albert Font, www.alberfont.com, Photo Stylist: Ino Coll, www.inocoll.com, **708-715** © Reto Guntli, www.zapaimages.com **2, 38-43, 52-63, 142-147, 220-227, 254-259, 410-415, 464-477, 624-629, 636-647, 672-687** © Reto Guntli, www.zapaimages.com, TASCHEN GmbH **544-549** © François Halard, www.francoishalard.com **168-175** © Hiepler, Brunier, www.hiepler-brunier.de **154-161, 378-385, 664-671** © Ditte Isager, www.edgereps.com **508-515, 538-543**© Christoph Kicherer, TASCHEN GmbH **524-531** © Vincent Knapp **416-421** © Nikolas Koenig **162-167, 184-197** © Nathalie Krag; Production: Tami Christiansen **86-91, 334-339, 386-393** © Ricardo Labougle, www.ricardolabougle.com **108-115, 394-401, 600-607** © Ricardo Labougle, www.ricardolabougle.com, TASCHEN GmbH **64-69, 340-363, 364-377** © Eric Laignel, www.ericlaignel.com, TASCHEN GmbH **268-275, 656-663** © Åke Lindman, www.lindmanphotography.com **14-21, 130-135** © Thomas Loof, www.trunkarchive.com **592-599** © Thomas Loof & Pernille Pedersen, www. trunkarchive.com **276-281, 316-321** © Daniela Macadden, www.surpressagency.com **392-399** © Toni Meneguzzo, www.tonimeneguzzo.com, GMAimages **440-447** © Michael Moran, www.moranstudio.com, TASCHEN GmbH **248-253** © Lorenzo Nencioni, Vega Mg **70-77** © Noshe, www.noshe.com, TASCHEN GmbH **578-585** © Matteo Piazza,www.matteopiazza.com **616-623** © Tuca Reinés, www.tucareines.com.br **586-591, 688-693** © Tuca Reinés, www.tucareines.com.br, TASCHEN GmbH **30-37** © Ioanna Roufopoulou, www. zapaimages.com **116-129, 176-183, 282-287** © Deidi von Schaewen, TASCHEN GmbH **136-141** © Jason Schmidt, www.jasonschmidtartists.com **422-429, 444-449**© Jason Schmidt, www.jasonschmidtartists.com, TASCHEN GmbH **502-507** © Mark Seelen, www.markseelen.com **198-213, 228-233, 322-333, 630-635** © René Stoeltie, TASCHEN GmbH **78-85** © Tim Street-Porter, TASCHEN GmbH **100-107, 648-655** © Vincent Thibert, www.vincentthibert.com **288-295** © Simon Upton, The Interior Archive **44-51** © Verne, www.verne.be, Production: Inés Daelman, www.inezz.com **92-99, 260-267** © Verne, ww.verne.be, Production: Marc Heldens, www. marcheldens.com **438-443, 458-463** © Paul Warchol, www.warcholphotography.com **310-315** © Pablo G. Zuloaga, Stylist: Inés Sentmenat

CONTRIBUTORS – 108-115, 394-401, 600-607 Ana Cardinale, Paris & Isabel de Estrada, Buenos Aires **116-129, 176-183, 282-287** Frederic Couderc & Laurence Dougier, Paris **254-259, 410-415, 464-469, 672-687** Alex Kerr, Bangkok & Kathy Arlyn Sokol, Tokyo **586-591, 688-693** Mônica Lima, Salvador **470-477, 624-629** Anita Lococo, Bali **38-43, 52-63, 220-227, 636-641** Daisann McLane, New York **340-377** Patricia Parinejad, Berlin **148-152, 214-219, 608-615** Julio César Pérez Hernàndez, Havana **14-21, 78-85, 130-135, 162-167, 184-199, 304-309, 316-321, 416-421, 478-585, 592-599** Ian Phillips, Paris **142-147, 642-647** Sunil Sethi, New Delhi **198-213, 228-233, 322-334, 630-635** Barbara Stoeltie, Brussels **422-463** Peter Webster, Brooklyn, NY **64-77** Ingeborg Wiensowski, Berlin **22-37, 44-51, 70-107, 136-141, 154-161, 168-175, 234-253, 260-275, 288-295, 310-315, 334-339, 378-393, 402-409, 616-623, 648-655, 656-671, 694-707, 712-715** Eva Zimmermann, Berlin

TRANSLATIONS – English translation: Mary Black (captions) for Locteam, S.L. Barcelona / Pauline Cumbers, Frankfurt am Main / Michael Hulse, Warwick / Alayne Pullen for First Edition Translations Ltd, Cambridge / Iain Reynolds, Berlin / Anthony Roberts, Lupiac / Julie Street, Paris / Dennis Wright for Locteam, Barcelona **– German translation:** Stefan Barmann, Cologne / Anne Brauner, Cologne / Christiane Burkhardt, Munich / Franca Fritz & Heinrich Koop, Straelen / Ingrid Hacker-Klier, Hebertsfelden / André Höchemer (captions) for Locteam, S.L. Barcelona / Dr. Thomas Kinne, Nauheim / Magdalena Nowinska for Locteam, Barcelona / Simone Ott Caduff, Pasadena, CA / Marion Valentin, Cologne **French translation:** Pascal Durand (captions) for Locteam, Barcelona / Christèle Jany, Cologne / Philippe Safavi, Paris / Michèle Schreyer, Cologne

Page 2 Sitting room in David Tang's residence in Hong Kong. The acid-green armchair and embroidered pink velvet curtains display Tang's preference for bold, intense colors and his love of rich detail. **Seite 2** In David Tangs Wohnzimmer in Hong Kong. Der giftgrüne Sessel und die bestickten Samtvorhänge in Pink offenbaren Tangs Vorliebe für kräftige, intensive Farben und seinen Hang zu opulenten Details. **Page 2** Le salon de la résidence de David Tang à Hong Kong. Le fauteuil vert acidulé et les rideaux brodés en velours rose fuchsia témoignent du goût de Tang pour les couleurs fortes et intenses, ainsi que de son amour des détails raffinés.

IMPRINT

EACH AND EVERY TASCHEN BOOK

PLANTS A SEED! TASCHEN is a carbon neutral publisher. Each year, we offset our annual carbon emissions with carbon credits at the Instituto Terra, a reforestation program in Minas Gerais, Brazil, founded by Lélia and Sebastião Salgado. To find out more about this ecological partnership, please check:
www.taschen.com/zerocarbon
Inspiration: unlimited. Carbon footprint: zero.

To stay informed about TASCHEN and our upcoming titles, please subscribe to our free magazine at www.taschen.com/magazine, follow us on Twitter and Facebook, or e-mail your questions to contact@taschen.com.

TASCHEN ARBEITET KLIMANEUTRAL.

Unseren jährlichen Ausstoß an Kohlenstoffdioxid kompensieren wir mit Emissionszertifikaten des Instituto Terra, einem Regenwaldaufforstungsprogramm im brasilianischen Minas Gerais, gegründet von Lélia und Sebastião Salgado. Mehr über diese ökologische Partnerschaft erfahren Sie unter:
www.taschen.com/zerocarbon
Inspiration: grenzenlos. CO_2-Bilanz: null.

Stets gut informiert sein: Fordern Sie bitte unser Magazin an unter www.taschen.com/magazine, folgen Sie uns auf Twitter und Facebook oder schreiben Sie an contact@taschen.com bei Fragen oder Lob zu unserem aktuellen Programm.

Consulting Editor
Margit J. Mayer, Berlin

Project Management
Stephanie Paas, Cologne

Production
Thomas Grell, Cologne

Design
Birgit Eichwede, Cologne

Layout
Tanja da Silva, Cologne

Printed in China
ISBN 978-3-8365-5726-9

UN LIVRE TASCHEN, UN ARBRE PLANTÉ!

TASCHEN affiche un bilan carbone neutre. Chaque année, nous compensons nos émissions de CO_2 avec l'Instituto Terra, un programme de reforestation de l'État du Minas Gerais, au Brésil, fondé par Lélia et Sebastião Salgado. Pour plus d'informations sur ce partenariat environnemental, rendez-vous sur:
www.taschen.com/zerocarbon
Inspiration: illimitée. Empreinte carbone: nulle.

Si vous souhaitez être informé des prochaines parutions TASCHEN, abonnez-vous à notre magazine gratuit sur www.taschen.com/magazine, suivez-nous sur Twitter et Facebook, ou contactez-nous par e-mail à l'adresse contact@taschen.com pour toute question concernant notre programme de publication.

This book is in large part a compilation from TASCHEN's previously published Interior & Lifestyle titles.

London, UK 288-303
Hamwood, IE 206
Paris, FR 478-577
Biarritz, FR 86
Madrid, ES 310
Loulé, PT 304
Carvalhal, PT 130
Essaouira, MA 176
Marrakech, MA 322

422-463 New York City, USA
190 Fire Island, USA

Beverly Hills, USA 78

340-377 Miami, USA
608 Santiago de Cuba, CU
416 Naguabo, PR
148 Cojímar, CU
214 Havana, CU

Acapulco, MX 14
Mexico City, MX 334

Barcelona, ES 44
Ibiza, ES 234

Mérida, MX 328

Milan, IT 378-393

688 Trancoso, BR

616 São Paulo, BR
586 Praia do Forte, BR

184 Faro José Ignacio, UY
276 La Barra, UY
316 Manantiales, UY
600 San Isidro, AR
394 Monte, AR
108 Buenos Aires, AR